# ECO-WARS

*Power, Conflict, and Democracy:*
*American Politics Into the Twenty-first Century*

ROBERT Y. SHAPIRO, EDITOR

*Power, Conflict, and Democracy:*
*American Politics Into the Twenty-first Century*
ROBERT Y. SHAPIRO, EDITOR

This series focuses on how the will of the people and the public interest are promoted, encouraged, or thwarted. It aims to question not only the direction American politics will take as it enters the twenty-first century but also the direction American politics has already taken.

The series addresses the role of interest groups and social and political movements; openness in American politics; important developments in institutions such as the executive, legislative, and judicial branches at all levels of government as well as the bureaucracies thus created; the changing behavior of politicians and political parties; the role of public opinion; and the functioning of mass media. Because problems drive politics, the series also examines important policy issues in both domestic and foreign affairs.

The series welcomes all theoretical perspectives, methodologies, and types of evidence that answer important questions about trends in American politics.

# ECO-WARS

POLITICAL CAMPAIGNS AND SOCIAL MOVEMENTS

RONALD T. LIBBY

COLUMBIA UNIVERSITY PRESS

NEW YORK

Figure 2.1 copyright © *The Gene Exchange*, December 1991, National Wildlife Federation. Reprinted by permission.

Figure 3.1 copyright © 1991 Dr. William Rempel. Reprinted by permission.

Figure 5.1 from Begay, Traynor, and Glantz, in "The Twilight of Proposition 99," IHPS March 1994. Reprinted by permission.

Figure 6.1 copyright © 1995 Random House, Inc. Reprinted by permission.

COLUMBIA UNIVERSITY PRESS
Publishers Since 1893
New York      Chichester, West Sussex

Copyright © 1998 Columbia University Press
Library of Congress Cataloging-in-Publication Data
Libby, Ronald T.
Eco-wars : political campaigns and social movements / Ronald T. Libby.
   p. cm. — (Power, conflict, and democracy)
   Includes bibliographical references and index.
   ISBN 0–231–11310–2 (cloth). — ISBN 0–231–11311–0 (paper)
   1. Pressure groups—United States. 2. Social movements—Political aspects—United States.
3. Consumer protection—United States. 4. Animal rights movement—United States.
5. Environmentalism—United States. I. Title. II. Series.
JK118.L53 1999
324'.4'0973—dc21
                                  98–39826

c 10 9 8 7 6 5 4 3 2 1
p 10 9 8 7 6 5 4 3 2 1

*For my brilliant and lovely daughter, Erin Kristin, with love*

# CONTENTS

# FIGURES AND TABLES

# ■ PREFACE ■

I got the idea for this book in 1993 while I was teaching at Southwest State University in Minnesota. I had just completed a book on the politics of the world grain trade and in the process had become personally acquainted with representatives of the food industry in the state and the Midwest. In the course of numerous conversations, farmers and industry representatives lamented their inability to cope with criticism and attacks by animal rights, environmentalist, and food safety activists that ranged from protests at agricultural fairs to the distribution of pamphlets, ads, and newspaper reports condemning the alleged abuse of and cruelty to food animals to the dangers of pesticides and herbicides in food production and water quality.

I was struck by industry's widespread perception that it is under attack and powerless to do anything about it. Farmers adamantly maintained that they are humane and responsible stewards of their livestock and are extremely careful in the use of farm chemicals. They said that such care is necessary for the safety of their families who live on and work the farms and for the commercial viability of their businesses. They also pointed out that farm chemicals are expensive and potentially dangerous and that farmers therefore exercise extreme care when using chemicals. Industry representatives were at a loss to explain the public's fear of chemicals in food production except to say that ill-informed political activists have been exploiting that fear in order to advance their careers.

The CEOs of large food companies and trade associations repeated the refrain—that they are unfairly criticized by activists and the media and that they are unable to defend themselves against these attacks. They claimed that environmental, food safety, and animal rights activists have a virtual lock on public consciousness and that the industry is constantly placed on the defensive. Public opinion is so hostile to the industry that in most cases its representatives do not even try to defend themselves, let alone undertake political campaigns to counteract the criticisms, they told me.

My initial response was skepticism. My training as a social scientist, plus the widely shared societal perception that large corporate interests dominate the political landscape, made me doubt the sincerity of these comments. I thought perhaps that industry was hypersensitive or was exaggerating what could be little more than a nuisance. Besides, were the corporate giants in these industries not prospering? However, when farmers explained that they are forced to devote hundreds of hours every year to complying with onerous and, in their view, unnecessary government safety and health regulations pertaining to the use of farm chemicals, that they could not get drugs for the medical treatment of their farm animals, and that the only public response of trade representatives to any criticism of food safety has been to withdraw questioned products from food stores, I began to take their comments seriously.

What intrigued me was their description of their political opponents. When I asked them to identify organizations or leaders spearheading the attacks, they were unable to name them. Indeed, with the exception of vague general references to well-known animal rights organizations such as People for the Ethical Treatment of Animals or high-profile consumer and food safety advocates such as Ralph Nader and Jeremy Rifkin, they were unable to identify their critics. Indeed, when I asked about specific instances of activist campaigns against the industry, they could not name their political opponents or describe their resources, strategies, or tactics.

This raised an intriguing question. If the industry's perception is correct—that it is beleaguered by environmental, consumer, and food safety activists—how are we to explain the political success of these groups? In terms of the conventional view of interest-group politics, they do not have the vast resources necessary to challenge large-scale corporate interests. But if such groups had indeed been able to put agribusiness on the defensive, scholars would need to reconceptualize the political influence of voluntary, grassroots, activist organizations. Social scientists also would have to reconsider the conventional wisdom about the dominance of business interests in capitalist democracies. This book represents an effort to explore these questions.

I addressed these issues by carrying out original field research on five major political campaigns by activist groups against business interests. I hope that by comparing these case studies, I will be able to illuminate the political resources, tactics, strategies, and leadership of voluntary grassroots organizations. My analysis should also help explain the circumstances in which activist groups are able to challenge the political influence of corporations in democratic policy making.

In the course of researching and writing the book I incurred many debts. Laura Woliver, David Vogel, William Browne, and Don Hadwiger read several drafts and made many helpful comments and suggestions for revision. I am particularly indebted to Woliver for her detailed and insightful comments. Her deep knowledge of the literature on social movements is a rarity for a political scientist. Jeffrey Berry and Theodore Lowi made helpful comments about the introductory section. My colleagues Francis Graham Lee and Tom Kane also read and commented on the book. Sanford Thatcher recognized the promise of the work and encouraged me to develop and refine it during its early stages. John Michel, my editor at Columbia University Press, appreciated its value and encouraged me throughout the review process. I am indebted to him for his continued faith in the book.

Industry, environmental, consumer safety, and animal rights groups were generous with their time and assistance. I never could have written this book without their cooperation. Although space does not allow a complete list of those who assisted in the research, I mention those who provided extraordinary assistance. Hugh S. Johnson, Stanley E. Curtis, Carolyn L. Stull, Steve Kopperud, Bill Rempel, Michael Fox, and Pam Comstock helped me understand the animal rights issue; Michael Hansen, John Stauber, Bradley Miller, and Don Colleton helped with the biotechnology and animal rights campaigns. John K. Van de Kamp, David Cameron, Richard S. Woodward, Charles Rund, Paul B. Holm Jr., and Kirk West provided invaluable assistance in regard to the Big Green campaign. Stanton Glantz, Lee H. Stitzenberger, and Jack Nicholl assisted in the secondhand smoke campaign, and Robin and Sole Libby helped gather data on the campaign. Michael Bean, Stephen Meyer, Jim Jontz, Nikos Boutis, Robert E. Gordon Jr., Chuck Cushman, Myron Ebell, Ike C. Sugg, Richard Manning, and J. Jon Dogett were important resources in the endangered species campaign. To these individuals and numerous others I wish to express my deep appreciation for their kindness and generosity in sharing their knowledge and insights.

I am indebted to Southwest State University for several faculty improvement grants, which permitted me to travel to California and Washington, D.C., for research. Dean Judith Chapman of Saint Joseph's University also generously provided a grant for final preparations of the book. Rosanne Jennings prepared the graphics and artwork, and Anne Szewczyk helped me meet Columbia University Press's computer formatting requirements. I thank Christopher Dixon, Mary Martinson, and other members of the Interlibrary Loan Department of the Drexel Library of Saint Joseph's University for their assiduous efforts to locate numerous obscure references needed for the book. As always, my younger daughter, Kathleen Elizabeth, inspired me to write this book.

# ECO-WARS

# ONE

# INTRODUCTION

Expressive Interest Groups

We see them all around us—abortion opponents blockading clinics, environmentalists protesting the cutting of old-growth forest and consumer groups condemning pesticides and chemically treated fruits and vegetables. They get a lot of attention in the media, so one might suppose that they have a powerful effect on society and help change attitudes and even, Congress willing, laws. But do these groups really have such power? Many experts who have studied interest groups believe they do not.

The purpose of this book is to examine the strategies and political influence of the most recent generation of interest groups in American politics.[1] They are sometimes called public interest groups, citizen groups, single-interest groups, cause groups, and externality and alternative groups. They are organized and seek to achieve their objectives through government policy. Typically, they have a passionate commitment to such causes such as abortion, civil rights, gun control, the environment, women's rights, animal rights, food safety, disarmament, and homosexuality. Unlike conventional interest groups, they are not primarily motivated by material benefits such as improved working conditions, wages, services, profitability, and economic well-being for their members.

They tend to be embedded in social movements such as environmental safety and cleanup, animal rights, and property rights. Unlike conventional interest groups, these groups do not rely primarily on lobbying, bargaining, and compromise to achieve their ends. They tend to have deep, often intangible, roots in society that constitute a major source of political support in their efforts to change public policy. In other words, these groups are like the proverbial tip of the iceberg, with a vast body of citizen supporters that is largely invisible to the student of conventional interest groups.

Choosing an appropriate term to describe these groups is problematic. Theodore Lowi, for example, notes that "any definition will bleed at the edges" (personal communication, November 15, 1997). Nevertheless, because the range of interest groups is wide, it is necessary to define this particular category of interest group for meaningful analysis.

E. E. Schattschneider (1960:23–46) discusses the hallowed distinction in political theory between public and private interest groups. *Public interests* refer to general interests widely shared in a community, whereas *special interests* are shared by only a few people or a fraction of the community. The implication is that special interests exclude members of the community and may even oppose them. However, Schattschneider acknowledges that agreement on any given interest is never 100 percent. The distinction between public and private interest is subjective because it is based on inferences about people's motives, intentions, and desires (p. 25). The term public interest is also incomplete because it excludes privately organized groups, such as property rights advocates who champion a strict reading of constitutional guarantees for all citizens.

The term *citizen group* is also inappropriate for describing these groups because it excludes many food safety and animal rights organizations that do not have grassroots memberships. For example, the Foundation on Economic Trends, a food safety group, and the Humane Farming Association, an animal rights group, have no members, no boards of directors, no elected or appointed officials or terms of office. The term *single-interest group* also does not accurately describe the multiple objectives of mainstream environmental organizations such as the Sierra Club or the National Wildlife Federation, both of which cover a wide range of concerns, including the use of pesticides, protecting endangered species, and holes in the ozone layer.

I shall use a more all-embracing term, *expressive group,* to designate these interest groups. This term has parallels with *social regulatory policy making,* a term proposed by Tatalovich and Daynes (1988). Such a policy is concerned with conduct that is good or bad in itself, instead of conduct that is good or bad in terms of its consequences. Social regulatory policy contrasts with standard regulation or regulatory policy, which denotes channeling or constraining policy in order to reduce injuries or increase benefits arising from those policies. Social regulatory policy has an intrinsic moral orientation, designed as it is to eliminate unethical or immoral policy. Moral policy issues tend to be dominated by interest groups and social movements and not political parties. These groups are more prevalent at the state than the national level. Moral considerations radicalize standard types of national regulatory policy. Examples of moral regulation include both sides of such issues as school prayer, pornography, crime, gun control, affirmative action, abortion, and basic property laws. Interest groups associated with moral regulation tend to be grassroots, single-issue, and social movements. Finally, social regulatory policy is not merely symbolic—it involves real efforts to radically transform social policy.

Advocates of expressive interest groups argue that they constitute a vital historical link in the democratic process by converting the wishes of ordinary citizens into government policies. Indeed, such groups have a long history in American politics. The original peace groups were formed in the United States in 1828, and the first women's organizations were established in the midnineteenth century. The temperance, antislavery, and civil rights movements profoundly affected government policy making and made politics more open and accessible to new participants.[2]

By contrast, critics argue that expressive groups threaten the political process. They tend to be single-issue groups that are unwilling to compromise and tend to paralyze the democratic process. Such groups can destroy the careers of good politicians who do not agree with their highly emotional issues, and the groups promote the selfish interests of particular segments of society at the expense of the common good. Indeed, some observers have even associated the decline of the party system in the United States with the emergence of expressive interest groups (Hershey 1993).

Despite the controversy over expressive interest groups, there is no consensus on their political influence. For example, Berry (1996:2) asks whether the growth of expressive groups since the 1960s has had any real effect on government policies. His litmus test is whether these groups have become effective opponents of business. If not, he speculates, business interests will continue to dominate interest-group politics in the United States. This proposition was first advanced by Schattschneider in the late 1950s. He argued in his important book, *The Semisovereign People,* that interest-group influence in Washington favors business and the wealthy, not the poor and the broad public interest of the country.

More than four decades later his observation is still the received wisdom. In his 1977 classic, *Politics and Markets,* Charles Lindblom argues that business enjoys a "privileged position" in American politics. It is not simply one among many powerful organized interests. The critical importance of business to capitalist societies gives corporations unrivaled political influence.

Lindblom acknowledges that business does not win every political battle. However, in the end, business will prevail because politicians understand that to be reelected they need a prosperous economy. Lindblom calls this form of politicoeconomic system *polyarchy*, a liberal democracy that is a private-enterprise market system.

Economic recession, high inflation, and unemployment can bring a government down. Therefore, in a market economy government accords business leaders extensive "inducements" to ensure that business performs well. Government inducements to business include favorable tax and monetary policies as well as favorable rail, highway, air, and tariff policies. Inducements to business include "income and wealth, deference, prestige, influence and power, and authority" (Lindblom 1977:174). Therefore, if the CEOs of large chemical companies say they need government support for research and development in the form of tax relief or tariff breaks, or need confidentiality in research tests, government will acknowledge this need and provide assistance. Thus business elites are more than simple representatives of special interests: they perform a quasi-public function that political leaders regard as indispensable. In other words, business elites are first among equals in the world of interest-group politics.

Following Lindblom, Vogel argues that despite the decline of business power during the 1960s and 1970s, expressive groups cannot match business's resources. Thus business enjoys "disproportionate influence over the political process" (Vogel 1996:156). And in a book widely read in the 1980s Schlozman and Tierney describe the dominance of business interest groups as greater than ever, constituting a threat to public welfare (1986:68).

However, some analysts have questioned the conventional wisdom that business dominates American politics. Walker (1983) argues that the mobilization and politicizing of citizen groups since the 1950s has enabled new participants to influence government policy. Boyte refers to this development as "a renaissance in citizen activism" (1980:3). Hadwiger (1982) examines conflicts between expressive and economic groups and finds that they achieve a political balance. Browne (1988:130–49) finds that the proliferation of expressive groups has effectively destroyed the traditional way of making agricultural policy in the United States. Berry contends that expressive groups "have made the political system more dynamic, open, and participatory" (1996:1). Even Schlozman and Tierney equivocate on the question of business dominance. They conclude that interest-group politics is now "less exclusive and skewed" toward business interests

(1986:75). However, they do not say how much less skewed government policy is toward business today than it was in the 1950s.

This book is designed to partially address this question by examining political campaigns carried out by expressive groups. It is an effort to understand how they campaign, the circumstances in which their campaigns are successful, and why they succeed.

### Expressive Interest Groups

The first theorist to describe expressive groups as a distinct type was T. Alexander Smith (1969). In proposing this new category of interest group, Smith drew on the pioneering work of Lowi (1964). Lowi argues that patterns of cooperation and conflict among interest groups differ according to the nature of the policy at issue. There are three different kinds of domestic policy, each with a unique set of institutional relationships, bargaining style, and structure of organized interest activity (termed *arena*). Lowi called them *distributive, regulatory,* and *redistributive* policies. Smith added a fourth category, -which he called *emotive symbolic.*

In order to understand emotive symbolic interest groups, it is necessary to briefly discuss the other arenas in which interest groups attempt to influence government policy. The distributive type is the most common policy-making arena and is characterized by little conflict between interest groups. Examples of distributive policies include government patronage and the provision of such services as highway and waterway beautification and agricultural subsidies. Usually, there is enough government largesse to satisfy all major interest groups.

The regulative arena is characterized by direct interest-group confrontation, which typically occurs in legislatures. Examples of regulative policies include the granting of a radio or television license, adopting a food packaging law, and imposing regulatory restrictions on cigarette advertising. According to Smith, most of what is called the "interest-group approach" to American politics fits this category of policy making.

The redistributive arena is not as prevalent as the distributive and regulatory types. It is characterized by a high level of conflict and a winner-take-all outcome. It involves large "peak" associations such as the National Association of Manufacturers and their trade-union counterparts such as the American Federation of Labor–Congress of Industrial Organizations. Interest-group conflict over redistributive policy involves intense ideological rhetoric from contestants who fear they may suffer major losses in the policy outcome. Free-enterprise or free-trade doctrines, as well as a living wage and worker security, are commonly evoked in this context. This type of interest-group conflict is rare and usually cannot be contained by a legislature or political elites because of the many people affected and the scope of the policy's effects.

The fourth category of interest-group conflict is emotive symbolization. This interest-group arena is also characterized by high levels of ideological conflict involving many people. Emotive symbolization evokes people's strong opinions about the ethics or correctness of an issue. Unlike other policy-making arenas, however, emotive symbolization tends to be noneconomic. It too produces such intensity of feeling that legislatures and government elites try to avoid it. As a result, emotive symbolic issues tend to be decentralized. Emotive issues usually land in the laps of individual legislators or go directly to voters through the initiative and referendum at the state level. In the ensuing conflict editorial boards tend to stake out a position. Examples of emotive symbolic issues include abortion, the death penalty, the environment, food safety, animal rights, women's rights, religious issues, employment and civil rights for gays and the disabled, and the many other causes championed by expressive interest groups. Berry contends that the "most enduring and vital" expressive groups have been environmental and consumer advocates (1993:31).

## The Origins of Expressive Groups

Expressive groups first emerged as a force in American politics during the Progressive era of the 1920s. This new organizational form of interest-group politics was based on specific issues or policy demands and supported by "extrapartisan voting blocs" (Clemens 1997). Interest groups became directly involved in legislative activity, monitoring the legislative process, acquiring technical expertise in policy, and mobilizing public opinion. This new pattern of organizational behavior was not guided by party loyalty. It enabled voters to directly intervene in policy making and hold representatives accountable at the polls. According to Clemens (pp. 3–4), this new organizational capability, which is termed the *people's lobby*, complemented traditional electoral politics and protest movements.

Between the 1890s and 1930s nonpartisan interest groups achieved major changes in government policy making. They innovated primary elections, the initiative and referendum, and the creation of government agencies and programs in order to achieve their policy goals. The Progressive movement also is credited with professionalizing city governments by introducing city management systems, civil service exams, and nonpartisan local elections. These interest groups set in train three processes that transformed American politics. First, competitive national parties began to decay; second, growing societal discontent in the guise of immigration (which created a demand for new forms of organizational protest or reform), labor unrest, and feminist demands led to new organizational models of participation that constituted an alternative to the party system; and, third, during the next three decades these alternative organizations shifted the center of national political power from electoral competition by the political parties to legislatures, administrative agencies, and public opinion.

Expressive interest groups continued to function with renewed vigor through the 1960s as a powerful force in American politics. According to Berry (1989:16–43), a wide range of new expressive groups emerged in the wake of the success of the civil rights and antiwar protest movements.[3] Interest-group surveys by Walker (1983:390–406) and Schlozman and Tierney (1986:75–76) from 1960 to 1980 showed that expressive lobbying organizations in Washington, D.C., had increased dramatically. Berry (1989:34) also found that about half the "public interest" groups he surveyed were established between 1968 and 1972. The growth of these groups has been even greater at the local level. For example, the National Commission on Neighborhoods listed eight thousand grassroots organizations and the U.S. Department of Housing and Urban Development compiled a list of fifteen thousand such groups toward the end of the 1970s (Berry 1977:22).

Expressive groups can be understood in terms of a deeply rooted reform tradition in American politics, the "good government reformers" who came out of the Progressive era. During the 1890s local political movements emerged from the middle class to eliminate political corruption, counteract the power of city bosses, and rewrite city charters (McFarland 1984:23–37). The movement quickly gained local, state, and nationwide support during the presidencies of Theodore Roosevelt, William Howard Taft, and Woodrow Wilson. During much of this period democratic reform dominated public discourse. Progressive politicians sought to make government more responsive to the public will by restricting the powers of big city bosses and placing monopolies or "trusts" under public control.

The outbreak of World War I temporarily displaced from the public agenda the interest in progressive reforms; nevertheless, the movement continued. For example, New York City's Citizens Union, established in 1897, continued to campaign for such democratic reforms as voter registration, reorganization of city government, local autonomy, and air pollution control (McFarland 1984:24–25). The Charter Party of Cincinnati and the League of Women Voters—along with hundreds of other more recent reform organizations such as Common Cause, Ralph Nader organizations, the Environmental Defense Fund, Consumers Union, and countless others—have continued to campaign for good government. The late 1970s saw the emergence of conservative groups such as the Moral Majority, the Christian Coalition, and the Concerned Women for America. These groups are largely motivated by the perception that the traditional family is threatened by the influence of liberal groups on society.

The rise of a new wave of expressive groups in the 1960s and 1970s added a new dimension to the progressive reform movement. This generation of reform groups emerged in response to widespread suspicion of government during the Vietnam War and the Watergate scandal, both of which tended to undermined public authority. These groups had an advantage that their predecessors did not. The communications revolution has lowered the costs of communicating the reform message to the public (Berry 1997:208). Thus conducting media campaigns on the Internet and by fax has dramatically enhanced the ability of expressive groups to mobilize public support for their cause.

Another difference between the traditional progressive reform movement and contemporary expressive groups is their political orientation. Expressive groups have been influenced by what Vogel terms the *New Left ideology* (1996:149), which calls upon the federal government to give the poor and disadvantaged the legal, financial, and organizational resources necessary to counteract the political dominance of business. The election of Lyndon Johnson advanced the cause of expressive groups with his War on Poverty, and Jimmy Carter supported environmental and consumer reform groups. However, unlike New Deal liberals, expressive groups do not wish to establish a large bureaucratic state apparatus to regulate business. Instead, they want to form a large number of private groups strong enough to compete with business in the formulation of public policy. However, the emergence of conservative expressive groups such as the Christian Coalition, with a "New Right" ideology emphasizing individual or family autonomy, also fits the category of expressive group. McFarland (1993:10–11) goes so far as to imply that the objective of expressive groups is to achieve a form of democratic corporatism or "middle-level corpo-ratism"—albeit on a limited or policy-by-policy basis. In this conception economic policy should be a product of negotiation between expressive groups, business, labor, and government.

### Expressive Groups: Marginal or Influential?

Vogel (1996:141–65) argues that expressive groups are the leading force in reg-ulating corporate activity. He goes so far as to compare the influence of expressive groups on business to the influence that trade unions had on cor-porations during the 1930s. These groups tend to campaign for what Inglehart (1977) terms postmaterial or quality-of-life concerns. Expressive groups pursue issues such as the environment, abortion, consumer protec-tion, animal rights, civil rights, education, equality, and religious rights. According to Inglehart, the affluence of Western industrial societies after World War II ushered in an unprecedented era of economic security that made possible the pursuit of postmaterialist goals of environmentalism, equality, and public morality. These issues differ significantly from the objec-tives pursued by economic interest groups such as business, trade unions, and the American Association of Retired Persons.

Despite the growth in the number of expressive groups and their unde-niable influence on American politics, theorists have tended to see them as of secondary importance. In doing so, the theorists have tended to follow the hallowed tradition of James Madison in *Federalist* 10. Madison argues that society is divided into subgroups or classes based on the distribution of property and the possession of capital. Propertied and nonpropertied groups and creditors and debtors constitute distinct political interests in society. Thus political subgroups in American society are defined primar-ily in terms of conflicting economic interests.

Theorists have tended to accept Madison's insight but have branched off in two directions. The first is called *pluralism* and is characterized by the work of Bentley (1908), Truman (1951), Key (1958), and Polsby (1980). Pluralists have tended to elevate interest-group competition in regard to public policy to the status of the master process that guarantees democra-tic governance. In this approach the role of government is that of honest broker or umpire, mediating interest-group conflict to ensure that no sin-gle interest dominates the political marketplace.

The second approach is comprised of critics of pluralism and is termed *polyarchy.* It is represented by the work of Schattschneider (1960), Lowi (1969), Lindblom (1977), and Dahl (1982). These critics seek to revise pluralist theory by emphasizing Madison's admonition on the dangers of "factional mischief." Of particular concern to them is the threat to the Republic posed by business's dominance of public policy. Lindblom (1977:35) asks, for example, whether the political influence of large corporations is compatible with true democracy. Thus Lindblom and Dahl use the term polyarchy to describe interest-group competition for the political influence that favors business over other interest groups.

However, both pluralists and their critics have tended to focus on the political competition between economic interest groups and have, relatively speaking, neglected expressive groups. Although pluralists have examined political causes such as the civil rights and suffrage movements, the expressive interest groups representing these movements have not been incorporated in interest-group theory. For example, instead of treating civil rights groups as interest groups and evaluating their competitive position vis-à-vis other interest groups in influencing government policy, the theorists have analyzed the movement largely in terms of its influence on public opinion and the historic expansion of voting rights in the United States (Tesh 1984:29).

In fact, civil rights, women's rights, animal rights, health and safety, abortion, gun control, religious rights, and a plethora of other expressive interests do compete with one another as well as with economic interests for control of government policy (Browne 1990:447–509). Heinz and colleagues (1993) point out that expressive and economic groups compete in all four policy domains, with neither group achieving ascendancy. Vogel (1996:155–60) argues that although expressive groups seek to counter the influence of business in public policy arenas, their influence has had the unintended consequence of increasing the expressive groups' dependence upon government regulation.

The principal motivation for expressive groups is not economic. Rather, it is deeply held beliefs about the justness or ethics of a cause. Therefore, by omitting expressive interest groups from analysis, traditional interest-group theory has acquired a skewed or biased perspective. Pluralists and their critics have given us an economic theory of interest groups, not a theory of interest groups. Thus it is not surprising that conventional interest-group theory predicts that the most powerful economic groups will have disproportionate influence on government policy.

I believe that the inclusion of expressive groups in the study of interest groups in general would lead to a very different theory. We should question the assumption that the only important political subgroups in society are those with economic interests. Likewise, we should reexamine the belief that business tends to dominate public policy. Indeed, a careful reading of Madison's *Federalist* 10 suggests that he does not rule out the emergence of factions arising from the "zeal for opinion" that causes people to disagree about even trivial matters. Therefore, "ideological" or expressive groups should be included in interest-group theory.

## Conventional Wisdom About Interest Groups

To incorporate expressive groups in interest-group theory we must first understand how their political strategies differ from economic interest groups.' I shall discuss the conventional wisdom regarding interest groups and then contrast it with my research findings on expressive groups. The literature reveals several areas of consensus regarding traditional interest groups:

1. Money is the primary political resource for interest groups.
2. The tax status of interest groups determines their political approach.
3. Unlike wealthy interest groups, expressive groups cannot afford to hire public relations firms to conduct media campaigns.
4. Interest-group campaigns that appeal to public fear, prejudice, and ignorance by exaggerating and misrepresenting facts are counterproductive.
5. Political parties are not critical to interest groups' efforts to influence public policy.
6. The traditional antagonism between business and labor is overshadowed by enmity between business and environmental and consumer groups.
7. Business groups have a political advantage over expressive groups insofar as economic groups offer material benefits to their members.

The conventional belief is that money is essential for interest groups to survive, let alone have any influence on public policies. The importance of money is its convertibility into political resources. This includes campaign contributions, mass mailings to members of organizations, hiring technical experts, lobbying government officials and politicians, and conducting media campaigns. The importance of money is such an article of faith among observers of interest groups that the failure of expressive groups to raise large sums of money is itself taken as a sign of failure. For example, Schlozman and Tierney (1986:112) argue that raising money is so critical to expressive groups that it interferes with their goals. And Bosso (1995:125) claims that environmental groups must compromise their ideals to get the money they need simply to survive.

The tax status of interest groups is also believed to determine their approach to politics. The conventional wisdom is that the ability of interest groups to attract private donations and gifts is powerfully affected by their tax status under the Internal Revenue Code. For example, Section 501 (c)(3) exempts about 467,000 U.S. nonprofit interest groups from paying taxes. Individuals who contribute to these groups are also able to partially deduct their donations to these groups from adjusted gross income. As a result, private foundations give sizable grants to nonprofit interest groups. This is said to constitute a vital financial resource for expressive interest groups.

However, the Code places severe restrictions on the political activity of nonprofit groups. A 501(c)(3) group is not permitted to campaign for, or against, legislation or mobilize its members to support, or oppose, legislation. The Code does allow such groups to "educate" the public and politicians with technical information. However, if the advocacy becomes too overt, these groups risk losing their tax-exempt status. Berry claims that the loss of an expressive group's nonprofit status "can be a matter of life and death" (1977:48). And Vogel argues that the tax-exempt status of expressive groups increases their power vis-à-vis business interests (1996:157).

According to Schlozman and Tierney (1986:161, 171), interest groups with "plenty of money" mount public relations campaigns and mobilize members at the grassroots level. However, it is commonly believed that expressive groups cannot afford the high price of public relations firms. Television and mass media campaigns are said to be beyond their reach. Therefore, expressive groups are forced to rely on press conferences, demonstrations, and free media coverage. This is assumed to place them at a disadvantage in competing with business to influence public policy.

The conventional wisdom is that interest groups that exaggerate and misrepresent the facts of issues in political campaigns lose credibility. The reputation of interest groups for honesty and trustworthiness is one of their most important assets. Interest groups make their case in the policy arena based on scientific facts and technical analysis of data. If a public official acts on the basis of flawed information and is embarrassed, the group that supplied that information is discredited in the eyes of policy makers. Therefore, the surest way to undermine a group's cause is to distort and misrepresent the factual basis of its case.

According to Schlozman and Tierney (1986:103, 298), an interest group's reputation for honesty and trustworthiness in dealing with those inside and outside government is essential for influencing policy. Berry (1993:38) notes in this regard that expressive groups have a great deal of credibility with the press. As a result, if an interest group presents bad information or distorts the facts in making its case, it will lose important political contacts and channels of communication.

Political parties are seen as not being important to interest groups in achieving their policy objectives. Although business and expressive groups are inclined to support different parties, the linkage between the groups and parties is said to be weak (Schlozman and Tierney 1986:200–20). To the extent that a linkage exists, interest groups and party organizations are believed to overlap and compete with one another.

Both interest groups and political parties have policy preferences, participate in selecting candidates for office, and campaign for the candidates' election. However, they differ insofar as interest groups wish to influence public policy, whereas parties seek to win control of government. Indeed, many observers believe that expressive groups are responsible for the atrophy of political parties because interest groups provide alternative outlets for citizen demands on issues of importance to them. Berry (1980:42–48) argues that expressive groups offer ordinary citizens a more attractive channel of expression for their views than do political parties.

The conventional wisdom is that the historic tension between business and trade unions in capitalist societies is now overshadowed by conflict between business and expressive groups. When challenged by expressive environmental and consumer groups in particular, business has tended to unite with labor in opposition. One explanation for this is the changed regulatory climate. Until the 1960s government regulation, such as freight rates or drug safety, tended to be industry specific. However, during the 1970s regulation in the areas of occupational safety and health and environmental preservation affected all business activity (Schlozman and Tierney 1986:286).

Berry (1993:32) notes that business organized a whole generation of new business interest groups in the 1960s in response to the success of liberal expressive groups that demanded new social regulation of business. The perception by business is that these groups seized control of the political agenda and business mobilized to counteract their influence.

Another widespread assumption is that business groups have a political advantage over expressive groups because business groups offer specific material benefits to their members. The leading proponent of this argument is the economist Mancur Olson in his 1965 work, *The Logic of Collective Action*. Olson argues that members of business or trade associations participate because they expect to receive such material benefits as favorable policy from Congress, business contacts, or valuable business information. The larger the group, the more members prefer to "ride free" on the efforts of individuals whose interest in the "collective good" of the organization is strong enough to pursue it. According to Olson (1965:51), to overcome the free-rider problem organizations must provide "selective incentives" to members to induce their continued membership. For example, workers must be offered collective goods such as increased wages, health care insurance, pension plans, and child care programs to ensure their continued participation in a union.

By contrast, supporters of expressive groups do not join these organizations in order to receive selective material benefits. Indeed, Olson raises the issue of free riders as an obstacle to what he calls "ideological lobbying." From his perspective, it is irrational for citizens to actively support expressive groups when they can enjoy the fruits of the labor of such organizations as the Sierra Club, Environmental Defense Fund, or the Humane Society of the United States without joining them. It is this reasoning that presumes that business has a political advantage because large businesses offer their employees selective economic benefits that expressive group do not.

Students of social movements, however, question Olson's thesis. McCarthy and Mayer Zald (1973, 1977) argue that although Olson's collective goods theory applies to social movements, the greater prosperity and widespread availability of skills in modern society have provided a solution to the dilemma. Societal resources are now available to organizers whom McCarthy and Zald call "movement entrepreneurs." Movement entrepreneurs are not motivated by having a stake in an organization's collective goods; rather, these professionals have the resources and skills to mobilize citizens to air their grievances in protest movements, which McCarthy and Zald call social movement organizations (SMOs).

Tarrow (1994:15–16) rejects Mancur Olson's thesis altogether. He claims that people join organizations for a wide variety of reasons, many of which are not economic. For example, they join for a feeling of group solidarity or commitment to a cause as well as for material benefits. Although such reasons may make organizing an expressive group more difficult, they also mean that members have a variety of noneconomic resources to contribute. Olson's criteria of success for economic organizations also do not fit social movements. The size of an organization's budget or membership rolls or its number of dues-paying members is not a reflection of the influence of a social movement. A movement does not have strict membership criteria but does have deeply rooted societal support, which is difficult to measure. Finally, unlike economic associations, social movements tend to be comprised of loosely coordinated coalitions of informal groups and sympathizers.

**Expressive Political Campaigns**

In order to evaluate the political influence of expressive interest groups, I have examined five of their campaigns. The first campaign, against biotechnology, illustrates the difficulty that expressive groups face in framing a campaign to mobilize social movement support when they ally with non-movement organizations. The second campaign, on animal rights, shows the weakness of not having broad-based social movement support as well as the consequences of not having political allies. The third campaign, against environmental pollution, illustrates the danger to an expressive group of having a political party take over leadership of a campaign. The fourth campaign, against secondhand smoke, demonstrates the importance of a well-organized grassroots infrastructure and financing. The fifth campaign, against the Endangered Species Act, illustrates the danger to an expressive group of compromising the principles of social movement organizations.

Feagin, Orum, and Sjoberg (1991) discuss the value of the case study approach to understanding the influence of interest groups. They point out that the case study is an extraordinarily useful research tool and strategy for social analysis. Indeed, analyzing several case studies is critical to continued progress in the social sciences. Feagin, Orum, and Sjoberg define a case study as "an in-depth, multifaceted investigation, using qualitative research methods, of a single social phenomenon" (1991:2). This contrasts with American positivism, which is preoccupied with statistical methods and attempts to copy social science research methods, such as random sample surveys of large population groups or opinion surveys.

Case studies, on the other hand, use both quantitative and qualitative data, and some of the best research involves case studies carried out in a comparative framework. One important case study method involves the history of social or political groups such as cities. *Middletown,* the classic 1929 case study by Robert and Helen Lynd on Muncie, Indiana, produced important theoretical propositions that have guided the research of several generations of scholars. For example, the work by Floyd Hunter (1953) on Atlanta and Robert Dahl's 1961 study of New Haven, Connecticut, were influenced by the Lynds' pioneering study.

Another example of a case study's generating concepts and theories is the 1956 pathbreaking work of Seymour Martin Lipset and his colleagues. They observed that labor unions tended to be dominated by a ruling oligarchy or clique. They found that among the unions they surveyed, only one, the International Typographical Union (ITU), was not controlled by a small ruling group. They then studied the ITU to learn why democracy was practiced in this union and not others. The result was a new theory of organizational democracy that has influenced generations of scholars. All these case studies focused on power structures and produced important theories of organizational politics. They provided an empirical basis for elaborating and testing the conventional wisdom of old social science concepts and theories.

Schlozman and Tierney (1986:162) point out that understanding interest-group influence requires a sample of policy controversies. They believe that a careful examination of parallel cases will yield generalizations about the political influence of interest groups. The cases in my study represent expressive group campaigns. Although it is not a representative sample, the campaigns I chose illustrate the tactics and strategies used by expressive groups in political campaigns.

To narrow the sample of campaigns I canvassed one hundred large and influential industry, environmental, and food safety lobbying organizations in the country. These included the American Farm Bureau Federation, the National Milk Board, the Animal Health Institute, and the National Livestock and Meat Board; campaign consulting firms such as the Charlton Research Company, the Tarrance Group, the Wirthlin Group, Woodward and McDowell, the Dolfin Group, and Nicholl and Knepprath; and environmental groups such as the Sierra Club, Environmental Defense Fund, National Resources Defense Council, Audubon Society, and National Wilderness Institute. The canvass also included animal rights and welfare organizations such as People for the Ethical Treatment of Animals, the Humane Society of the United States, and the American Society for the Prevention of Cruelty to Animals and federal regulatory agencies such as the U.S. Environmental Protection Agency, Food and Drug Administration, General Accounting Office, Fish and Wildlife Service, and Department of Agriculture.

Representatives of these organizations were asked to identify political campaigns by expressive groups that illustrate the groups' strategy and tactics.[4] The campaigns selected were not the most or least successful but those that best illustrate the political strategies of expressive groups and their opponents in political campaigns. Three campaigns—animal rights, Big Green, and secondhand smoke—were initiative or referendum campaigns. This reflects the the assumption that expressive group campaigns have grassroots social movement support. The fourth campaign, against biotechnology, occurred in the context of regulatory politics involving the Food and Drug Administration and represents the large number of regulatory campaigns by expressive groups. The fifth campaign, against the Endangered Species Act, took place in the context of congressional politics, which reflects the large number of expressive campaigns in Congress.

## Social Movements and Expressive Groups

To understand the influence of expressive groups in political campaigns I must place them in the context of the social movements that gave birth to them. Indeed, I believe that the failure of conventional interest-group theorists to understand that expressive groups are embedded in social movements has led these critics to underestimate the groups' political power. Industry groups and their supporters also have tended to underestimate the political influence of expressive groups and for the same reason.

Likewise, the failure of social movement theorists to appreciate the importance of expressive groups in political campaigns has led to an omission in the social movement literature. A void exists at the intersection of interest-group and social movement literature. The failure of interest-group theorists to understand that expressive interest groups have broad-based social movement support and the failure of movement scholars to appreciate the importance of the political strategies of expressive groups in political campaigns have created a blind spot in scholarly writing. Indeed, discussion of campaign strategies by expressive interest groups is virtually absent in the social movement literature.

For example, another widespread belief is that these groups find it easier to mount collective action in the streets than to influence public policy (Tarrow 1994:26). This implies that expressive groups are less effective in political campaigns than they are in mobilizing citizen protest. I question this assumption and argue that expressive groups can and frequently do outmaneuver their political opponents in competition for control of public policy.

Tarrow defines social movements as "collective challenges by people with common purposes and solidarity in sustained interaction with elites, opponents and authorities" (1994:3). Rucht (1996:186) argues that social movements have two basic components. The first is a network of groups called movement structures that mobilize citizens to demand social change; the second is individuals who join protests and contribute resources to the movement without formally joining it.

Mobilization is the process of creating movement structures and participating in protests. Movement structures are the organizational base of movements. They gather and use the movement's resources, including information, to mobilize citizens to protest. The second component involves individuals who provide the movement with resources such as money, expertise, and skills.

Kriesi (1996:152) also uses the term social movement organizations (SMOs) to describe the "mobilizing structures" of social movements. He argues that SMOs have two distinguishing characteristics: they mobilize their constituency for collective action, and they have political goals. Kriesi points out that social movements have other mobilizing structures, such as family, friendship, and informal relationships among activists. Four other formal types of mobilizing organizations are supportive organizations, movement associations, political parties, and interest groups. Supportive organizations are "service organizations" such as schools, churches, friendly media, and print shops that help build a constituency for collective action but do not directly carry out a protest. Movement associations are "self-help" organizations, associations, or clubs that provide for the daily needs of their constituents.

McAdam, McCarthy, and Zald (1996:2) argue that three factors determine the emergence of social movements: political opportunities, mobilizing structures, and framing processes. When these three factors come together, the preconditions for the emergence of a social movement have

been met. The first factor, political opportunities, was originally elaborated by Tilly (1978), McAdam (1982), and Tarrow (1983). Tarrow (1994:18)
explains political opportunity in terms of a political environment that
encourages or discourages people from undertaking collective action. In
other words, movements emerge in response to opportunities to gain
leverage over a political regime. Frequently, this occurs when a political
elite suffers a split or a government is unstable or vulnerable. This gives
the movement and its leaders the opportunity to gain access to elites and
influence policy. McAdam (1982:230) argues that the civil rights movement made major gains because of improvements in the "structure of
political opportunities" confronting blacks from 1930 to 1954. Weakened
opposition gave SMOs in the movement, namely, black churches, col-
leges, and NAACP chapters, greater political leverage with which to press
their demands. These successes in turn encouraged collective action
within the movement.

The second factor, mobilizing structures, refers to the social networks
that form the basis of social movements. For example, the civil rights
movement was rooted in the black churches, and the networks of "base"
communities of the Catholic Church in Latin America set in motion a
populist social protest against entrenched political oligarchies.

Rucht (1996:187) says that movements have three basic mobilizing
agents that are designed to influence public policy and bring about social
change. They are social movements, interest groups, and political parties.
Each agent uses a different mode of operation and resources. The chief difference between social movements, political parties, and interest groups is
that parties and interest groups are formally organized and hierarchically
controlled and social movements are not. Movements have no formal constitutions and therefore are based on informal networks that lack centrally
controlled rules and regulations. Rucht concedes, however, that in practice
the boundaries separating movements, parties, and interest groups are not
always clear. For example, interest groups and parties may protest government policy, but they may not have highly formalized rules or be centrally
controlled.

The organizations I term expressive interest groups intersect Rucht's
analytical boundaries. On the one hand, they have the properties of interest groups in the sense that they are formally organized; they have money,
expertise, a political agenda, and access to policy makers; and they mount
political campaigns to influence public policy. On the other hand, they
have the properties of SMOs in the sense that they mobilize citizens to

protest for social change. In other words, in some political campaigns they take a leadership role, designing strategies and tactics to influence public policy, whereas in others they take the secondary role of mobilizing citizen protest for social change.

Indeed, the overlap in expressive interest groups and their ability to act interchangeably with SMOs is a great source of political strength. It gives them great flexibility within movements. Sometimes they function as interest groups, mounting political campaigns to change public policy, while at other times they perform in the secondary role of SMO, supporting expressive groups in political campaigns.

Doug McAdam's 1988 work, *Freedom Summer*, also provides important insight into the interchangeability of SMOs and expressive groups in mounting political campaigns. McAdam notes that the political leaderships of three major social movements of the 1960s were interrelated. The free speech, antiwar, and the feminist movements were organized by many of the same leaders. The decision of the Student Nonviolent Coordinating Committee to bring white student activists to Mississippi in 1964, during the period known as Freedom Summer, was designed to awaken the national conscience by radicalizing the students. When they returned to their college campuses, many assumed leadership roles in the antiwar movement and later the feminist movement (McAdam 1988a:161–232). The fluidity of leadership and organizational roles in social movements makes it difficult for opponents to recognize, let alone counteract, the political leadership and strategies of social movements.

The third factor determining the emergence of social movements is what Snow and colleagues (1986:464) refer to as a *frame* or *framework*. Borrowing from Goffman (1974:21), they define framing as a "schemata of interpretation" that enables individuals "to locate, perceive, identify and label occurrences within their lifespace and the world at large." The idea is that the presence of the other two preconditions for collective action—political opportunities and mobilizing structures—is insufficient to account for collective action. A critical third ingredient is new ideas, or an ideology, which is necessary to mobilize people to take collective action. This ideology must appeal to people's perceived grievances and offer the promise of a solution to problems if people take collective action. For example, the women's movement reached a peak in the 1970s as a result of the ascendance of a "legal equality" versus "special needs" agenda within the movement (Costain 1992:77–99). Consensus within the movement was achieved during the height of support for the Equal Rights

Amendment (ERA) within Congress. Thus ideological consensus, coupled with political opportunities, coincided to bring the movement to a political peak.

To understand the relationship between expressive groups and social movements, I shall briefly examine the emergence of one movement—the hazardous waste movement.

### The Hazardous Waste Movement

The hazardous waste movement is an example of a social movement that has had a significant influence on public policy. Szasz (1994:99) argues that the movement was largely responsible for shifting pollution control policy from "waste regulation" to "waste reduction."

Before the mid-1970s industry was not required to report its waste practices. Therefore, no one knew how much chemical waste was produced or what happened to it. In addition, little was known about the effect of chemical waste on public health. Although some isolated local protests were held against waste sites, hazardous waste was not a national issue. Nevertheless, the public was becoming increasingly concerned that industrial production threatened the environment and public health. The popularity of Rachel Carson's 1962 book, *Silent Spring*, which warned of the danger of DDT, awakened the public to the dangers of toxic chemicals.

Public concern with industrial pollution, however, changed to a fear of toxic chemicals in 1978 following the massive media coverage of Love Canal, New York, and other chemical pollution disasters such as the dioxin spill in Seveso, Italy; PCB contamination of the Hudson River; Agent Orange; kepone contamination in Virginia, and others. For two years TV news saturated the airwaves with details of Hooker Chemical Company's dumping of toxic chemical wastes in Love Canal. The coverage included extensive reports of chemical contamination and its cancer-causing effects on humans and animals. The public was bombarded with reports that unregulated chemical waste could result in catastrophe.

The coverage of chemical disasters had a profound effect on the public. The stories emphasized that this was an unseen silent killer that was "seeping out of the ground" (Szasz 1994:43). This invisible killer was said to have caused cancers, miscarriages, and birth defects. Reports included heartrending stories of financial bankruptcy to families who were ill and could not afford to move. The news stories described communities destroyed by toxic waste with danger signs on abandoned schools, parks, and homes.

The stories suggested that Love Canal was not the only chemical time bomb. A deadly chemical ooze was waiting to seep out of the ground without warning in any community in the country. Walter Cronkite, the most credible news anchor at the time, said of Love Canal, "The problem of hazardous chemical waste drifts across this nation these days like a bad dream" (Szasz 1994:45).

The toxic waste stories fundamentally altered public opinion. For example, an ABC News/Harris poll conducted in June 1980 showed that 93 percent of those polled felt that federal waste disposal must be made "much more strict," and 86 percent said that the federal government should give high priority to cleaning up waste and toxic chemical dump sites.

Students of social movements would argue that "toxic waste" as a national grassroots issue had finally arrived. They note, for example, that the public mind associates an overturned chemical drum accompanied by "moonsuited" cleanup teams with cancer and birth defects. Indeed, by the 1980s this image had become a permanent fixture in Hollywood movies and remains instantly recognizable.

The massive media coverage of toxic waste disasters was accompanied by social movement activity. A sea change occurred in public awareness after 1978, and isolated toxic waste protest groups began to network, bringing in speakers who had combated similar waste disposal problems to explain their tactics and strategies. Within a decade a complex social movement infrastructure was created.

The scope of the hazardous waste issue expanded as the movement grew. It started out as a problem of community landfill contamination by chemical companies and expanded to include ozone depletion, pesticides, food irradiation, electronic pollution, global warming, oil spills, occupational health dangers, air pollution, acid rain, and others. Nevertheless, the theme was the same: in the pursuit of profits, industry—producers of petrochemicals, nuclear power and weaponry, microelectronics, and high-tech agriculture—threaten the public health and welfare.

The movement was also effective in framing the issue to mobilize citizens for collective action against toxic waste producers and dumpers. To appeal to movement supporters, Activists created a radical ideology that was an eclectic mixture of symbols, including the American Revolution, Bill of Rights, Judeo-Christian ethics, and populism, featuring the individual citizen confronted by large powerful polluting corporations. The movement also generated a wide range of supportive and association groups, as well as SMOs such as Lois Gibb's Citizens' Clearinghouse for Hazardous Wastes based in Arlington, Virginia. Citizen's Clearinghouse publishes an annual report of grassroots groups involved in the movement. In 1988 the organization reported 4,687 groups with affiliates in 162 cities in thirty states and the District of Columbia. Other antitoxics SMOs include the National Toxics Campaign and Greenpeace, which work with thousands of local hazardous waste protest groups throughout the country.

Despite the emergence of a potent antitoxics social movement, however, analysts have had difficulty demonstrating that the movement has had any real influence on public policy. For example, Szasz (1994:137–39) says that it is impossible to make a connection between successes in mobilizing citizen support for changes in pollution control policy and actual changes in the country's waste policy—because there is no real toxic waste cleanup.

This has led to a paradoxical conclusion. On the one hand, for example, Szasz argues that the combination of grassroots activity and legislation has shifted the country away from "pollution control" and toward "pollution prevention." On the other hand, after ten years of Superfund activity (the Superfund was established in 1972) and the expenditure of billions of dollars, the EPA has failed to clean up most hazardous waste sites. What is missing in this analysis are the political campaigns of antitoxics expressive interest groups. An examination of toxics campaigns would reveal which groups were involved, what their strategies and political agendas were, who their opponents were, and what success they had. In other words, the political strategies of antitoxics expressive groups, as well as those of their opponents, would help explain this apparent contradiction.

This lapse in the analysis of the toxics movement reveals a blind spot in the literature. Indeed, McAdam, McCarthy, and Zald (1988:727) observe that "movement outcomes" are a neglected topic. I believe that the reason for this neglect is that the final stage of social movement activity—political campaigns by expressive groups—is often omitted from the analysis.

Expressive interest groups, which are integral to social movements, perform the vital function of waging the political campaigns. Table 1.1 outlines the expressive groups, social movement organizations (SMOs), nonmovement allies, political allies, political opponents, framing processes, freerider problems, and outcomes of the campaigns I discuss.

TABLE 1.1  Expressive Interest-Group Campaigns

|  | Biotech | Animal Rights |
|---|---|---|
| Expressive groups | FET<br>HFA<br>CSPI<br>RV | CEASE |
| Social movement organizations (SMOs) | CU<br>NRDC<br>HSUS<br>FOE<br>NWF | HSUS<br>FARM<br>HFA<br>PETA<br>MSPCA<br>ASPCA |
| Non-movement allies | Dairy farmers (Co-ops) | United Farm Workers (AFL-CIO) |
| Political allies | Farm state congressional leaders, Wisconsin & Minnesota legislators | None |
| Political opponents | Drug companies | MFB<br>AFBF<br>Agribusiness companies |
| Framing process | Failed | Successful |
| Free-rider problem | No | No |
| Outcome | Mixed | Lost |

* Acronyms for groups in the biotech campaign are Center for Science in the Public Interest (CSPI), Humane Farming Association (HFA), Foundation on Economic Trends (FET), Consumers Union (CU), Rural Vermont (RV), and Natural Resources Defense Council (NRDC), Humane Society of the United States (HSUS), Friends of the Earth (FOE), and the National Wildlife Federation, (NWF). Acronyms for groups in the animal rights campaign are Coalition to End Animal Suffering in Experiments (CEASE), HSUS, Farm Animal Reform Movement (FARM), HFA, People for the Ethical Treatment of Animals, (PETA), Massachusettes Society for the Prevention of Cruelty to Animals (MSPCA), American Society for the Prevention of Cruelty to Animals (ASPCA), United Farm Workers, Massachusettes Farm Bureau (MFB), and the American Farm Bureau Federation (AFBF). Acronyms for groups in the Big Green campaign are NRDC, Sierra Club (SC), National Toxics Campaign (NTC), and the California League of Conservation Voters (CLOC), California

| Big Green | Secondhand Smoke | Endangered Species |
|---|---|---|
| Campaign California | Coalition for Healthy Californians | Grassroots ESA Coalition |
| NRDC<br>Sierra Club<br>NTC<br>Pesticide Watch<br>CLOC | ACS<br>AHA<br>ALA<br>CNA<br>CAH<br>ANR<br>SC<br>PCL | ALRA<br>NWI<br>CGN<br>SOR<br>APC<br>WMC<br>UFWDA |
| Hollywood celebrities | PTA<br>CWF | AFBF<br>ESCC<br>NESAR |
| California Legislature<br>  State Democratic<br>  Party | California Legislature<br>Governor, City &<br>county councils | Rural & western con-<br>gressional leaders |
| Chemical industry<br>CFB<br>CCC<br>Timber companies | Philip Morris | Endangered Species Coalition |
| Failed | Successful | Failed |
| Yes | Yes | Yes |
| Lost | Won | Mixed |

Farm Bureau (CFB), and the California Chamber of Commerce (CCC). Acronyms for groups in the ETS campaign are American Cancer Society (ACS), American Heart Association (AHA), the American Lung Association (ALA), California Nurses Association (CNA), California Association of Hospitals (CAH), Americans for Nonsmokers' Rights (ANR), SC, the Planning and Conservation League (PCL), Parent-Teachers Association (PTA), and California Wellness Foundation (CWF). Acronyms for the secondhand smoke campaign are the Grassroots Endangered Species Act (ESA Coalition), American Land Rights Association (ALRA), National Wilderness Institute (NWI), Committee for a Great Northwest (CGN), Stewards of the Range (SOR), American Policy Center (APC), Women's Mining Coalition (WMC), United Four-Wheel Drive Association (UFWDA), AFBF, Endangered Species Coordination Council (ESCC), and the National Endangered Species Act Reform Coalition (NESARC).

**NOTES**

1. An interest group is a number of people who have commonly shared goals and attempt to influence government policy. Interests and interest groups are different. Interests are more all embracing, involving people who share an occupation, class, ethnicity, language, or religion. By contrast, an interest group is organized and committed to influencing public policy. Interest groups include trade unions, professional and trade associations, environmental groups, corporations, and universities. Some interest groups, such as the American Legion and National Education Association, have memberships, and others, such as General Motors and public interest law firms, do not. When interest groups seek to influence government policy makers, it is called lobbying.

2. Talcott Parsons (1978:320–21) uses the term *expressive revolution* to describe a countercultural movement that challenges the rationalistic and utilitarian individualism of American industrial society. He describes it as a form of civil religion or collective solidarity that is part of the original Puritan ideal and that seeks to transform modern society. The expressive revolution is manifested as a rebellion against the Watergate scandal and other excesses of the Nixon administration, which Parsons believes are symbolic of the self-interested individualistic corruption of modern society.

3. Berry (1993:31) notes that although the most successful expressive groups—environmental and consumer protection—were formed during the anti–Vietnam War and civil rights movements, they were not protest oriented.

4. Among the controversies mentioned frequently was the spraying of apples with the chemical Alar in the 1980s. However, because this campaign has already been researched extensively, I did not include it.

# TWO

# THE ANTIBIOTECHNOLOGY CAMPAIGN

Farmers, Food Safety Groups, and Drug Companies

## The Antibiotechnology Movement

Since the 1970s the food safety and animal rights movements have campaigned against biotechnology. The term *biotechnology* is a catchall phrase that includes older biological knowledge based on the structure, functioning, and development of plants and animals in their ecological setting.[1] This includes the traditional breeding techniques for producing racehorses, fruit and vegetable varieties, and pedigreed dogs. However, these techniques are limited in the range and speed of genetic combinations. Newer biotechnologies are based on genetics and cellular and subcellular processes and make possible genetic combinations that could never have occurred naturally.

Genetic engineering can be loosely described as taking genes from one organism and inserting them in the genetic material of another organism. A gene is a series of lengths of deoxyribonucleic acid (DNA) that carries the code for a sequence of amino acids that make up a protein. DNA is the hereditary molecule in all living organisms. Microgenetic engineering has made possible what is called "transgenic manipulation," which means that totally unrelated species that cannot interbreed now can share each other's genetic composition.

As a result, genetic engineers have created viruses that are hybrids of two different viruses. Supertoxic bacteria have been created to replace chemical pesticides, make plants poisonous to insect pests, and prevent crops from freezing. Genetic material has been used in transgenic manipulation so that sheep can produce human proteins in their milk and pigs possess the genes for human growth hormone.

The commercial application of genetic engineering is enormous. For example, the gene for making the human insulin protein has been produced artificially in laboratories instead of taking insulin from pig or cow pancreases. Genetic engineering is also used to increase the productivity of crops and livestock. Crops have been engineered to retard spoilage, and fruit trees and vegetable plants have been made resistant to pesticides, pests, and herbicides. Large corporations such as Calgene and Monsanto have developed genetically engineered food plants such as the "super tomato," which does not rot.

The antibiotechnology movement has mounted campaigns against genetic engineering on three grounds: social and economic issues, bioethical concerns, and consumer health risks. The social and economic issues raised by technology include who is to benefit and whether consumers are being excluded. Competitive pressure to adopt biotechnology may benefit large corporate farmers but force small family farmers out of business. The monopoly structure of agribusiness may not necessarily lower consumer prices.

Bioethical concerns are reflected in the term *new creationism*. This refers to a subtle and dangerous attitude toward genetic engineering. It may not be safe to impose on nature a technocratic attitude toward biological systems. Rising technocracy in society values economic determinism, scientific imperialism, and secular humanism. This may be turning the natural world into an "industrialized wasteland" and food animals into biomachines (Fox 1990:92). The new creationism replaces God with humans who use the tools of molecular biology. The biotechnologists "create" improved animals and plants with an eye on short-term human benefits instead of letting animals and plants evolve naturally for thousands of years. This fosters a mechanistic view of animals and nature. The ethical question this raises is whether citizens should allow the natural world to be remade in the image of industrial efficiency and productivity. Alternatively, should we preserve the beauty, harmony, and diversity of the natural world?

Consumer fears of biotechnology are based on the risks that may be posed by new, genetically novel foods. For example, genetically engineered organisms released in the environment may be hazardous. If they are dangerous, controlling or eradicating these organisms may not be possible. Environmental risks include those posed by chemicals and toxic substances or dangerous bacteria or viruses.

Antibiotechnology activists campaign to strengthen government regulation of genetic engineering. In 1983, for example, Jeremy Rifkin, the director of the Foundation on Economic Trends (FET), sued the National Institutes of Health after it approved a University of California decision to release mutant bacteria. The bacteria were released into the environment without an environmental assessment or environmental impact statement, as required by the National Environmental Policy Act. However, Congress has never legislatively addressed the risks of genetic engineering. Many genetically engineered plants, animals, and microbes are not monitored or regulated.

## The Food Industry's Position on Biotechnology

Executives in the food industry believe that biotechnology will revolutionize agriculture in the twenty-first century. Although more than ninety companies are involved in biotechnology research, five major pharmaceutical companies—Monsanto, Elanco (a merger of Dow and Eli Lilly), Upjohn, American Cyanamid, and Pitman-Moore—have taken the lead. In 1987 these five companies formed a biotechnology task force within the Animal Health Institute (AHI), a trade association, to develop strategies to prevent political barriers from blocking the development and approval of products based on genetic engineering (AHI 1993).

AHI represents approximately 80 percent of all U.S. manufacturers of animal health products, including veterinary pharmaceuticals and biological products such as vaccines, serums, and feed additives. These companies are responsible for the bulk of the investment and basic research in biotechnology. Monsanto is the leading biotech company, with an estimated $1 billion invested as of 1990. Monsanto's objective is to be the leading biotech corporation in the world (AHI 1993).

Biotechnology is the third wave of technology, after the mechanical revolution of the nineteenth century and the petrochemical revolution that began in the 1940s and reached its zenith during the 1970s (Lasley and Bultena 1986). The mechanical revolution transformed agriculture by replacing human labor and animal power with the steam engine and tractors. In the petrochemical revolution chemical fertilizers such as nitrogen were introduced and insecticides and herbicides were developed. The third wave involves altering the genetic codes of plants and animals to increase production by enabling crops to grow in such harsh environments as cold snaps, prolonged heat, drought, and poor soil. Genetic engineering can also change the genetic material of crops and livestock to protect them from pests and disease and to increase production.

The agricultural industry acknowledges that biotechnology is in its infancy. However, the expectations for it are great. It is said to be the key scientific tool for feeding the global population, projected to double to ten billion people by the year 2030. Biotechnology can increase agricultural productivity by making food crops resistant to certain viral diseases that cause crop damage in the millions of dollars each year and that cannot be treated effectively with chemicals or any other means. Crops can also be made resistant to ravaging insects such as bollworm and tomato horn-worm. One example of how genetic engineering can increase agricultural productivity is the "super spud." Scientists have succeeded in altering a gene in potatoes to make them resistant to bacterial ring rot and soft rot diseases that cause millions of dollars in potato crop losses annually. By crossing the potato seed with an enzyme found in chicken eggs, they block the softening gene in the potato, thereby making it resistant to the disease.

The industry argues that genetic changes in crops will enable farmers to reduce both the amount of insecticide they use and their production costs. Genetic engineering can also increase crop tolerance of herbicides, which will enable farmers to apply them after a crop has emerged instead of using a blanket application shortly after planting, thereby reducing overall her-bicide use. Gene alteration in plants has a great variety of additional uses, such as controlling fungal diseases, providing resistance to drought, and even enhancing taste (Wheale and McNally 1990:3).

The potential for dramatic increases in productivity is also great in animal biotechnology. For example, most bulls used for semen production are produced through artificial insemination and embryo transfer. As a result, one cow can produce six bulls in a single year, whereas a cow left to breed naturally might never produce a bull. Selling embryos has increased farm-ers' income. Since 1972 embryo transfer has become a multimillion-dollar business, achieving roughly 100,000 pregnancies per year in the United States alone (National Association of Animal Breeders, 1986).

The most controversial recent development in animal biotechnology has been the mass production of animal growth hormones, which can increase milk and meat production. In the early 1980s the two growth hor-mones most likely to be approved for commercial marketing by the U.S. Food and Drug Administration (FDA) were bovine somatotropin (BST) and porcine somatotropin (PST). Somatotropin, the master hormone reg-ulating growth, occurs naturally in the pituitary gland of all mammals. Somatotropin is produced in a laboratory in much the same way that insulin is made (Deakin 1990:65).[2]

Dairy cows injected with supplemental BST increase their average milk output by as much as 15 to 20 percent. Pigs given supplemental PST yield 10 to 20 percent more lean meat. In 1985, when the FDA approved the commercial sale of milk and pork produced from the test animals receiving supplemental somatotropin, the milk was expected be the first biotechnological product to be widely commercially marketed (as opposed to treating a disease or ailment). Two years later the five drug companies that formed a biotechnology task force within AHI also formed the BST Working Group to develop a strategy to persuade the FDA to approve BST for commercial use.[3] (Only four companies were developing BST for commercial use—Monsanto, Elanco, Upjohn, and American Cyanamid [AHI 1993]).

According to the Office of Agricultural Biotechnology of the U.S. Department of Agriculture (USDA), the biotechnology revolution eventually will affect all aspects of American agriculture. The growth in U.S. agricultural productivity has averaged 2.5 percent a year since 1947. The continued growth in productivity depends upon the adoption of the new technology. However, since environmental concerns preclude continued reliance on agrochemicals, the use of biotechnology will be necessary to sustain these historical growth rates (Young 1990:264).

But food safety groups say using this technology has unacceptable social and economic costs. They say it has transformed American agriculture from family-oriented farms to highly centralized and vertically integrated producers controlled by a handful of large agribusiness corporations. According to the Office of Technology Assessment (OTA) (1986, 1990, 1992), technological change will cause the number of U.S. farms to drop from 2.2 million to 1.2 million by the year 2000. The technology office predicted that of the remaining farms, only about fifty thousand will account for approximately 75 percent of total production. Much of this change is directly attributable to biotechnological innovations, according to the technology office.

## The Antibiotechnology Campaign

The principal expressive interest groups in the antibiotechnology campaign were the Foundation on Economic Trends, the Humane Farming Association, Rural Vermont, and the Center for Science in the Public Interest. Social movement organizations (SMOs) supporting the campaign were the Consumers Union and the Natural Resources Defense Council. Nonmovement allies included small dairy farmers, the Humane Society of the United States, Friends of the Earth, and the National Wildlife Federation. Political allies in the campaign were the Wisconsin and Minnesota legislatures and congressional leaders from farm states. Arrayed against them were the large drug companies. The outcome of the campaign was a mixed victory for the expressive groups.

### The Campaign Against BST/BGH

Political opposition to biotechnology in general, and to BST in particular, emerged within the food safety, animal rights, and environmental movement in the United States in 1990. These organizations singled out BST for an all-out campaign, calling it bovine growth hormone (BGH) instead of bovine somatotropin to emphasize that it is an artificial biotechnological product. Food safety SMOs saw the drug as a beachhead for a general war against biotechnology because it is used to increase milk production, not to treat disease. SMOs believed that blocking its adoption by the FDA was essential because it was the first in a generation of genetically engineered drugs for commercial use.

The campaign against BST became a mission against biotechnology. Expressive groups took the position that genetic engineering poses inherent risks to health and therefore must be stopped or regulated out of existence. They argued that genetic engineering could change harmless substances into deadly organisms. They gave the splicing of human growth hormone into other species as an example of the unpredictable nature of this process. Such splicing produces giant mice but skinny cross-eyed pigs with arthritis and no increase in size (Vermont Biotechnology Working Group 1991:15).

One of the expressive groups opposed to BST, Rural Vermont, used its "Real Food Campaign" to mobilize public opinion, claiming that "genetic engineering is coming toward your table courtesy of food industry giants and chemical corporations—with virtually no oversight by the government" (Rural Vermont 1993:20). One eye-catching item in that winter 1993 issue of the newsletter *Rural Vermont Report* featured a mock menu that illustrated the nature of the attack on biotechnology (see figure 2.1). The menu was reprinted from the December 1991 issue of *Gene Exchange*, published by the National Biotechnology Policy Center of the National Wildlife Federation.

---

## MENU

### Appetizer

Potatoes with waxmoth genes
Tomato juice with flounder genes

### Entree

Fresh catfish with trout or virus genes
Scalloped potatoes with chicken and bacteria genes
Cornbread with firefly genes

### Dessert

Rice pudding with pea genes
Cantaloupe with virus genes and apples with bacteria

---

**FIGURE 2.1 Menu of Transgenic Foods**
Federal permits have been granted or are pending for all items on the menu.
SOURCE, GENE EXCHANGE, DECEMBER 1991.

Rural Vermont says that the "first wave" of genetic engineering has social, religious, and environmental implications that have not been examined (Rural Vermont 1993). The organization argues that genetically altered foods threaten the safety of the U.S. food supply and that the only beneficiaries are a handful of chemical companies and large food processors. Rural Vermont lists a number of risks it claims are associated with altered foods, including allergic reactions and the addition of contaminants or toxic agents to food. What will happen when wheat genes are added to potatoes, which are then eaten by consumers allergic to wheat and unaware of the potatoes' genetic engineering? The organization also is concerned about the presence in food of genes that are resistant to antibiotics. Rural Vermont further criticizes genetically altered food as being tasteless and less nutritious and argues that the technology violates religious and cultural traditions. For example, a tomato could contain pig genes, obviously a problem for Jews who keep kosher, especially if the tomatoes are not labeled.

Rural Vermont proposed that the FDA declare a moratorium on the sale of all transgenic (altered) plants and animals. According to Rural Vermont, the foods should be independently tested to the satisfaction of consumer groups, and all genetically engineered food should be labeled as such. The organization believes that the FDA should not treat genetically altered food in the same way that it regards common foods and food additives such as salt. If the FDA grants such products the status of being "generally recognized as safe," they can be marketed commercially without special testing for food safety (Doyle 1985:153, 502).

That was why Rural Vermont and SMOs opposed the FDA's policies regarding BST, singling out two FDA policies in particular: confidentiality and the sale of experimental food. Under the rules of confidentiality the FDA treats as confidential all information supplied by a company seeking approval for a new drug. This includes the location of field tests being conducted on animals and the results of drug safety tests.

The SMOs take the position that all test information about new drugs should be made public so that consumers can evaluate the drugs' safety for humans and food animals. According to FDA policy, such information is not publicly available. Food safety SMOs also say that before the FDA approves the sale of food that comes from animals being tested with a new drug, it should make public the data that demonstrate the food is safe for human consumption. The FDA allows certain food produced from test animals to be sold for human consumption after an initial battery of tests has found the food to be safe. For example, the FDA allowed the drug companies to sell milk from BST-treated cows, after BST had been tested for several years, although the drug did not meet the other requirements of the FDA, including the safety of the animals, until 1993 (Grassie interview 1998).

In the case of both BST and its porcine counterpart, PST, the FDA found no detectable difference in milk and meat from low-tech cows and pigs and BST-supplemented cows and PST-treated pigs (U.S. Food and Drug Administration [USFDA] 1993:73–74). Indeed, in the campaign against BST, SMOs exaggerated the drug's risks to human safety to gain maximum public support for their political campaign. At joint hearings of the U.S. Department of Health and Human Services's Food Advisory Committee and the FDA's Veterinary Medicine Advisory Committee in 1993, the former director of the veterinary committee, Gerald B. Guest, explained the confusion created by SMOs opposed to BST.

Guest said that one reason that BST had become one of the most highly publicized new animal drugs was the use of the words *hormones* and *biotechnology* to describe the drug and the social and economic implications of using it (USFDA 1993:73–74). He said that much of the controversy surrounding BST was related to its economic consequences for small-scale dairy farmers, which were beyond the authority of the FDA to consider. He underscored the scientific consensus that the milk produced by BST-supplemented cows is "indistinguishable from milk of non-treated cows" (USFDA 1993:59). Neither the milk nor meat from BST-treated cows was genetically altered in any way, and the animals' digestive tracts broke down the BST, rendering it inactive and harmless to humans who eat BST-supplemented beef, Guest said.

The evidence for this was research conducted during the 1950s in which BST was injected into children with dwarfism. BST had no effect on the children (USFDA 1993:72). Also, studies of rats show that when they are injected with BST, it stimulates growth, but when they are fed BST, it has no effect, no matter how much they receive (USFDA 1993:72). An SMO, the Consumers Union, questioned this research in a letter to the Food and Drug Administration, arguing that the research on rats' reaction to being fed BST was flawed because of the size of test groups and the levels of dosage (Hansen and Halloran 1993).

*Scientific Challenge to BST*

The only credible scientific challenge to BST came in a study by the U.S. General Accounting Office (USGAO 1992d) requested by members of Congress at the urging of SMOs opposed to BST. The study repeated the FDA's finding of a statistically significant increase in the incidence of mastitis (swelling of a cow's udder, the most common disease in dairy cows) in animals treated with BST. From this observation the GAO argued that BST posed an indirect threat to human health.

The GAO report reasoned that milk would contain elevated levels of antibiotic residues if farmers used more antibiotics to treat the higher incidence of mastitis in cows. The GAO and the SMOs argued that the Food and Drug Administration was underestimating the incidence of mastitis resulting from BST. They claimed that serious health hazards are connected with the unregulated and unmonitored use of antibiotics by farmers in treating the disease (Consumers Union 1993a; Center for Science 1990). The GAO is a congressional agency that is supposed to be a nonpartisan watchdog. But the story of its involvement in the BST controversy is fraught with politics.

The chair of the House Human Resources and Intergovernmental Relations Subcommittee was Ted Weiss, a liberal Democrat from New York, a major dairy state. Weiss's district encompassed the most liberal reform-minded neighborhoods in New York, including Greenwich Village and the Upper West Side (Dao 1992). He worked closely with SMOs in seeking to ensure the safety of food additives. Under Weiss's leadership the number of formal inquiries or investigations of the FDA's drug approval process tripled during the 1980s. He also used the GAO (which does not have expertise in animal drug research) to challenge the FDA's credibility. Indeed, in 1994 the GAO had at least thirty-five ongoing investigations of the FDA.[4]

Under Weiss's leadership the subcommittee's work on food safety issues focused on the levels of antibiotic residues in milk (Zeller 1993:1609). The committee turned to milk as the key food safety issue after a 1989 *Wall Street Journal* report on the results of two surveys of animal drug residues in milk (Ingersall 1989). The surveys were sponsored by the *Journal* and an antibiotechnology expressive group, the Center for Science in the Public Interest (CSPI). The CSPI is an SMO founded in 1971 with a membership of about 200,000 and a nutrition newsletter circulated to members. In response to the report, which found antibiotic residues in milk, Weiss asked the FDA to reassess the adequacy of the FDA's studies of antibiotic drug residues in milk, which were carried out in 1988 and 1990 and found that antibiotic residues were not a problem (USGAO 1990:1).

Because of milk's role as a nurturer of infants and children, expressive groups and SMOs targeted milk purity and especially BST for a political campaign against biotechnology. Weiss's subcommittee repeatedly asserted that the FDA was unable to ensure the safety of the milk supply. The committee took the position that the FDA could not guarantee that milk was free of dangerously high levels of antibiotic residues and claimed that such residues could produce allergic reactions and illness in humans. The committee reasoned that, given FDA drug approval procedures, the agency essentially approves drugs based upon a manufacturer's recommendations. The people making a new drug are naturally going to claim that it is safe, which may or may not be the case. Thus having new drug technology approved by the FDA is like having the fox watch the henhouse.

This theme was repeated time and again in congressional hearings and in a series of GAO reports requested by Weiss's subcommittee. The message from the subcommittee and the GAO to the public was that the country's milk supply might not be safe and that the FDA was responsible for this intolerable situation. This charge against the FDA is an article of faith among expressive groups and SMOs and was widely publicized in their campaign to mobilize citizen protest against FDA approval of BST.

### The Antibiotic Health Threat

In 1985 Weiss's subcommittee had issued a report that argued that "as many as 90 percent or more of the 20,000 to 30,000 new animal drugs estimated to be on the market have not been approved by the FDA as safe and effective and are therefore being used in violation of the Food, Drug and Cosmetic Act" (U.S. House 1985). The report went on to claim that as many as four thousand of these new animal drugs could have adverse health effects on humans and animals.

The basis of GAO's criticism of the FDA five years later was that, although as many as two hundred antibiotic drugs are given to dairy cows to treat infection, milk-testing technology enables the FDA and state agencies to test milk for only about twelve. Furthermore, because most of these drugs are not officially approved by the FDA for the treatment of cows, no one knows the safe tolerance levels for human consumption of milk with these drug residues (USGAO 1992d:6).

For economic reasons the drug companies cannot afford to test and gain FDA approval for drugs specifically earmarked for all six hundred animal species. Because of this since 1984 the FDA has tolerated the use of drugs for animals for whom the drugs are not specifically authorized. This is called the "extra-label" use of drugs for animals.

Weiss's subcommittee, the GAO, and SMOs strongly opposed the FDA's policy of allowing the extra-label use of drugs when few drugs are officially authorized for the treatment of disease in food animals. For example, hardly any therapeutic drugs are approved for the treatment of sheep, goats, and fish. In fact, a huge gap exists between drugs required for good veterinary medical practice and the drugs that the FDA has approved for use. Furthermore, the research on new animal drugs has dropped dramatically since the late 1980s because of the high cost of developing new drugs for small species and the long cumbersome FDA approval process, which can take ten years or longer. SMOs' influence on the FDA may have lengthened the drug approval process (AHI 1992).

In 1990, at the request of the Weiss committee, the GAO also challenged the safety of the nation's milk supply, arguing that the FDA had failed to provide leadership in this crucial area (USGAO 1990:1). This was the GAO report that cited the study involving two surveys of test samples, one conducted by Dr. Stanley Katz of Rutgers University on fifty retail milk samples from ten major cities for the *Wall Street Journal* in 1989, and one by the expressive group CSPI of twenty retail milk samples from the Washington, D.C. area; the GAO report supported the contention of Katz and CSPI that drugs were contaminating the milk supply. Katz found the presence of sulfamethazine, an antibiotic, in 22 percent of the samples. The FDA sought to replicate Katz's findings by using the same sample size and retail origin of samples. The FDA conducted the same tests and cross-checked the results with additional tests. But the FDA's replication found no drug contamination of the milk supply, and the agency therefore questioned the validity of the Katz and CSPI studies on the ground that the small amounts of drug residue in milk pose no serious health hazard (USGAO 1992b:15–16).

However, the FDA's response to the GAO report was not presented in the report. According to a source on the Senate staff, the GAO intentionally did not ask the FDA for written comments on the report. If the GAO had asked for comments, it would have been obliged to print the FDA's rebuttal. The practice of denying the FDA the opportunity to answer GAO criticism was part of a tactic of censorship by omission. The strategy of publicly criticizing the FDA without giving it the opportunity to respond in a public forum served the purpose of undermining the credibility of the agency. The FDA was also not allowed to submit written comments for inclusion in the three 1992 GAO reports questioning the FDA's ability to guarantee a safe milk supply and recommending against the approval of BST. The GAO repudiated the findings of three FDA studies on milk residues carried out between 1988 and 1990, in response to the media reports of contaminated milk, on the ground that they were incomplete, the Senate staff member said.

The FDA concluded on the basis of the three surveys—the Katz and CSPI surveys as well as FDA's attempt to replicate their findings—that the antibiotic residues it found in milk samples were within heath safety guidelines and that the U.S. milk supply was in fact safe. But the GAO criticized the FDA's findings, saying they were incomplete because the FDA's testing methods were inadequate. The GAO went on to say that new tests for all antibiotics in milk were necessary before anyone could rule on the safety of the milk supply. In other words, the GAO was arguing for absolute guarantees of milk safety.

In January 1992 the GAO issued another report (USGAO 1992a) that reiterated the thesis advanced in the 1985 Weiss subcommittee report (U.S. House 1985) and the 1990 GAO study: that the FDA was incapable of protecting public health from harmful animal drugs such as antibiotics in milk. The GAO said that recently hired FDA officials were not adequately trained nor did they have the time and resources to protect the public from potentially fraudulent data on new test drugs, including BST, submitted to the FDA by the companies developing the drugs (USGAO 1992b:12). The implication of this study was that the FDA was biased toward its principal clientele, the drug companies, and therefore could not adequately serve the public interest. The FDA strongly disagreed with the GAO's contention, however, saying that its procedures were adequate to vouchsafe the accuracy of drug trial data submitted by the drug companies.

The GAO released three more reports in August 1992 (USGAO 1992b, 1992c, 1992d). On August 5, at the request of the Weiss subcommittee, the GAO published a follow-up to the 1990 study on antibiotics in the milk supply (USGAO 1992b). On the same day the agency published a separate report containing the testimony of the director of the larger GAO study (USGAO 1992c). The thrust of these two reports was to restate the thesis elaborated by the Weiss subcommittee, the GAO, and SMOs. They repeated the claims made by Katz and CSPI, that the country's milk supply might be contaminated by antibiotic residues. The GAO also argued that the FDA had failed to provide leadership in examining the safety of the nation's food supply (USGAO 1992c:15–16).

However, the reports acknowledged that in the two years since the GAO's first critical report, the FDA had improved its monitoring and testing of the country's milk supply. For example, beginning in January 1992 the FDA sampled all milk tank trucks and tested their raw milk for beta-lactam drugs (a class of antibiotics that includes beta-lactamase drugs such as sulfanamides and tetracyclines) as the trucks entered dairy plants (USGAO 1992b:23–24). The FDA also was requiring the milk industry to test for other drugs when there was reason for concern about their residues. The GAO concluded that the FDA still had not done enough to guarantee the safety of the country's milk supply. The FDA agreed to expand its milk testing and monitoring programs within the resources granted by Congress. However, the FDA firmly maintained that the U.S. milk supply was safe (USFDA 1990:23).

On August 6 the GAO released its third report, a study of BST (USGAO 1992d:1–2). The agency said it had studied the substance for two reasons: that "a number of individuals and groups" were opposed to BST in the belief that the genetically engineered product was a threat to human health and that it constituted a danger to animal health. The GAO recommended that approval of BST be withheld because of concern about the safety of the country's milk supply and the possibility of its contamination by antibiotic residues.

Increased milk production in cows resulting from the use of BST was said to lead to increased incidence of mastitis and this, in turn, would lead to higher levels of antibiotic residues in milk and meat from dairy cows. And, consistent with past GAO-FDA confrontations over the milk safety issue, the FDA disagreed with the conclusion of the report on the ground that BST did not constitute a threat to human food safety. The FDA continued to maintain that the higher incidence of mastitis was manageable and that the FDA and the states adequately tested and monitored the safety of the country's milk supply.

What is significant about the scientific debate about the FDA's approval of BST is that it is unrelated to the issue of biotechnology and hormones that expressive groups emphasized in their campaign against the drug. Hormones are a normal component of milk, which includes protein. In fact, milk has thirty known hormones, including the vitamin D that is added to it. Furthermore, the milk produced by BST-treated cows is not a biotechnology product. Although BST itself is produced through biotechnology, the milk from these cows is not a genetically altered food.

### Nonmovement Allies

A key factor in the campaign against BST was the role of small-scale dairy farmers and their political representatives in the effort to block FDA's approval of the drug. They sought to do this by adding a fourth hurdle to the FDA's traditional scientific drug approval process.[5] The fourth hurdle was a social needs test, that is to say, a marketplace test of economic demand and social and cultural acceptance of a new drug. According to this reasoning, if consumers or producers object to a new biotech product for reasons of employment, fashion, habit, religious or cultural preference, or special interest opposition, the technology should not be developed. Although how to carry out such a test is undefined, it includes a wide range of social, cultural, and economic factors that tend to displace the established scientific procedures of the FDA.

But under Section 512 of the Federal Food, Drug, and Cosmetic Act, which is the enabling legislation for the FDA that took effect in 1969, the agency is prohibited from considering the social and economic effects of new drugs (U.S. House 1993b:106–26).

The approval process has two stages. The first is that any company seeking approval of a new drug must submit an Investigational New Animal Drug Application (INAD) to the FDA's Center for Veterinary Medicine. The INAD must outline how the company proposes to test a new drug for food animals such as cattle or poultry. The tests are to be designed to determine the safety of human consumption of animals that have received the drug, the drug's safety for animals, and whether the drug works in the way it is intended.

Once the studies have been completed, the company requests final approval to sell the drug by submitting a New Animal Drug Application. The second application consists of a compilation of investigational studies carried out during the INAD stage of the process (called pivotal studies) that demonstrate the safety of the drug for humans and animals, its effectiveness for the purpose intended, and whether it can be reliably manufactured.

To these traditional scientific criteria members of Congress from dairy states sought to add the fourth criteria, the social and economic effects of the drug on dairy producers. In other words, to gain approval from the FDA for the use of BST drug manufacturers would also have to meet the test for adverse social and economic effects.

The strongest congressional opponent of BST was Senator Russell Feingold, a Wisconsin Democrat elected in 1992. He had become concerned about the adoption of BST in 1986, when he was a state senator. Several small dairy farmers from his district had warned him of the potentially damaging economic consequences the drug would have on them and the state's dairy industry (Stauber interview 1993). His opposition to the drug was based upon the concerns of small-scale dairy farmers (fewer than one hundred dairy cows) about the economic consequences of BST.

Dairy farmers with small herds were already suffering from low milk prices due to surplus production. Greater production through new technology would impose a labor problem on small producers, and the additional milk production could further lower the price of milk. This is a classic case of a small owner-operated business trying to compete with a large retail chain operation. The large diary farms in California and Texas have a thousand or more cows.

The senator gave three reasons for his opposition to the drug (USFDA 1993:100–106). The first was the adverse economic consequences that BST would have for the small- and medium-sized dairy farms that predominate in Wisconsin. He cited a 1988 study by the University of Wisconsin that estimated a decline in the net income of Wisconsin dairy farmers of $100 million annually. The loss of income would force large numbers of dairy farmers out of business.

The second reason was that consumers' fears of BST would reduce their consumption of milk, thereby further depressing prices. In this regard, Feingold argued that, at the very least, if the FDA approved BST, it should also require labeling so that consumers could distinguish between BST- and non-BST–produced milk. Expressive groups favored this approach because it would provide a means of identifying, and boycotting, BST milk. Feingold's third reason was that the increased production of milk resulting from the adoption of BST would increase the already sizable milk surplus. This would cost the federal government millions of dollars in subsidies and add to the country's budget deficit.

Andrew Kimbrell, the chief legal counsel for the Foundation on Economic Trends (FET), an expressive group led by Jeremy Rifkin and supported by a Wisconsin-based consumer, environmental, and dairy farmer group called the Coalition for Responsible Technology, reinforced Feingold's theme of preserving the small family dairy farmer at an FDA hearing in 1993 (Stauber interview 1993). The coalition included the Wisconsin Farm Unity Alliance, Wisconsin Farmland Conservancy, Wisconsin Democratic Party, and the National Family Farm Coalition's Dairy Committee. The National Family Farm Coalition is comprised of more than forty grassroots farm and rural organizations in thirty states with a combined membership of more than two hundred thousand (U.S. House 1990:794).

Kimbrell said that there were social and cultural reasons to oppose the drug. He noted that two states, Minnesota and Wisconsin, had approved moratoriums on the use of BST because people in those two important dairy states did not wish to destroy the "cultural icon of America"—the small family farmer (USFDA 1993:137–41). Rep. Bernard Sanders, an independent from Vermont who was also an outspoken opponent of BST, argued that BST would be an "economic disaster" for dairy farmers (USFDA 1993:106).

The Humane Society of the United States (HSUS), an animal welfare SMO, also opposed BST, saying it threatened animal welfare. Michael W. Fox, an HSUS vice president, argued that the decision to approve BST should not be judged solely on the basis of science. Social, economic, environmental, and animal welfare considerations must also be considered, he said. Fox compared the FDA's "science-based view of reality" to a "flat-earth world view." He said that the consuming public had the right to determine what farmers produced and, indeed, should control the entire food production system.

Second, Fox argued that the FDA should back farmers who opposed the use of BST. He said that this was consistent with backing farmers who practiced "humane sustainable animal husbandry including low-input and organic methods."[6] In this connection, Fox highlighted the results of a 1987 survey of 270 Wisconsin dairy farmers carried out by the University of Wisconsin. He noted that only 11 percent of those surveyed approved BST, whereas 56 percent opposed it (Fox 1992:65). The third point was that cows given BST would also be given high energy feed, which lessens natural forage production and consumption by cows. According to Fox, this is a big step backward in terms of sustainable agriculture (ecological farming that includes crop rotation [USFDA 1993:257]).

Fox also repeated Rural Vermont's unsubstantiated claims of stillborn deaths and deformity in calves from cows treated with BST. He also argued that because of the high cost of genetic engineering, designing "factory farms" to serve the animals' welfare would be costly. However, in the case of BST, there is virtually no additional outlay required in terms of equipment or capital aside from the drug itself.

Michael Hansen, who represented the Consumers Union, a food safety SMO, summed up the fourth hurdle that expressive groups, SMOs, and nonmovement allies sought to use to block FDA approval of BST (Consumers Union 1993b:9–10). Hansen said consumers wished to avoid BST-treated milk for philosophical, ethical, or moral reasons. Some wished to avoid it because the injections of the drug led to increased disease, which constitutes cruelty to animals. Some wished to avoid it because of the socioeconomic effect it would have on small farmers. Still others wished to avoid BST milk because it would add to the already sizable surplus production of milk and would therefore add hundreds of millions of dollars to the cost of the USDA price support program for milk.

## The Expressive Group Campaign

The principal expressive interest groups in the antibiotech campaign were the FET, CSPI, and Humane Farming Association (HFA), an animal rights organization based in California. SMOs supporting the campaign were the Consumers Union, Rural Vermont, Natural Resources Defense Council, Friends of the Earth, National Wildlife Federation, and HSUS. Nonmovement allies were small dairy farmers and milk cooperatives in Wisconsin, Minnesota, and Vermont. The political allies in the campaign were farm state congressional leaders and the Wisconsin and Minnesota legislatures. The principal political opponents of the campaign were the drug companies. The outcome of the campaign was a mixed victory for the expressive groups.

Opposition to BST initially began in 1986 with protest action by small-scale dairy farmers against depressed milk prices and the failure of the government to provide them with economic relief. Indeed, the leaders of the movement were dairy farmers. As this populist movement gained strength, particularly in Wisconsin, Minnesota, and Vermont, the scope of the protest expanded to include BST. However, the overarching concern of the movement was with the economic effects that the drug, which increases milk production, would have upon small-scale dairy farmers. Indeed, as late as 1990, when the state legislatures of Wisconsin and Minnesota established moratoriums on the commercial use of BST, the objective of the movement was to protect the precarious economic status of dairy farmers in those states. At this point, BST was an economic issue.

Only after the state moratoriums against BST were adopted did major expressive groups become involved. After 1990 the BST issue became one of food safety and animal rights, which expressive groups hoped would capture national attention and advance their political agendas. The issue that united the farmers and expressive groups was their opposition to genetically engineered food and cruelty to farm animals. Because consumers had strong concerns about the purity of milk, and the Weiss subcommittee was already campaigning against the FDA's alleged failure to guarantee the safety of milk, BST was an ideal political issue.

Although campaigns were conducted in several states (especially Vermont and Minnesota), the political opposition to BST in Wisconsin was the key to its becoming a national political issue. Other dairy states had long looked to Wisconsin, which was the top dairy state in the country at the time, for leadership. Indeed, Minnesota's moratorium on BST was triggered by the Wisconsin decision. In April 1990 the Minnesota legislature passed a one-year moratorium on the use of BST on the condition that Wisconsin enact a similar ban. However, of even greater significance was the role played by then–state senator Feingold in the political campaign against BST in Wisconsin and later in the U.S. Senate.

The campaign against BST followed the pattern outlined by Shabecoff (1993:233). He notes that although legal and congressional victories by national consumer safety groups benefit their local and state counterparts, the political activities of national groups have little immediate relevance to state organizations. This was the case with the expressive group campaign against BST. The anti-BST campaigns were initiated by state political organizations in Wisconsin, Minnesota, Vermont, New York, and California. Each organization was different, and each campaign was based on the unique characteristics of each state's politics, including public opinion, the timing of elections, and political leadership.

For example, in the case of Wisconsin, the predominance of small-scale dairy farming, Feingold's bid for the U.S. Senate as the BST issue was heating up, the state's tradition of populism, and Governor Tommy Thompson's run for reelection in 1990 all played a role in the political strategy to defeat BST. Indeed, Feingold was a pivotal figure in the effort to defeat the drug in Wisconsin.

Beginning in 1986, the state senator met regularly with representatives of a loose coalition of small-scale dairy farmers in his district as well as representatives of consumer and environmental groups. These groups had gathered under an umbrella organization called the Coalition for Responsible Technology. Their chief task was to coordinate opposition to the approval of BST in Wisconsin. The coalition's leadership included John Kinsman, the founder of the Wisconsin Family Farm Defense Fund; Glenn Stoddard, legislative director of the Wisconsin Farmers Union; and John Stauber, a consultant and later the coordinator of Jeremy Rifkin's expressive group, FET. The coalition also included representatives of the Wisconsin Rural Development Center; Northern Thunder, an environmental organization; a farm lobby called Agricultural Price, Inc.; the Madison Institute (the food research and policy center at the University of Wisconsin); the Department of Rural Sociology at the University of Wisconsin; Lea Zeldin of Health Writers; and dairy farmers.

According to Stauber, members of the coalition met every month with Feingold to develop a strategy to defeat BST in Wisconsin. This included mobilizing members of their organizations and voters to write and call state representatives who supported the sale of BST in Wisconsin (Stauber interview 1993). Feingold took a direct personal interest in the issue and the growing public debate about BST. He was the hub of a network sponsoring legislation to ban BST in Wisconsin, supported by the chair of the Senate Agriculture Committee, state senator Rod Moen, and state representative Barbara Gronemus, chair of the Assembly Agriculture Committee.

Feingold's role in getting the one-year moratorium banning the drug was considerable. His display of independence in championing the interests of small dairy farmers in opposition to the major drug companies, large dairy farming interests such as the Wisconsin Federation of Cooperatives, and major corporate processors such as Kraft aided his campaign for the U.S. Senate eight years later.

The economic plight of small dairy farmers was the focus of Feingold's anti-BST campaign. In a 1991 press release, for example, he said that dairy farmers were receiving only 1978 prices for their milk and that this financial pressure could force four thousand of Wisconsin's thirty-four thousand farmers off the land in that year alone. He said that, given the low prices for milk, rising costs, and surplus production, a moratorium on the sale of BST was one way to help dairy farmers. Feingold continued to press for a moratorium on BST in Congress after his election to the U.S. Senate in 1992.

In June 1993, as a member of the U.S. Senate Agriculture Committee, Feingold insisted on a one-year national moratorium on the sale, marketing, or use of BST through September 1994. He made the moratorium a condition for his vote for President Bill Clinton's budget reconciliation package, which ultimately passed by a one-vote margin when Vice President Al Gore was forced to vote to break a tie in the Senate. In a press release Feingold gave as his reason for his stance the same one he had given for pushing the 1990 moratorium in Wisconsin—"our seven-year-long struggle to protect consumers and dairy farmers from BGH." Feingold added an economic reason: if the administration placed a moratorium on BST, U.S. taxpayers would save $15 million in price supports. He also said that imposing the moratorium would stave off the loss of export markets in Europe. The European Union had imposed a moratorium against BST-supplemented dairy products, which would shut U.S. producers out of European markets.

The congressional budget reconciliation negotiations in August 1993 led to a three-month moratorium on the sale of BST, if and when it was approved by the FDA. Although the SMOs saw this as a defeat, Feingold and his supporters, including dairy-state senators Patrick Leahy (D-Vt.) and Herbert Kohl (D-Wisc.), saw this as a victory—there was hardly any support in Congress for a moratorium on BST. They also felt that three months would be enough time for expressive and dairy groups to sue in U.S. District Court to contest FDA approval of BST and to allow opponents to produce another study of the effects of the drug on dairy cows and milk safety. Opponents hoped that this would mobilize public opposition to BST, according to a Senate staffer.

### Reframing the Campaign Issue

The major expressive groups opposed to BST—FET, HFA, and CSPI—campaigned against BST after the state moratoriums were adopted in 1990. When these groups entered the campaign, the debate shifted from an economic issue at the state level to one of food safety and animal rights.

At that point the campaign ceased to be an issue of concern primarily to dairy farmers and became a battle to prevent the contamination of milk by adding genetically altered hormones to it and the infliction of cruelty to dairy cows. A large number of environmental SMOs also supported the campaign but played a more passive role. These included Friends of Earth, Citizens' Action, National Wildlife Federation, and the Natural Resources Defense Counsel.

The 140,000 dairy farmers in the United States, many of whom had been campaigning against BST approval, were caught in the middle of this battle. On the one hand, they feared that if they did not adopt the new technology, they would not remain competitive. On the other hand, they feared that if they did use BST, the milk safety and animal rights campaign would trigger a consumer backlash against milk. In either event, dairy farmers feared, they would be forced out of business.

The expressive groups coordinated their campaigns only informally. The two most active expressive groups were Rifkin's FET and the HFA. Both groups waged high-profile media campaigns to mobilize citizen protest of the drug. The FET, which has no membership, took the lead in opposing BST by coordinating the national and international campaign against it. Rifkin created the International Coalition Against Bovine Growth Hormone and launched a "Pure Food Campaign" against BST. Rifkin appointed Stauber, a consultant who was allied with the Wisconsin Family Farm Defense Fund, to head the national BST campaign. Stauber had played a key role in engineering the moratorium against BST in Wisconsin in 1990. The Pure Food Campaign was designed to block the commercial development of all genetically engineered food, with initial emphasis on BST, which Rifkin described as the "flagship" biotechnology product.

In 1993 Rifkin claimed that his Pure Food Campaign had mobilized five thousand food professionals against genetically engineered foods, including BST. He said that the public wanted to avoid the addition of artificial hormones to food and wanted organic food. He also said that 2,000 chefs, 1,000 growers, 800 food stores, 300 processors, more than 100 companies—including Gerber Foods, Bristol Myers, Wyeth, and Ross Labs (all of which produce infant formula)—had joined the campaign. Some of the biggest dairy companies, such as Altadena, had also signed pledges not to use BST milk (USFDA 1993:135). Rifkin claimed that the Pure Food Campaign had twenty thousand activists in nine hundred cities who would petition consumers at stores to protest the use of BST milk if the FDA approved the drug (USFDA 1993:135).

Rifkin said that if the FDA approved BST for sale, his organization would conduct a national advertising and telephone campaign against the drug. FET would emphasize the danger that BST posed to human safety and would organize a boycott against the use of the drug among farmers, processors, and retailers. In effect, the strategy involved raising concerns about the safety of BST and then threatening a consumer boycott against any producer or retailer who handled BST-treated milk products. For example, one Rifkin anti-BST ad, which ran in *Time* on May 17, 1993, showed a child with a glass of milk with the caption, "Was there a dose of artificial growth hormone in her milk this morning?"

The HFA also carried out an ad campaign to raise safety concerns about BST. Speaking at the campaign launch in 1991, Bradley Miller, HFA executive director, said that the ads were the opening salvo against genetically engineered hormones in milk (Tesconi 1991:1). One ad ran in the November 18, 1991, issues of *Time* and *U.S. News & World Report*, which then had combined circulations of 6.5 million readers.

The advertisement consisted of a stark black-and-white photograph with a huge needle penetrating the flank of a cow. The copy said that dairy cows "can't say no" and argued that the drug is a genetically engineered growth hormone that forces cows to produce unnaturally high levels of milk. It also said that BST leads to increased disease in cows, which increases the demand for antibiotics supplied by drug companies to treat the disease. It concluded by saying that the agridrug companies were selling hormones that harmed animals and endangered the food supply.

Not only were the expressive groups effective in elevating public concern about BST, but they indirectly sued the industry to prevent the companies from publicly responding to the ads. In November 1990 FET brought suit in U.S. District Court against the USDA's National Dairy Board on the ground that it was illegally promoting BST.[7] Based on information the FET obtained through the Freedom of Information Act, the foundation charged that the Dairy Board had illegally spent $1.1 million in a three-year pattern of collusion with Monsanto to influence the FDA's decision on BST. According to the suit, the Dairy Board did this by promoting the drug before it was officially certified by the FDA as safe.[8] Rifkin also petitioned the FDA commissioner to immediately stop all marketing promotion of BST by Monsanto, Eli Lilly (Elanco), Upjohn, and American Cyanamid until a final decision had been made by the FDA; promoting a product before it receives FDA approval is illegal.

Although the court dismissed the suit against the Dairy Board, the board discontinued its efforts to counteract food safety ads against the drug. The FET then launched a "Dump the Dairy Board" campaign to pressure the board of directors to withdraw its support of BST. And in response to Rifkin's petition to the FDA, the agency officially ordered the companies to discontinue their BST advertising.[9] This blocked one of the companies' efforts to counteract the campaign against BST (Guest 1991; Rural Vermont 1991:3). Monsanto also successfully lobbied legislators in Minnesota, Wisconsin, and Vermont to adopt legislation that protected any milk producer or supplier from lawsuits such as the one Monsanto filed in February 1994 against an eastern Iowa dairy cooperative that refused to buy milk from BST-treated cows.

### Boycotting BST at the Supermarket

The FDA ultimately approved the commercial use of Monsanto's BST drug under the trade name of Posilac in November 1993. The ninety-day congressional moratorium on the sale of the product expired in February 1994. However, the expressive, SMO, and farm groups had secured an FDA ruling that permitted stores and dairies to label milk that does not come from BST-treated cows. Therefore, although the consumer groups failed to block FDA approval of the drug, labeling milk that does not come from treated cows gave them a political weapon against BST in the marketplace. Their strategy is to pressure dairies and supermarket chains into labeling or segregating milk that comes from non-BST cows.

Kroger, the country's largest grocery chain with 1,277 stores in twenty states and 944 convenience stores in seven states, asked its suppliers to provide milk from non-BST cows. Lucky Stores in California also requested written assurances from its suppliers that milk in its 429 outlets in California and Las Vegas would come from untreated cows. And in Arkansas, Maryland, Virginia, and the state of Washington large dairy cooperatives have agreed not to use BST.

These political successes, however, may be short lived. Consumer boycotts are notoriously difficult to enforce. The reason is that ultimately the individual consumer decides the outcome of such campaigns. In the case of BST, not only is there no scientific evidence that BST-treated milk is any different from non-BST milk but non-BST milk is more expensive. The cost of collecting, bottling, shipping, and labeling BST-free milk adds 15 to 20 cents to the price of a gallon of milk (University of Wisconsin 1990). In the absence of a government-imposed restriction on BST milk, the consumer may soon lose interest in the boycott.

## Conclusion

The outcome of the antibiotechnology expressive group campaign against BST was mixed or partially successful. The limited success was largely the result of an informal political coalition of expressive groups, SMOs, and nonmovement allies that included expressive food safety and animal rights groups as well as dairy farmers. This political alliance resulted in state moratoriums against the new biotechnology drug. It also gave expressive groups political leverage over congressional committees that had oversight of the FDA, which was empowered to approve new drugs. Without the political alliance with nonmovement allies, however, the expressive groups and their SMOs would not have been able to slow down or qualify the FDA's approval of BST.

The expressive groups allied with dairy farming groups because it was an issue on which they could coalesce. Farmers allied with expressive groups in order to broaden their economic protest movement. However, their political agendas were different. Expressive groups were opposed to genetically engineered food and cruelty to animals, and farmers were opposed to a technology that threatened their economic status.

However, their differing objectives made it hard for the coalition to frame the campaign issue. Expressive groups framed the issue in terms of contaminating the food supply and cruelty to animals. Farmers and their political representatives framed the issue in terms of technology's adverse economic effect on society. This made it difficult to mobilize citizen protest against biotechnology. The resulting ambivalence enabled the agridrug industry to divide the coalition. The drug companies argued that there were two separate issues in the campaign against BST. One was economic and the other was food safety. The industry dismissed the economic issue by using the legal-constitutional argument that extraneous socioeconomic factors cannot be included in the FDA's scientific drug approval process. This enabled the industry to focus upon the expressive groups' claim that the technology contaminated the food supply.

In this debate the drug companies had an advantage over the coalition. They had what Lindblom (1977:172–78) calls the "privileged position of business." The FDA's confidentiality rules enabled the industry to make an unchallenged scientific claim that the new technology was safe. Although the companies prevailed on this issue, they did not have sufficient political influence to prevent the labeling of food products not produced with the drug. This created the potential for consumer boycotts against the technology.

## NOTES

1. *Bio* refers to biology, which is the science of life, including all living things. *Technology* refers to tools and techniques, including animal breeding, embryo transfer, genetic engineering, fermentation, and tissue culture. *Biotechnology* applies scientific tools to living organisms to improve the health and efficiency of plants and livestock, including the quality of food products derived from them.

2. BST can be manufactured in commercial quantities by using recombinant DNA technology. The naturally occurring BST in dairy cows is isolated and transferred to ordinary *E. coli* cells in the laboratory. The bacteria ferment, producing large amounts of BST. The bacteria are then killed and separated from the BST. The BST is injected in the animals daily or weekly. Laboratories use similar techniques to produce insulin and human growth hormone for human treatment.

3. As of 1990 about twenty thousand cows, or about 1 percent of all U.S. dairy cows, had received BST on an experimental basis in the United States. Monsanto's BST product, Posilac, was approved by the FDA for commercial use in November 1993. In the first six months Monsanto sold 6.8 million doses of the product at $5 each, for a total income of $34 million (*Feedstuffs*, November 14, 1994:8).

4. When Ted Weiss died in September 1992, Rep. Bernard Sanders (I-Vt.), along with John Conyers Jr. (D-Mich.), chairman of the House Government Operations Committee, sought to continue the campaign against BST. In this undertaking they

were joined in the Senate by the chairman of the Agriculture Committee, Patrick Leahy (D-Vt.) and senators Russell Feingold (D-Wisc.), Herbert Kohl (D-Wisc.), Paul Wellstone (D-Minn.), and Harris Wofford (D-Pa.), all from major milk-producing states.

5. The term *fourth hurdle* has also been used in connection with the European Union's ban on the use of growth hormones in beef. The ban has been used as a trade barrier for U.S. beef imports to the EU for social and economic reasons—to protect European producers from the economic consequences of U.S. competition. In 1993 the European Community extended an existing moratorium on BST for seven years (i.e., until the year 2000), ostensibly to protect the safety of dairy cows.

6. Fox has also advanced an antimeat, vegetarian agenda in lobbying on behalf of the Humane Society. He argues that society must break its "addiction to meat" (Fox 1992:4).

7. Congress established the Dairy Board in 1983 to help promote dairy products. Its board of directors consists of thirty-six dairy farmers, all of whom are appointed by the secretary of agriculture. Under federal law all U.S. dairy farmers must pay a mandatory annual "check-off" amount (15 cents per hundredweight of production). The board collects more than $75 million from the check-off each year. However, federal law forbids the use of check-off funds to influence government policy or action in any way.

8. One additional criterion is considered under the terms of the National Environmental Policy Act, the President's Council on Environmental Quality regulations, and FDA's supplemental regulations. Under the terms of these regulations the Center for Veterinary Medicine examines the procedures used by investigators to prevent and control accidental spills or occupational exposures. However, the FDA has never identified any significant environmental impact stemming from the use of food animal drugs (AHI 1992:3).

9. After Rifkin's lawsuit was thrown out of court, Representative Sanders and Senator Feingold joined in the effort to take punitive action against Monsanto for promoting its BST product before receiving FDA approval. The company had sponsored a seminar on BST for diary producers at Louisiana State University just before the drug's approval in November 1993. The U.S. Department of Health and Human Services found no justification for taking action against Monsanto. For a discussion of the efforts of Sanders and Feingold to sanction Monsanto, see U.S. Department of Health and Human Services (1994).

# THREE

# THE ANIMAL RIGHTS CAMPAIGN
## Agribusiness and Animal Rights Groups

### The Animal Rights Movement

Since the 1970s new animal rights SMOs have emerged within the more traditional animal welfare movement. These groups have not only given new life to the more traditional SMOs such as the Humane Society of the United States (HSUS) and the American Society for the Prevention of Cruelty to Animals (ASPCA) but they have transformed the entire movement. Jasper and Nelkin (1992:3) estimate that by 1990 thousands of animal welfare organizations and several hundred animal rights groups had formed. Ten to fifteen million people make financial contributions to these SMOs. The movement was inspired by the successes of the civil rights, feminist, ethnic, and other movements. Animal rights advocates have adopted the language of rights for animals and see them as another oppressed group in society.

Supporters and activists in the movement are baby boomers. They were raised during a period of transition from rural to urban society in which the population lost contact with food animals and had contact only with pets. This was also a period of economic prosperity and affluence. The movement questions the use of science as a technical means to fulfill moral ends in society. Technical efficiency, or "instrumentalism," is rejected as an adequate basis for making social choices. The movement protested instrumentalism for its exploitation of humans by corporations and the state. These organizations assert that the pursuit of profits ignores quality-of-life considerations and human needs (Jasper and Nelkin 1992).

The animal rights movement is also influenced by the New Age movement derived from Eastern mystical religions. This philosophy emphasizes the interdependence of humans and the natural world. It includes holistic philosophies with its concern for how products are produced and what effect they have on the natural world. For example, did animals suffer in the production of food, the discovery of new medical drugs, or the production of new products or entertainment? Thus the New Age movement adds consumer strategies to produce a worldview that is congenial to the animal rights movement (Jasper and Nelkin 1992).

Ironically, however, supporters of animal rights tend not to be religious. For example, 65 percent of the readers of a major animal rights magazine, *Animals' Agenda,* who responded to a questionnaire claimed they were atheists or agnostics. This compares to the general population, which, according to a 1984 Gallup poll, found that 90 percent say they believe in God, 70 percent belong to a church, and 60 percent attend church services at least once a month (Jasper and Nelkin 1992:38).

The animal rights movement frames political campaigns with ideas from two sources. The first is the traditional eighteenth- and nineteenth-century bourgeois sympathy for animals, which sees them as sentient creatures that therefore should be protected from cruelty and unnecessary suffering. The second is the 1970s emphasis on individual moral rights to life. The movement has justified animal rights on the basis of tradition, moral principles, and nature, and its adherents compare animal rights to human rights. This moral vision of animal rights is inspired by feminist and environmental movements (Jasper and Nelkin 1992).

All three movements are based on a societal critique of instrumentalism that says that technology, production, and profits override moral values and societal needs. According to this doctrine, instrumentalism reduces humans to things and tools rather than valuing life as an end in itself. Thus animal rights activists campaign against animal exploitation for human gain in the same way that environmental activists oppose the exploitation of nature for profits (Jasper and Nelkin 1992).

However, although the environmental movement is ideologically compatible with animal rights, the two movements have areas of disagreement that inhibit the formation of coalitions. For example, vegetarianism, experiments with animals, and hunting, fishing, and trapping for sport alienate environmentalists who are meat eaters. Likewise, some feminist groups support the animal rights movement, and an estimated 70 percent or more of the movement's adherents are women. However, animal rights–feminist political coalitions are rare.

## Animal Rights and Farm Animals

The animal rights movement in the United States has only recently focused its attention on the treatment of farm animals. Until the humane farming referendum in Massachusetts in 1988 that was designed to protect farm animals, the movement lacked political focus and coordination on farm animal issues. Indeed, with the exception of isolated attempts by a handful of animal rights SMOs such as the Humane Farming Association of California (HFA), People for the Ethical Treatment of Animals (PETA), and the Farm Animal Reform Movement (FARM) to pass state and federal legislation, most animal rights groups in the United States do not address the issue of the humane treatment of farm animals at all. In fact, the SMOs that concentrate on farm animals were formed only in the 1980s.

Historically, animal welfare organizations in the United States have concentrated on eliminating the use of animals in laboratory research, ending the hunting and trapping of wild animals for sport and clothing, and, more recently, opposing the use of animals for entertainment and educational purposes in zoos, circuses, aquaria, rodeos, and breeding, and for companionship as pets.

The most contentious farm animal rights issues are the raising of veal calves, confining laying hens to wire cages, confining pigs to steel stalls or cages during pregnancy, using hormones to increase the productivity of food animals, using antibiotics to increase resistance to disease, and genetic engineering to produce superior food animals.

The reason that animal rights groups have only recently campaigned against animal agriculture is their recognition that most people who have grown up with a meat diet are not going to give it up. Indeed, only about 6 percent, or 12 million in the U.S. population of 265 million, are true vegetarians (Yankelovich, Skelly, and White 1992:3). Furthermore, because less than 2 percent of the population lives on or near farms, most people have no contact with or knowledge of farm animals except when they purchase meat at the supermarket. Therefore, the older animal welfare organizations such as HSUS, with a membership of 930,000, have taken a moderate line, encouraging people to reduce their consumption of animals and to purchase "free range" animal products instead of those that result from what animal rights groups call *factory farming* (Harrison 1964).

In the late 1970s, however, HSUS shifted its focus. Under the leadership of the British animal rights activist and veterinarian Michael W. Fox,

HSUS turned its attention to what it regards as the inhumane treatment of farm animals created by modern intensive farming practices.

*Factory Farming*

The term *factory farming* was first brought to public attention in a 1964 book by the British author Ruth Harrison. In *Animal Machines: The New Factory Farming Industry* Harrison argues that modern farming methods for the production of human food have become so intensive that animals live out their entire lives in factory-like buildings that are extremely crowded. The animals are denied sunlight, the opportunity to graze for natural food, and are given unhealthy doses of antibiotics to control disease. They are forced to endure an unnatural, painful, and miserable life, Harrison says. The book became famous in England soon after its publication, and it inspired an official British inquiry called the Brambell Committee on the treatment of farm animals. The committee was named after its chairman, F. W. Rogers Brambell, an eminent zoologist (Shurland 1990:2; Garner 1993:109–17; Crabo 1991; Humane Society 1989:245).

The inquiry resulted in the 1965 Brambell report, which called for sweeping reforms of the animal agriculture industry. This report became a model for U.S. animal rights groups in their efforts to reform the industry. The Brambell report had several important outcomes in Great Britain. The first was that the British government created the Farm Animal Welfare Council to advise the minister of agriculture, fisheries, and food on the humane treatment of farm animals. Second, in 1968 Parliament made it illegal to cause farm animals "unnecessary pain or unnecessary distress." Third, the British government adopted specific codes of practice for each farm animal species and gave the state veterinary service responsibility for implementing the codes, although it withheld enforcement powers. And fourth, the government banned the use of crates in raising veal calves.

From the British reform legislation emerged what activists term the "five fundamental freedoms" for food animals: freedom from hunger and malnutrition, thermal and physical discomfort, injury and disease, and fear, and freedom to express most normal patterns of behavior.[1]

The freedom from fear and freedom to express normal patterns of behavior are controversial. Industry representatives say no scientific evidence exists that livestock or poultry can be free of fear or, indeed, that they even experience fear in the sense that humans do. The industry also says that no one knows what constitutes normal patterns of animal behavior in the raising and production of food animals or that normal behavior is even possible in the production process (Curtis interview 1993).

Fox brought the British animal rights agenda to the United States in a 1984 book, *Farm Animals: Husbandry, Behavior, and Veterinary Practice*. Fox argues that "factory farming" methods are dangerous to the health and well-being of farm animals as well as human health. Fox posed four questions about the welfare of farm animals:

Are the animals experiencing stress, frustration, or suffering as a result of restrictions placed on their "range of experiences and activity," such as cutting birds' wings and raising veal calves in wooden crates?

Are animals that do not show symptoms of stress because of poor health or disease able to respond to stress?

Which husbandry practices cause stress and suffering in animals?

Is it ethical to raise food animals in a way that denies their "intrinsic nature" (which Fox termed "natural rights")? (1984:202–204)

Animal science can address the first three questions. However, the ethics of denying farm animals' "natural rights" is a moral question that science cannot answer. The answer to this question is found in individual and societal judgments about the economic merits of large-scale intensive farming versus the animal rights philosophy that farm animals, like humans, have a moral right to live according to their "natural behavior," free of fear, suffering, and pain. It is on this question that the politics of animal rights turns. Thus the real issue for animal rights SMOs is not one of improving the welfare of animals by, for example, providing more comfortable bedding for livestock, improving their diets, allowing them more space to lie down or move around in a pen, or giving livestock the opportunity to run or play in the fields. Science is incapable of understanding how an animal feels.

## The Relationship Between Humans and Animals

According to Caplin (1990), there are four major approaches to understanding the relationship between humans and animals. First is the so-called mechanistic approach of the French philosopher René Descartes. He argues that because animals are incapable of experiencing pain, it is morally acceptable for humans to use animals in any way they choose. This position is not widely supported at present.

Second is the Judeo-Christian view, which assumes that animals exist to serve people and that humans have an absolute moral right to subjugate animals and use them to satisfy human needs. However, humans also have a moral responsibility to be good stewards of their livestock and care for the needs of their animals, including a duty to minimize pain and suffering. This position is the most widely held in society and is the one endorsed by the animal agricultural industry.

The third perspective is represented by the work of Peter Singer ([1975] 1990). He argues for a utilitarian perspective, that animals have a moral right to be free from pain and suffering and that this right is comparable to human rights. In Singer's view the pain and suffering of animals can be justified only if it serves the greater good of society and animals by minimizing the suffering of both species. This position calls for a highly restricted use of animals. It is the most popular view within the animal rights movement. Organizations such as HSUS and the ASPCA subscribe to this view.

The fourth position is articulated by the U.S. animal rights philosopher Tom Regan (1983). He argues that animals have an absolute right to be free from pain and suffering regardless of the benefits to society, such as medical experimentation on animals to find a cure for AIDS or cancer. He rejects Singer's limited-use proposition, saying that because animals are vulnerable to human control (comparable to the status of human babies and the mentally incompetent), humans have a moral responsibility to protect animals from pain and suffering. This represents an extreme position vis-à-vis the mechanistic view of Descartes and calls for a complete ban on the human use of animals. Only the more aggressive and militant SMOs such as PETA and the Animal Liberation Front endorse this view.

The event that exploded in the political imagination of animal rights groups was the publication of Singer's 1975 book, *Animal Liberation*. The influence of Singer's book on the animal rights movement has been compared to the influence of Rachel Carson's celebrated 1962 book, *Silent Spring*, on environmentalists.

Singer's is the most widely read and influential book in the animal rights movement.[2] In the chapter on farm animals Singer argues that the use of animals for food is the most exploitative form of what he terms *speciesism*, which he defines as the belief that nonhuman animals exist to sustain and support human life. Singer asserts that nonhuman animals or species have the same rights as humans to be free from pain and suffering and that they have a moral right to live free of domination by humans. This includes the right to be protected from slaughter and confinement for human food production.

Singer goes so far as to say that "there will surely be some non-human animals whose lives, by any standard, are more valuable than the lives of some humans" (1990:19). The example he gives is a chimpanzee, pig, or dog that has "greater capacity for more meaningful relations with others" than a severely retarded infant or person of advanced senility. In fact, as far as Singer is concerned, on a moral plane at least, the only real difference between human and nonhuman animals is their species. For humans to deny that animals have a moral "right to life" is simply a matter of prejudice, comparable to the logic that a racist uses to justify discrimination.

Therefore, the only way to eliminate speciesism is to give up a meat diet and become a vegetarian. It is interesting to note in this regard that a sizable segment of the American public believes that animals "are just like humans in all important ways." This surprising finding was reported in a national survey of 1,612 adults conducted from December 4 to 7, 1993, by the *Los Angeles Times* (Balzar 1993:A1). The survey found that 47 percent of respondents felt that animals were like people. They believed that the emotions and reasoning ability of animals and humans are comparable. Some believed that animals are equal to humans in that they are entitled to basic rights derived from God or society.

Singer sees speciesism, along with famine, poverty, war, racism, sexism, unemployment, and protecting the natural environment, as a major problem facing the world. He points out that the oppression of nonhuman beings by humans in providing food, clothing, and entertainment is "gigantic" compared with the suffering inflicted by humans upon one another (1990:220). More than 100 million sheep, cattle, and pigs and billions of chickens suffer intense pain and endure unnecessary cruelty and death each year in the United States as a result of human oppression, he says. Further, Singer notes that unlike war, racial inequality, poverty, and unemployment, ending the suffering of animals is politically feasible. In effect, Singer's book is a call to arms to end animal agriculture.

This message has a potent political appeal, especially to members of animal rights SMOs. They are concerned with the so-called quality-of-life issues, such as protecting the natural and physical environment and eliminating all forms of societal "oppression" and victimization of women, children, and minority groups. However, as Guither and Curtis (1983) point out, animal welfare is a major political issue only in countries that are affluent, where the food supply is adequate, and where political groups actively campaign on ethical and moral issues concerning animals. Western European countries lead the rest of the world in this regard, with the emergence of Green parties forcing the issue onto their political agendas. While Great Britain was the pioneer in guaranteeing rights for farm animals, Germany, Holland, Sweden, and Switzerland have taken the lead in adopting protective legislation that has real enforcement power.

The credibility of the animal rights movement is strengthened by two widely held societal beliefs. One is the need to be kind to animals, and the other is the need to "save planet Earth." The failure of the food industry to challenge the animal rights groups by arguing that animal agriculture is equally committed to these beliefs has yielded this political terrain to animal rightists.

## The Argument Against Animal Rights

Despite the industry's reluctance to join the debate with animal rights SMOs, producers, animal scientists, and industry organizations have strong views on animal rights issues. For example, Bill Rempel (1991b:7–8), a research scientist at the Department of Animal Science at the University of Minnesota, offers three arguments against the animal rights position. First, to concede that animals are beings, not machines, because they experience pain and pleasure is not to say that animals are the same as humans. The single-criterion thesis of animal rights groups is that if humans are truly different from animals, all humans should have one trait in common that is absent in animals. Animal rights groups reject this argument by pointing to severely retarded and mentally incompetent humans. However, Rempel points out that it is easy to demonstrate the existence of such a trait in human species, which is the sum total of human achievement, from cave drawings to space exploration and heart transplants.

Second, Rempel argues that speciesism is a logical extension of unequal rather than equal relationships such as that between a mother and child. He rejects Singer's thesis that speciesism, civil rights, and feminism are connected, pointing out that civil rights activists and feminists are able to organize politically to correct an unjust situation. Animals, on the other hand, are incapable of perceiving, let alone correcting, a societal injustice. Furthermore, it is implausible to suggest that nonhuman animals wish to achieve equality with humans. And it is presumptuous for animal rights groups to assume that they are the only voice for animals or that they have a special understanding or insight into animals' needs. Rempel explains that species are simply units of evolution and that Homo sapiens has evolved as the highest form of life on earth. This has been achieved through social cooperation and organization.

Third, Rempel rejects the animal advocates' "borderline argument." According to this thesis, some humans are less competent mentally and physically than some animals. And, if such humans are accorded rights, it follows logically that animals should be given the same rights. Rempel rejects this on the ground that rather than comparing extremes in the competencies of humans and animals (the low end for humans and the high end for animals), it is necessary to compare the average for both groups. Furthermore, he argues that no rights inhere to humans or animals. The basis of human rights is religion and philosophy, which are beyond the intellectual capability of animals.[3] Indeed, Rempel concludes that the very notion of animal rights is religious. Therefore, the animal rights movement is a religious movement. Singer's attempt to equate human and nonhuman species and Regan's attempt to equate the rights of humans and nonhumans only degrade human life. It does not elevate animals.'

### Industry's Perception of Animal Rights Campaigns

Rempel (1991a:6) has sought to conceptualize the animal food and production industry's perception of the political influence of animal rights groups. He argues that political influence has four stages: development of an issue, politicizing the issue, legislating the issue, and litigating the issue (see figure 3.1).

The industry believes that as an issue advances through the four stages, the influence of the animal rights group increases, making it more difficult to combat that influence.[4] The industry hews to the religious view of animals discussed earlier: that they exist to serve people and that humans have an absolute moral right to subjugate animals.

At the first stage in the process, the development of an animal rights issue, advocates seek to make the political case that animals have rights. At this point, if the industry does not challenge animal rights SMOs and the concept gains public acceptance, the industry will face a more difficult task in coping with these groups in the future. For example, if the animal industry had challenged the 1990 campaign in Aspen, Colorado, to ban fur sales, and the biomedical industry had challenged the antivivisection campaign against the use of animals for research as soon as these were advanced, the industry could have easily defeated these campaigns and would not be on the defensive.

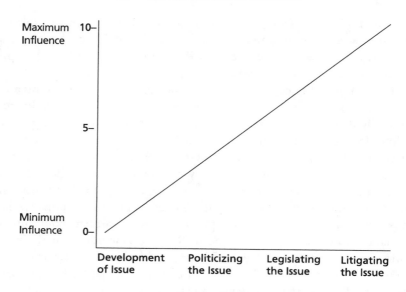

**FIGURE 3.1 The Four Stages of Political Influence**
SOURCE: REMPEL (1991A).

Animal rights proponents, however, reject the grouping of all animal rights campaigns in a single category. They take the position that each issue should be considered on its merits. For example, in Singer's limited-use perspective, the suffering and pain of animals can be justified only in terms of the greater good of society. Using this standard, testing new cosmetics by placing irritating substances in rabbits' eyes and experimenting on animals to find a cure for cancer are substantially different. Animal experimentation to find a cure for cancer serves the larger good of society, whereas experimentation to develop cosmetics does not.

Rempel underscores the industry's point of view by reference to Ovid's *obstra principiis*, which says that one should take a firm stand on a matter of principle and avoid the "slippery slope" of making concessions. Rempel urges the industry to act early and present its position if it wants to influence an animal rights issue. Another animal scientist, Brian Crooker (1990), supports this argument, contending that the industry's reluctance to enter the political debate with animal rights groups is misguided. He attributes the industry's failure to challenge these SMOs in the public arena to ill-advised recommendations from political consultants. Compounding this failing is a tendency among "insiders," including agricultural producers and veterinarians, to dismiss animal rights criticism, saying it is based on emotion and lack of knowledge and not on science (Grommers 1988:5).

However, this represents an extreme and dogmatic point of view. It is an all-or-nothing position that ignores circumstances in which the pain and suffering inflicted on animals by the industry is excessive and unnecessary.

### Industry's Reaction to Animal Rights Advocates

The initial reaction of animal agriculture in the United States to the animal rights movement was shock and surprise. The leaders of animal agriculture believe that they are devoted to the good health and welfare of their animals. They are personally insulted by the criticism of animal rights SMOs, which they regard as uninformed. Hence, their initial reaction was to deny the criticism and ignore animal rights groups altogether (Curtis interview 1993).

The food animal industry decided to ignore the animal rights groups after commissioning several public opinion surveys (see Wirthlin Group 1989 and Colleton and Curtis interviews 1993). For example, in 1989 the Wirthlin Group, a Virginia-based consultancy, carried out a national survey of consumer attitudes for the National Cattlemen's Foundation (established by the National Cattlemen's Association). Wirthlin found that only a few respondents were critical of the industry's treatment of livestock and its use of the natural environment, including land and water. Wirthlin (1989) concluded that because it found little public concern about the treatment of food animals, campaigning against animal rights groups would be counterproductive for the industry. Such a campaign would only draw public attention to the charges made by animal rights SMOs, thus giving them credibility, which they did not have.

This became the standard modus operandi for the animal agricultural industry. Don Colleton, an attorney representing the National Livestock and Meat Board in Chicago, explained that animal rights groups are free to make any charge or accusation about the health risk of food without scientific proof (Colleton interview 1993). Likewise, they can level charges of cruelty to food animals against the industry in mass circulation magazines and newspapers without any evidence. This places the industry in the difficult position of proving a negative. Invariably, animal advocates will be able to find one example of farm animal abuse, typically involving a novice who has no business raising livestock. The animal advocates then publicize the case as a typical example of animal neglect by the farm industry as a whole.

Because animal rights groups have the ability to wage high-profile public relations campaigns, the industry faces a daunting task in answering the criticism. Colleton said the industry is in the position of a man trying to respond to the charge that his wife is a prostitute. How does one prove the negative? The industry's traditional response to criticism has been to present complex scientific arguments to the public, which is at best only semiliterate in science and skeptical of the scientific claims for societal advances resulting from technology.[5] Of course, the industry's claim of scientific neutrality is an example of Lindblom's "privileged position of business" (1977:170–88). It implies that industry understands better than scientists in the animal rights movement what constitutes the most humane and safest treatment of animals.

The industry has tended to assume that if it publicly counters animal advocates, doing so will only give the opposition publicity and credibility (Crooker 1990:295–97). Crooker argues that this strategy is ill advised. If the biomedical community had not adopted an "ostrich approach" to the antivivisection campaign against the use of animals in laboratory research, it would not now find itself in an uphill battle to conduct experimental research. In other words, if the industry had explained to the public that almost every advance in medical science during the twentieth century has been the result of animal experimentation, it could have combated the antivivisection campaign.[6] However, many scientists concede that with recent developments in computer technology, many medical experiments formerly conducted on laboratory animals can now be simulated.

The second stage of animal rights groups' influence is politicizing an issue. Once they have developed a public issue, the next step is public legitimation. Typically, this is achieved through public demonstrations and marches, which often become media events featuring prominent Hollywood personalities and celebrities. The objective at this stage is to reframe the animal rights issue as a political issue that expressive groups can use to mobilize grassroots support .

Rempel (1991a:8) notes that at this stage the industry has significantly reduced its ability to influence an issue. In other words, once animal rights groups have the political initiative, the industry faces a difficult task in trying to stop the momentum. Of course, those in the animal rights movement argue that the public has the right to express itself on any major societal issue. The infliction of unnecessary pain and suffering on animals for profit is clearly one of these issues.

The third stage in the political process is legislation. After the issue has become political, animal rights groups seek to gain legislation to support the issue. However, as of early 1998 animal rights groups had failed to secure any major legislation. For example, the antifur initiatives in Colorado, the animal rights campaign to protect farm animals in Massachusetts, and several efforts in Congress to ban the use of wooden crates to raise veal calves have all failed. Nevertheless, the initiatives gained significant public support during those campaigns.

The industry has only reluctantly and belatedly entered political campaigns against animal rights groups when it has faced the imminent threat of legislation deemed hostile to industry. In other words, the industry responds when in a crisis. It has not developed coherent and coordinated political strategies to cope with the growing number of animal rights campaigns.

The fourth stage of animal rights influence is litigation. Once legislation is passed, for all practical purposes the industry has lost the issue. The only recourse left to industry at this point is the courts, and suing is very time consuming and expensive. It also places the industry in the negative position of challenging a law that legislators and the courts believe has popular support.

Rempel (1991a) argues that animal agriculture is close to losing the battle with activists. He says that the power equation between animal rights advocates and the industry is about midway up the trend line in figure 2.1, specifically between the political and legislative stages. If animal rights groups succeed in gaining legislation, the industry will lose, and animal advocates will gain maximum influence in what Rempel calls the animal rights war. Animal rights proponents reject this analysis, calling it is alarmist. They say the movement has not progressed beyond Rempel's first stage (figure 2.1) and that no evidence exists that the industry would be adversely affected by a more humane treatment of farm animals.

Nevertheless, a grassroots movement has emerged to challenge the animal rights movement. This countermovement emerged in schools, churches, and businesses in the 1980s and is supported by trade associations, producers, and companies. The movement is committed to the traditional religious, or dominion, view of using animals to serve society (Kopperud interview 1993a).

Regardless of the merits of the philosophical dispute between the animal rights groups and supporters of the traditional use of food animals, the conflict is fundamentally social and political. The outcome turns on the question of who decides the use of food animals. Is it the consumer, as the industry believes, or is it the state, as the animal rights SMOs believe?

## The Massachusetts Animal Rights Campaign

The expressive group that carried out the animal rights campaign in Massachusetts in 1988 was the Coalition to End Animal Suffering in Experiments (CEASE; the organization later became the Coalition to End Animal Suffering and Exploitation). The SMOs supporting the campaign were HSUS, FARM, HFA, PETA, the ASPCA, and the Massachusetts Society for the Prevention of Cruelty to Animals (MSPCA). Nonmovement allies in CEASE's campaign included the United Farm Workers (AFL-CIO). CEASE had no political allies, but its opponents included the Massachusetts Farm Bureau, the American Farm Bureau Federation, the drug companies, large agribusiness corporations, and Massachusetts farmers. The animal rights campaign was defeated.

The American agricultural industry has historically opposed efforts by the government to regulate the industry. For example, the largest farm organization in the United States, the American Farm Bureau Federation, has taken an unequivocal position against efforts to regulate animal agriculture. The Farm Bureau's policy statement reads, "We oppose legislation that would give animal-rights organizations or any public agency the right to establish standards for the raising, handling, feeding, housing or transportation of livestock, poultry, aquaculture and fur-bearing animals" (AFBF 1997:74).

That policy was directly challenged in Massachusetts. An expressive animal rights group waged a campaign to enact a law that for the first time would establish government standards and rules for the humane treatment of farm animals. The initiative would have led to a fundamental change in the way farm animals are raised, transported, and slaughtered. Although various campaigns have sought to protect whales from extinction and dolphins from becoming ensnared in tuna-fishing nets, this was the first time that an animal rights group had brought to the voters its conception of how farm animals should be raised. Equally important, it galvanized farmers to conduct a grassroots campaign against the animal rights groups.

### Framing the Animal Rights Issue

The veal industry has always been the first target of expressive groups. Animal advocates have historically appealed to the emotions of urban consumers by showing them photographs of veal calves raised in wooden stalls.

Veal is a small, expensive, specialty industry. Few animal farmers raise veal calves, and some oppose the use of crates. Thus animal agriculture as a whole has tended to distance itself from veal production. The industry believed, incorrectly as it turned out, that the animal rights agenda did not extend to it (Cheatham 1991).

The Massachusetts campaign changed all that. Animal advocates conducted a broad-based campaign on what they regarded as the inhumane treatment (intensive confinement) of all farm animals. As in the past, animal rights SMOs focused media attention on the veal industry. However, the legislation proposed for Massachusetts included all farm animals. This shocked the agricultural industry.

Animal rights advocates hoped that the referendum would become a model for the country (CEASE 1988a). They regarded Massachusetts as the ideal place to launch an animal rights campaign because the state had a small population, the electorate had the reputation for being among the most liberal in the country, it was predominately urban, and it had a tiny agricultural sector. In other words, Massachusetts provided the most hospitable political climate in which to introduce animal rights legislation.

According to Troy Soos, a representative of CEASE, the animal rights organization that launched the campaign, Massachusetts was a good place to begin setting humane standards for farm animals because the state's agricultural sector was so small that humane standards could be introduced without having a "devastating effect on agriculture." Less than 15 percent of Massachusetts's food is produced in the state so, regardless of the outcome, experimenting with Massachusetts's tiny livestock industry was politically expedient because doing so would not disrupt the supply, or the price, of food in the state (Nelson 1987).

In 1988 Massachusetts had fifty-one hundred farmers, who represented only one-tenth of 1 percent of the state's population of five million. The farmers worked on 6,200 farms, which employed 4,500 people and included 3,188 livestock and poultry farms. Most of the state's farms were small family operations (Nelson 1987). There were 512 farms producing $100 million annually in dairy products, poultry farms producing $27.4 million in chicken and turkey products, cattle operations producing $12.7 million in beef and veal, hog farms producing $4 million in pork, and sheep operations sending $500,000 in products to market (Comstock 1988).[7] The Massachusetts Department of Food and Agriculture estimated that livestock farms netted only $130 million in 1988. If this is added to so-called indirect revenue (including the price of fuel, feed, bedding, clothing, veterinary services, and machinery), the figure increases to only $2.6 billion annually.

Massachusetts had only two small veal farms in 1989, with 26 calves in one and 160 in the other. Both farms supplied a kosher market in New Jersey and were inspected every six months by the Massachusetts Department of Food and Agriculture. Of the sixty-four poultry operations in the state, only three were commercial hatcheries. With the exception of one small egg farm, the practice of grinding or suffocating unwanted male chicks had been discontinued fifty years earlier. And the farm that used that practice discontinued it in 1988 (Comstock 1988). One significant dimension of the animal rights campaign—because it appealed to voters' concerns about the environment—was that Massachusetts farms accounted for about 360,000 acres of open space.

### Expressive Group Strategy

Expressive groups charged that the Massachusetts Farm Bureau, backed by the large pharmaceutical companies and veal packers from other states, waged an inflammatory campaign to defeat expressive groups' challenge to large-scale chemical-intensive farming practices that dominate American agriculture. Animal advocates claimed that the industry had no concern for the welfare of farm animals or the family farm. Industry argued that the initiative was part of a secretive "vegetarian conspiracy" waged by the animal rights movement to force vegetarianism on the general public and to eliminate the human use of farm animals.

Franklin Loew, the influential dean of Tufts' School of Veterinary Medicine, saw the initiative as a classic case of culture clash between Cambridge and Berkeley and agrarian America. As he saw it, a few animal rights groups were playing on the sympathies of an urban intelligentsia that had an unrealistic view of animals ("People Are Looking" 1988). Most voters' only real experience with animals was owning a cat or a dog. Many believed that farm livestock deserved to be treated like pets. For example, animal rights advocate Evelyn Kimber made the following analogy: "If your neighbor had a dog chained into a 22-inch-wide crate in the basement for his entire lifetime, unable to turn around, you'd consider it socially unacceptable. But we have hundreds of cows being treated that way every year" ("Diary Farmers Fewer" 1988).

Chris Hurn, a sociologist at the University of Massachusetts, noted the extraordinary nature of the campaign. He observed that a campaign to get an initiative on the ballot usually reflects a popular concern among a large segment of the population. However, the petition to protect farm animals was sponsored by a small group of animal advocates without widespread public awareness of the issue ("People Are Looking" 1988). Nevertheless, because the concept that animals had rights had popular support in Massachusetts, advocates were able to tap this belief in mounting their campaign.

The animal rights proponents who initiated the referendum, called Question 3, on the Massachusetts ballot in November 1988 belonged to a small obscure organization called the Coalition to End Animal Suffering and Exploitation (CEASE). The organization was comprised largely of volunteers. At the height of its political influence it had no more than about a thousand supporters. Its total campaign budget was about $50,000. CEASE was originally established in 1979 in Cambridge to combat a variety of animal rights abuses (Japenga 1989).

In 1979 the most important issue to CEASE was to end animal experimentation in laboratories. In fact, the original name of the group was the Coalition to End Animal Suffering in Experiments. However, as the group evolved, it widened the scope of its activities to include issues such as the buying and wearing of fur, genetic engineering, abandoned pets, and the protection of wildlife preserves (Japenga 1989:38). The group changed its name from "experiments" to "exploitation" to reflect the expanded scope of its objectives.

CEASE's campaign headquarters were in Somerville, short subway ride from downtown Boston. The organization had one full-time employee, the office manager. In addition, Mark Sommer, the president of CEASE and a freelance journalist, was paid for ten weeks during the campaign to coordinate the drive to gather enough signatures to place Question 3 on the ballot. Stephen Ronan, a New York transplant, was the principal author of the petition. Ronan was a chef at elegant restaurants in Boston and held an undergraduate degree from Harvard in psychology. He volunteered his time and took the first steps in developing the issue. Ronan explained that what prompted him to draft the initiative was his experience as a chef. He said that he became particularly concerned about the treatment of veal calves when he saw slabs of cold meat in restaurants (Japenga 1989).

The CEASE initiative was drafted in 1987 after a bill designed to protect the welfare of veal calves died in the Committee on Natural Resources and Agriculture in the Massachusetts House of Representatives (Shurland

1990:5). The bill was sponsored by mainstream animal welfare SMOs, including the MSPCA, ASPCA, HSUS, and Animal Rights International. Supporters of the bill argued that it was defeated because it was poorly written and because the major animal welfare organizations did not campaign hard enough for the bill, fearing they would risk their political reputations in a losing cause.

The lesson to Ronan and other CEASE members was that an animal protection bill had few prospects for passage in the Massachusetts legislature. Their only recourse would be to follow the unconventional path of taking the issue directly to voters through the referendum process. Ronan produced the original draft of the initiative in June 1987, patterning it after the British Brambell report, except that the Massachusetts initiative had real enforcement powers, comparable to the Swedish, Norwegian, and Icelandic animal protection acts.

The initiative went through several rewrites by CEASE members in June and July and was finally completed and submitted to the Massachusetts attorney general for approval in August 1987. The CEASE members who participated in the various stages of drafting the initiative were those who showed up at the meetings. In fact, the chaotic nature of the CEASE organization contributed to the failure to negotiate a compromise bill that might have passed the legislature (Shurland 1990:5).

CEASE's representatives changed from meeting to meeting, and no one seemed to have the authority to speak on behalf of the organization. According to CEASE representatives, the legislature failed to approve a farm animal protection bill because CEASE refused to compromise on its demands that veal calves be raised in group pens with space to lie down and groom themselves instead of the traditional method of placing them in individual crates or stalls (Shurland 1990:5). The Massachusetts Farm Bureau disputes this interpretation, however, arguing that other issues were more important but that CEASE was either not able to compromise or was not serious about negotiating an acceptable bill (Shurland 1990:5).

A loose coalition of animal rights and animal welfare SMOs also supported the campaign. In August 1988 CEASE formed Citizens for Humane Farming to mobilize the vote. The coalition involved eighteen other groups, including the Humane Society of Cape Cod, Homes and Rights of Animals, Concerned Citizens for Animals, the South Shore Humane Society, the People for Animals in Wakefield Society, and student animal protection groups at Wellesley, the University of Massachusetts at Amherst, Brandeis, Harvard, MIT, and Tufts. It also had the backing of the United

Farm Workers union (AFL-CIO), its president, César Chavez, and celebrities such as the author and education activist Jonathan Kozol. In the early stages of the petition campaign some farmers supported the initiative, including members of the Massachusetts Grange. However, after the state and national Grange opposed the initiative, the local chapter withdrew its support.

For the initiative to qualify for the November 1988 ballot in Massachusetts, CEASE had to collect 62,203 certified signatures in a petition drive (3 percent of the previous election turnout) by November 1987. CEASE had ten weeks to complete the petition drive, easily exceeding its goal with 72,580 signatures.[8] CEASE had an easy time collecting signatures because of the wording of the initiative. All CEASE had to do was circulate petitions at shopping malls and supermarkets that asked whether voters favored the humane treatment of farm animals. The Massachusetts Farm Bureau wryly declared in an April 1988 press release that only Jack the Ripper would oppose such an high-sounding and innocuous petition.

However, behind the animal rights initiative was an ambitious political agenda. The initiative was designed to place all animal agriculture (defined as any animal or animal product for food and fiber valued at $500 or more) in the state under the supervision of an unpaid five-member scientific advisory board. According to Section 54 of the initiative, the advisory board would include the director of the state Division of Animal Health and four members appointed by the governor; the four had to be specialists in veterinary medicine or animal science and nominated by at least two nonprofit humane animal welfare organizations. No provision was made for farmer representation on the board, and the committee would become part of the Department of Food and Agriculture.

The perception was of an unbalanced committee biased against farmers. Opponents of the initiative said that the committee should reflect the interests of farming, public health, animal science, and medicine as well as animal welfare (Hiscock 1988:6).

Farmers were alarmed. They feared the committee could become a powerful regulatory body, issuing directives for the raising, housing, feeding, health care, transportation, and slaughter of all livestock in Massachusetts. For example, the advisory committee would have to approve all new housing for livestock that cost $10,000 or more. And the state director of animal health would be empowered to enforce committee regulations. Anyone caught violating the new regulations could be fined as much as $1,000.

They feared existing animal housing on farms would have to be altered to meet the new regulations. The dairy industry alone estimated that 60 percent of its existing housing would have to be replaced. The cost of replacing the older stanchion-type barns (in which cows are tied together in long rows during the winter), at $250,000 per 100-head barn, was estimated at $90 million. Enforcement of the initiative could cost farmers more than $750 million, and the Massachusetts legislature had said nothing about authorizing new taxes to pay it. The industry feared that, if approved, the measure could shut down farming.

Farmers were also concerned that the regulations would be unworkable and financially onerous. For example, most farmers purchase local anesthetic at $2 to $3 a bottle for dehorning about ten head of cattle. Under the new regulations only a veterinarian could dehorn cattle. But veterinarians then charged about $25 dollars to visit a farm, $50 an hour to dehorn, and another $7 per animal dehorned. If Massachusetts livestock farmers had to call a vet every time they needed to dehorn or castrate livestock, or were required to anesthetize every time they debeaked a chicken (which involves removal of one and one-eighth inches of the top beak) or performed a minor surgical operation, many would go out of business. In addition, anesthetizing animals for minor operations might even be dangerous to their health.

The animal rights groups tried to soften the advisory committee's potential influence by saying that the committee only had the power to recommend to the commissioner, who represented the agricultural industry. They pointed out that the initiative included a proposal for state money to help farmers absorb the financial burden of the new regulations and provided an eighteen-month renewable exemption for farmers who had difficulty competing with out-of-state farmers. However, the farmers were not convinced and remained adamantly opposed to the advisory committee. Farmers argued that although the advisory committee's only power was to recommend, the initiative allowed any citizen to bring legal action against the commissioner for failure to carry out the regulations called for in the initiative. Animal rights groups were certain to use this provision as a way to force the commissioner to follow the recommendations of the advisory committee. Farmers also had no guarantee that the legislature would allocate anything approaching the real cost to farmers of implementing the regulations. And even if the money were made available, many farmers would rather go out of business than conform to the new regulations, which they regarded as time consuming, costly, and unnecessary.

During the campaign animal rights groups stressed that the initiative was intended to produce four major changes in animal husbandry. The first was a ban on the veal crate and traditional milk-fed-veal production. The second was requiring anesthetics for castrating and dehorning livestock. The third prohibited grinding or suffocating unwanted male chicks. And the fourth was humane standards for raising all farm animals, which the advisory committee would impose.

Consistent with other farm animal rights campaigns, banning the veal crate was the most symbolic feature of the Massachusetts campaign. Banning the raising of veal calves in wooden crates with no straw bedding, no solid food, and the use of antibiotics to keep the animals healthy was by far the campaign argument most effective for the animal advocates.[9] In effect, CEASE and its supporters campaigned primarily on this issue. Indeed, their campaign used pictures of veal calves chained in wooden stalls or crates in dimly lit barns without straw bedding and fed nothing but liquid milk during the sixteen weeks of their lives to shatter the public mythology of bucolic scenes of cows and their calves grazing in the pasture.[10] The small pens or crates prevent the calves from moving around, enabling growers to keep them clean and monitor their health and development.

There is no scientific evidence that raising veal calves chained indoors in wooden crates or individual stalls and fed liquid milk is less healthy or more stressful than raising them in group pens and with solid feed. The only comprehensive study of the effects of raising "special-fed" veal in individual crates was conducted by Carolyn Stull and Duncan A. McMartin of the School of Veterinary Medicine of the University of California at Davis. Their study was carried out over eighteen months ending in 1992. It included 550 bulls calves at ten commercial special-fed veal facilities. The diets, health, and stress levels of the calves were carefully monitored through regular on-site visits and 'round-the-clock videotaping. They found that the traditional method of raising special-fed veal calves is no less healthful or more stressful than other methods (Stull and McMartin 1992).

However, animal rights groups have rejected the validity of the study, claiming it was tainted by special interests. They argue that the California Assembly funded Stull and McMartin's study to prove that raising veal calves in crates is humane. In other words, the study was designed to take the heat generated by the animal rights SMOs off political elites. The University of California at Davis provided $50,000 toward the cost of the study, and the American Veal Association matched that amount.

Nevertheless, the publicity about the raising of veal calves in crates shocked the general public. CEASE exploited this. Its brochures, slides, and newspaper ads featured a three-year-old picture of a veal calf that had fallen down while chained in a two-foot-wide wooden crate in an unidentified barn that was dimly lit and filthy (Luttrell 1988a).[11] CEASE said that milk-fed veal is produced by making a calf anemic. Instead of receiving mother's milk, the calf gets an antibiotic-laced formula that leads to diarrhea. These calves are forced to lie in their own excrement, choking on the ammonia gases. According to CEASE, they are chained in dark buildings with hundreds of other calves suffering the same fate.

This had a powerful effect on the public and gave animal rights groups an initial advantage in the campaign. Indeed, the industry conceded that if it had to fight the animal rights initiative on the veal issue, it would lose (Curtis interview 1993; Cheatham 1991:2).

The industry spent most of its war chest on print, TV, and radio advertising. Because CEASE received a great deal of free print and air time, the estimated $50,000 that CEASE spent significantly understated its actual resources in the campaign. Indeed, CEASE spent most of its money to collect petition signatures because it did not have to wage a media campaign to influence public opinion. Voters supported the initiative even before the campaign began.

Although the Federal Communications Commission officially revoked its "fairness doctrine" in 1987, the media felt morally obliged to honor it and provided CEASE with free air time to counter the industry's advertising. And regular news coverage included the rebroadcast in the Boston area of a 1986 five-part syndicated CBS-TV series entitled *Misery on the Menu.*

In 1988 the ASPCA followed up on *Misery on the Menu,* producing its own video, *The Other Side of the Fence,* which stresses cruelty to veal calves. The ASPCA distributed this video free of charge to schools, members of Congress, the news media, and Massachusetts state legislators. CEASE members also appeared on TV news programs to promote their campaign, and Boston TV stations showed slides of veal calves and laying hens in close confinement and described this treatment as cruel.

By contrast, the industry had to pay for most of its print, TV, and radio air time because its representatives were rarely given voice during news reports. Because of the high cost of TV ads in the Massachusetts market (especially during the 1988 presidential campaign), and the industry's meager campaign resources, the industry could afford to run TV spots opposing the initiative only during the last ten days of the election campaign.

Alex Hershaft, president of the Farm Animal Reform Movement, discussed another advantage that animal rights groups had in the campaign. He said that although the industry had more money than the activists, animal rights SMOs had "thousands and thousands of troops on our side who are willing to work for nothing" (Japenga 1989:43).

Two other major elements of the initiative were outlawing grinding or suffocating chicks and minimizing pain in castrating or dehorning livestock. However, these issues did not have the same emotional effect on the public that the veal issue did. Indeed, the animal rights groups acknowledged that grinding and suffocating chicks was not currently practiced in Massachusetts.

Mabel Owen, the director of the state agriculture department's Division of Animal Health, explained to a reporter the reasons for the current methods of raising farm animals. For example, farmers remove chickens' beaks because chickens are highly cannibalistic and would otherwise seriously injure each other. Laying hens are kept in pens off the ground to ensure that eggs are clean and to stop the spread of disease that can be transmitted by their feces. Veal calves are kept in small pens for health and safety reasons and to monitor their development. Furthermore, under her agency's $1 million annual program, state veterinarians visited veal farmers every six months and had never received a complaint about the inhumane treatment of farm animals (Nelson 1987).[12]

This suggests that CEASE activists were concerned about more than the welfare of farm animals in Massachusetts. They were also engaged in a political campaign to advance the rights of animals and hoped that the campaign would have national significance. CEASE acknowledged that Massachusetts farmers were responsible and humane. In fact, CEASE even argued that the passage of the initiative would emphasize that Massachusetts farmers already treated their animals humanely. CEASE claimed that the initiative would give Massachusetts farmers a competitive advantage over farmers in other states who did not treat their animals as humanely (CEASE 1988b:5–6).

For its part, the industry badly fumbled its response. CEASE wrote a 150-word argument for Question 3, which appeared on the ballot and was not challenged by the industry. This enabled CEASE to frame the issue, forcing the industry to respond to that interpretation of the initiative. This was a critical mistake. It meant that the industry had forfeited its opportunity to frame the issue by entering the public debate before it became political. Thus from the very beginning the agricultural industry was behind in the campaign, and it struggled to catch up and overcome CEASE's early success.

## Political Opposition to the Initiative

The Massachusetts Farm Bureau led the opposition to the animal rights initiative. Although the bureau represented 92 percent of all Massachusetts farmers, only forty-eight hundred were paid-up members. The bureau had four staff members and an annual budget of about $255,000. In effect, the bureau's meager financial resources dictated that it rely on large out-of-state agribusiness companies for money to campaign against the initiative. Although all major agricultural industries gave their verbal support to the bureau's efforts to defeat the initiative, they did not provide adequate financial resources to launch a campaign. More than two hundred individuals and organizations made financial and nonfinancial commitments to the campaign.[13]

The Massachusetts Farm Bureau's public relations consultants estimated that a major campaign against the initiative would cost $2.4 to $4.2 million in the expensive New England media market. The cost estimates depended upon whether the consultants would actually conduct the campaign or merely advise. Jay Slattery, the executive director of the state Farm Bureau, created a political action committee and served as its treasurer to raise money for the campaign. He met with representatives of more than thirty national business organizations in March 1988 to solicit campaign funds. However, his appeals went largely unheeded. Although the industry was eventually forced to conduct a last-ditch campaign effort, it contributed only about $640,000, far short of the amount the consultants had deemed necessary.

This contradicts claims made by animal rights groups about who was funding the opposition and how much funding the opposition had. For example, CEASE charged that the drug companies had made major campaign contributions to defeat the initiative. In fact, the pharmaceutical companies contributed only $1,000 to $5,000 each, although the Farm Bureau had requested a minimum contribution of $5,000 to $10,000 from each company. The American Veal Association promised $250,000 but contributed only about $62,500, and the National Milk Producers made no financial contribution at all (Kopperud 1988a, 1988b; Slattery 1989).

By the end of the first week of October 1988, four major commitments to the state Farm Bureau, each involving $100,000 or more, had not materialized. With one month to go in the campaign the Farm Bureau had received and spent about $400,000 and was in debt with no money to run an expensive media blitz during the last two weeks. In late October, for example, with one week to go before the referendum, the bureau did not have the $70,000 it needed to run a print ad in major Boston newspapers (Kopperud 1988b).

### The Industry Strategy

The first thing the industry did when it recognized that an animal rights initiative would be placed on the ballot was to meet with CEASE to try to persuade the organization to abandon its petition. At the first meeting in July 1987, attended by CEASE, the state Farm Bureau, the Massachusetts Poultry Association, the state Department of Food and Agriculture, and other industry representatives, the industry tried to persuade CEASE that Massachusetts farmers were humane and that any attempt to legislate animal welfare reform through referendum would be counterproductive. The industry representatives pointed out that a better course would be to introduce the petition in the form of a bill for consideration by the legislature (Slattery 1989).

The state Farm Bureau argued that CEASE's failure to follow the conventional legislative process would only alienate and anger key legislators on the Committee on Natural Resources and Agriculture, which would have to vote on the referendum petition in any case. In addition, the petition was vague in key respects, and the Department of Food and Agriculture was hostile to it and would not implement its provisions without resistance. Furthermore, if the electorate approved the initiative, the legislature could not modify it to iron out any ambiguities in it. Legislators were almost certain to overturn the initiative in 1989, the industry said (McCarthy 1989).

CEASE members dismissed the industry's arguments, however, and insisted that the failure to secure approval of the recent state veal protection bill revealed lawmakers' hostility to any animal welfare bill. They also said that although most Massachusetts farmers were well intentioned, the intensive confinement of animals was inhumane and a major legislative overhaul like the initiative was necessary. CEASE members said that even if voters rejected the initiative, the attempt to get it passed would bring the issue to the public's attention (Japenga 1989; Shurland 1990).

From July 1987 until January 1988 the industry took no positive action to stop the petition. During this crucial six-month period CEASE submitted its petition to the attorney general, the attorney general certified it, the petitioners wrote a summary of the petition that ultimately appeared on the ballot (without challenge by the industry), and CEASE gathered 50,525 signatures supporting the petition. This forced the Massachusetts legislature to vote on the bill (see note 8). In early 1988, faced with a threatening piece of legislation, the industry finally reacted to the growing momentum of the CEASE initiative. But by that time the petition's appearance on the ballot in November was virtually a foregone conclusion because of the number of signatures proponents had gathered, no matter how the legislature voted.

In January 1988 about fifteen industry representatives, including the Massachusetts Farm Bureau, the Grange, United Cooperative Farmers, United Egg Producers, National Milk Producers, and the American Feed Industry Association, met to discuss a course of action. At the meeting these representatives interviewed four public relations firms specializing in corporate campaigns about how best to cope with what had become a serious problem. One firm was from New York, another from California, and two were from Boston. Although the industry representatives made no decisions at that meeting, they agreed to meet weekly to discuss the petition and work out a common strategy (Slattery 1989).

At a subsequent meeting the industry made three important decisions. The first was to establish a political action committee (PAC) to raise money for a campaign against the initiative. The PAC was initially named The Friends of Massachusetts Agriculture but later was renamed The Committee to Save the Family Farm to reflect the political strategy that the industry adopted. Clearly, the industry had decided to reframe the debate by recasting the initiative as an attack on the family farm and mobilize citizen opposition to the animal rights initiative. The PAC was chaired by the president of the Massachusetts Farm Bureau Federation, Gordon Price, and the treasurer was James Slattery, its executive director (Slattery 1989).

Pam Comstock, the state Farm Bureau's director of information, was responsible for organizing and coordinating seventeen hundred of Massachusetts's farmers in the campaign. The PAC was designed to involve the Farm Bureau's membership in any major legislation, constitutional issue, or initiative likely to affect the agricultural community. The campaign's strategy was to raise money; encourage the writing of letters to newspaper editors; distribute pamphlets and documents at train stations, business centers, conventions, and fairs; address public meetings; get out the vote; make signs and artwork for the campaign; organize telephone banks; and monitor the activities of CEASE and its supporters, including TV and radio appearances, newspaper articles, and public speeches (Comstock 1989).

The second decision was to hire two Boston public relations firms to map out the farm bureau's campaign strategy. They were BMc Strategies, a public relations company, and Cambridge Reports, a firm that conducts opinion polls. BMc Strategies had long experience working on political campaigns in Massachusetts, including those involving farm issues and referenda. Cambridge Reports was to help the industry figure out how to effectively communicate with a nonfarm public if the issue went on the ballot. The PAC allocated $45,000 for Cambridge Reports to carry out a baseline public opinion poll to determine what public opinion was on the animal rights initiative. BMc Strategies received $50,000 for consulting work in designing a strategy (Vanderbeek 1989).

The third decision was to hire a law firm specializing in election law to determine whether CEASE's petition process complied with Massachusetts law. The law firm chosen was Cosgrove, Eisenberg, and Kiley. Thomas R. Kiley was a former first assistant attorney general with eighteen years of election law experience. The industry hoped the lawyers would find a legal technicality that would invalidate the petition. This cost the Farm Bureau $24,000. Kiley concluded that the petition was legal and admonished the bureau for not organizing and securing legal counsel until the petition process was nearly complete.

### The Industry's Campaign Theme

The industry's first reaction to the initiative's qualifying for the ballot was that it should challenge CEASE's claim that farm animals in Massachusetts were not treated humanely. In other words, the industry wanted to challenge the expressive group on its own terms and demonstrate that farmers treated their animals humanely. However, BMc Strategies and Cambridge Reports strongly advised against such a strategy based on the results of an opinion survey done from February 18 to February 22, 1988, that showed most voters favored the initiative (Cambridge Reports 1988).[14]

Respondents were read the summary of the initiative as written by CEASE and as it would appear on the November election ballot. They were asked if they would vote yes or no. Seventy-five percent said they would vote yes, whereas only 14 percent said they would vote against it. Seventy-six percent of those giving a firm yes said that they would vote that way to ensure the humane care of animals (Cambridge Reports 1988).

The survey also found that 65 percent of the respondents agreed that animals had the same rights as humans when it came to pain and suffering, whereas only 28 percent disagreed. Asked whether the initiative would stop the needless torture of animals in Massachusetts, and whether the law would stop large corporate agribusiness and drug companies from putting profits before the humane treatment of animals, 52 percent of the respondents agreed, and only 3 and 6 percent disagreed. Thus the consultants concluded that the industry could not win an animal rights issue (Cambridge Reports 1988).

The consultants stressed that the industry was facing a tough campaign. They felt that the only way the industry could prevail was to reframe the issue. In other words, without an alternative context in which to interpret the initiative, voters would approve it.

The consultants recommended redefining the initiative in terms of three arguments that had the highest anti-initiative support. The first was that placing more regulations on Massachusetts farmers could eliminate all animal farming in the state. Fifty-one percent said that if that were the case, they would vote against the initiative; 29 percent said they would vote for it. The second was that the disappearance of farming would leave thousands of acres of scarce land open for more development. Forty-eight percent of the respondents said they would oppose the initiative in order to thwart developers, and only 5 percent would still vote to approve the initiative. This argument had the appeal of attracting environmentalists who might otherwise support the animal rights initiative. The third argument was based on an appeal to fairness. Forty-seven percent of the respondents said that the exclusion of farmers from the Scientific Advisory Committee was unfair to the industry, and only 5 percent said it was not unfair (Cambridge Reports 1988).

These three arguments—the elimination of farms, the exploitation of open space, and the fairness issue—formed the basis of the industry's campaign. The industry's strategists felt these arguments could defeat the initiative for two reasons. The first is what pollsters called a "blank slate" in the electorate on the initiative issue. Asked whether they had heard or read anything about a ballot measure dealing with farm animals, 95 percent of respondents said they had not or were not sure. An open-ended question asked respondents to list the most important problems facing Massachusetts; farming was not even mentioned among the twenty-two major issues, which included high taxes, pollution, and poverty (Cambridge Reports 1988).

Thus, at least at an emotional level, absent any specific knowledge of what the animal rights issue entailed, 75 percent of respondents expressed support for it. The consultants concluded from this that the industry had to separate the public's emotional support for the humane treatment of farm animals from Question 3 on the ballot. In other words, if the public believed that the initiative was unnecessary to ensure the humane treatment of animals but that it threatened farmers and eliminated scarce open land, voters would reject it (Cambridge Reports 1988).

The survey also found that farmers in Massachusetts were held in high public esteem. Sixty-eight percent of respondents said that farmers treated their animals humanely; only 4 percent felt they did not. When this response was coupled with a question about the credibility of people and organizations on the issue of humane treatment of farm animals, farmers were rated highly believable (Cambridge Reports 1988).

The respondents rated the state's farmers as second only to veterinarians as the most believable on issues related to the treatment of farm animals. Forty-four percent felt that farmers were very believable; another 44 percent said they were somewhat believable. This compares with 31 percent who felt that CEASE was very believable and 35 percent somewhat believable. However, the Massachusetts Farm Bureau received ratings of only very believable from only 32 percent and somewhat believable from 48 percent. The consultants concluded that the most credible representatives for the industry were farmers themselves (Cambridge Reports 1988). Indeed, the direct participation of Massachusetts farmers in the campaign ultimately led to the defeat of Question 3 in the November ballot.

### Farmers Turn the Tide

Despite the industry's greater financial resources, agriculture was losing the campaign until two weeks before the election. This was reflected in the only other poll the industry conducted.[15] The second poll was carried out in September, and on the surface it was almost as discouraging for the industry as the February poll. For example, the September 1988 survey found that 65 percent of respondents said they would vote for the initiative, whereas only 16 percent said they would vote against it. With little more than a month to go in the campaign, the industry's own pollsters said that support for the initiative was overwhelming.

Table 3.1 gives the results of polls on Question 3 carried out by a Boston TV station during the campaign. What is interesting is the major shift in public opinion that occurred in October before the industry's media blitz. The only significant campaign activity during October was conducted by

TABLE 3.1 **Polling Results for Animal Rights Initiative**
Percentage Response

| Date of Poll | Yes | No |
|---|---|---|
| February 19–22 | 75 | 14 |
| September 3–5 | 65 | 16 |
| October 5* | 55 | 22 |
| October 19* | 49 | 34 |
| October 29–30* | 38 | 47 |

*The Boston Herald/WBZ-TV polls were carried out by K.R.C. Research and were based on samples of 400 likely voters.

Source: The Boston Herald/WBZ-TV polls, February and September, 1988.

Massachusetts farmers who volunteered their time and money to urge a no vote on the initiative. Not until October 28, ten days before the election, did campaign money become available to the industry for limited broadcast advertising (AFBF 1991:42). Seventy-three TV spots ran from October 28 to November 7 on WNEV (Channel 7), WCVB (Channel 5), and WBZ (Channel 4)—all major Boston TV stations—at a cost of about $200,000. The industry spent $68,000 more on newspaper ads that ran November 3 to November 7 and about $8,000 on thirty-second radio spots that ran November 8. However, most of the advertising appeared after public opinion had shifted from supporting to opposing Question 3.

From February to June the Farm Bureau strategy had been to persuade CEASE to withdraw the initiative from referendum. The industry held several meetings with CEASE representatives and tried to line up a coalition of farm and nonfarm organizations—including Governor Michael Dukakis, the Audubon Society, and the MSPCA—that were against the initiative in order to persuade CEASE (Slattery 1989).

The industry also sought to use to its advantage the April 1988 hearings on the initiative held by the state legislature's Joint Committee on Natural Resources and Agriculture; the hearings were required by the state's referendum procedures. The Farm Bureau mobilized more than six hundred farmers to attend the hearings and successfully lobbied legislators to get a near-unanimous vote in the House and Senate against the initiative. After the hearings the chairman of the committee brought the

Farm Bureau, CEASE, the MSPCA, the Animal Rescue League, and Tufts' School of Veterinary Medicine together to negotiate a compromise that would keep the initiative off the ballot. But these efforts failed, and CEASE refused to negotiate changes in the wording of the initiative (Shurland 1990:11–12).

After June 1988 the industry found itself in a very difficult position. All the polls showed that the initiative would pass by a large margin (Vanderbeek 1989). Meanwhile, the farm lobby did not have even the minimum financial resources necessary to mount a media campaign; at the time the industry had less than $500,000 in its war chest. And the industry felt that even if it had the $2.4 million for such a campaign, it would still have to concentrate all its money on TV and radio advertising close to election day, which might be too late (McCarthy 1989).

But then in late October a sea change in public opinion finally occurred, registered in the Boston Herald/WBZ-TV poll carried out from October 29 to 30 and made public on November 1 (see table 3.1)—before the industry's media blitz.

Massachusetts farmers knew that they did not have the money for a major media campaign. So they took their case directly to the voters. The polls show that only after farmers became directly involved in the campaign in the major cities did public opinion shift against the initiative. This suggests that media advertising in itself could not have achieved what the farmer-volunteers achieved. Indeed, the journalists who witnessed this unprecedented political mobilization of farmers compared it to Shays' Rebellion more than two hundred years ago. Instead of revolting against taxes and the foreclosure of farms, farmers protested an animal rights initiative.

Farmers took time out from their busy harvest season in September and October to distribute pamphlets and put up posters in the state's urban centers to persuade voters to reject Question 3. Beginning at 6 A.M. and continuing until early evening, farmers were at the Boston train stations, which handle 600,000 to 1.2 million commuters daily. They handed out leaflets and asked for support to defeat the initiative. Farmers were also at the mouth of the Callahan tunnel, traveled by 250,000 commuters daily. To get to the cities many farmers drove their tractors, trucks, and trailers, plastered with signs reading "Save the Family Farm—Vote No on Question 3." One turkey producer spent the entire weekend before the election atop of his trailer truck in a major shopping center. He had a flock of birds and a microphone and addressed large crowds urging the defeat of Question 3. In fields along major highways farmers erected huge signs calling for a no vote on Question 3 (Kopperud 1993b:21).

Although agribusiness and the Massachusetts Farm Bureau contributed to the success of the campaign, the farmers were decisive. On November 8, 1988, the animal rights initiative went down to a resounding defeat, losing by a margin of 42 percent.

### Conclusion

Expressive animal rights groups lost their campaign in large measure because they did not have the support of major SMOs and they did not have political allies. The groups that mounted the campaign were united under the leadership of the Coalition to End Animal Suffering and Exploitation (CEASE), but the major animal rights SMOs did not support CEASE's campaign.

For example, the largest movement organizations, HSUS and the ASPCA, supported CEASE's goals but disagreed with the strategy of circumventing the state legislature by sponsoring a popular initiative. Political elites opposed the use of the initiative largely because it was beyond their control. The animal rights SMOs did not want to jeopardize their relationship with political leaders by supporting the initiative (Shurland 1990:5).

The CEASE campaign was highly effective in framing the election issue, tapping into a widespread and popular belief that farm animals, like domesticated animals, should be treated humanely. Survey research persuaded the industry that it could not counter CEASE on this ground, which led the large agribusiness firms to withdraw most of their financial commitments to campaign against the initiative.

Free riders were not a factor in this campaign. CEASE had no formal membership, no officers, and no dues required for participation. Indeed, CEASE's lack of formal leadership made it virtually impossible for industry opponents to negotiate concessions to the animal rights groups, business's traditional strategy, which placed the companies at a disadvantage. The business strategy was to make concessions to CEASE in order to persuade the organization to withdraw the initiative. However, when different representatives of CEASE turned up at negotiating sessions, reaching any agreement became impossible. The industry's attempts to arrange negotiating sessions simply weakened its response to the campaign.

Only the last-minute farmer protest saved the day. Farmers recognized that the agriculture industry would not finance a campaign. The corporations feared that if they sponsored a losing effort, they would expose their vulnerability and encourage similar campaigns throughout the country. That left the farmers with no recourse but to try to save their own bacon. And they did.

### NOTES

1. Twenty other European countries have also adopted sweeping reforms to protect farm animals. For example, the Swedish Parliament adopted legislation in 1988 that covers all animal housing (Crabo 1990 and 1991). It requires, for example, that cattle in sheds be allowed to graze outdoors, the phasing out of battery cages for laying hens within ten years, that sows no longer be tethered, that bedding be provided for cows and pigs, slaughterhouses use new humane methods, and that new more stringent restrictions be placed on genetic engineering. Similar laws have been adopted in Denmark, Switzerland, Norway, and the Netherlands. The European Union also has endorsed some of these laws.

2. Although Singer has had arguably the greatest influence on the animal rights movement in the United States, he explicitly rejects the concept of animal rights on the ground that it is a cliché or little more than political rhetoric. Instead, he emphasizes the notion that animals are "sentient," or feeling, beings with the ability to suffer and as such have an interest in their own well-being, which humans are morally obliged to honor.

3. According to Regan (1983), the philosophical basis of animal rights lies in the fact that animals are beings and not things. All living beings have certain basic moral rights because they are "subject of a life." Regan lays out seven criteria for a subject of a life: that beings can perceive and remember; have beliefs, desires, and preferences; intentionally pursue goals; have feelings and emotions; a sense of their future; a psychophysical identity of maturing and aging; and that they understand the importance of their individual welfare, independent of others. According to this logic, all animal agriculture is unjust, believers must become vegetarians, and it is the duty of individuals to oppose or protest the violation of animal rights by industry or government. In addition, hunting and trapping should be banned, and the use of animals in scientific laboratory tests or research should be outlawed.

4. However, according to John Kingdon's criterion (1984:147–50), no consensus on animal rights issues is emerging within the political elites. Indeed, no evidence exists

that policy makers have even identified animal rights as a unique policy category comparable to health care, transportation, or welfare.

5. According to study by the American Federation of Teachers (AFT 1994) only 4 percent of U.S. high school students are able to pass a high-level achievement test in biology that requires deep knowledge and skills.

6. Crooker (1990:296) notes that since 1901, fifty-four of the seventy-six Nobel Prizes awarded to scientists in physiology and medicine were for discoveries based on animal experimentation.

7. Massachusetts also had one hundred small farms that produced nontraditional livestock such as llamas, alpacas, angora and mohair rabbits and goats, and aquaculture. The state also had several hundred operations that raised, boarded, and trained horses.

8. According to the state constitution, after a referendum petition is certified by the attorney general, the legislature must hold hearings on the initiative, and both houses must vote on it by May 4. If the legislature fails to approve the initiative, the petitioners must collect an additional one half of 1 percent of the last vote for governor, or eighty-five hundred signatures in 1988. These additional signatures had to be obtained after the legislature's vote and submitted for certification fourteen days before the filing deadline (ten days for Boston), which was June 18 in Boston and June 22 in the rest of the state.

The Massachusetts Legislature held hearings in April 1988, and the House of Representatives voted 2–150 against the initiative on May 2; the state senate voted against it on May 3, 0–34. These votes triggered the need for more signatures, which the petitioners collected easily, submitting 100,000 more by the deadline. State law makers did not like the petition process because they could not modify an initiative once voters approved it.

9. Contrary to claims by animal rights groups, certain drugs have been approved by the U.S. Food and Drug Adminstration for use in formula-fed veal. And the Food Safety and Inspection Service (FSIS) of the U.S. Department of Agriculture, which has responsibility for testing for drug residues in special-fed veal carcasses, reports that the veal supply is safe (FSIS 1992). Animal rights groups challenge the validity of these tests and point out that there is no monitoring of farmers' use of antibiotics.

10. There are three categories of veal: "Bob," "grass-fed," and "special-fed" veal. Because veal calves are a by-product of the dairy industry, veal production is located in the major dairy states. The veal industry is based upon the availability of surplus male or bull calves, usually the off-spring of Holstein cows. The male calves sent directly to slaughter within a few days of birth are called Bob veal calves and usually weigh less than 150 pounds. Grass-fed veal is produced from calves raised partly on pasture or grain as well as milk, and they are slaughtered between six months and one year of age.

The so-called special-fed veal calves, also known as "formula-fed," "milk-fed," "prime," "fancy," or "white-veal" calves, are fed only enriched milk. They are typically kept immobilized in individual wooden stalls or crates inside a barn until they are slaughtered at about sixteen weeks of age and weigh 350 to 400 pounds. The special-fed veal supplies a consumer demand for a gourmet product and is served in exclusive restaurants. This veal is prized for its tenderness, and the meat is identified by its pale pink color, in contrast to the red coloration of the other two categories, Bob and grass fed.

11. Animal rights groups have used the same unidentified picture of a downed veal calf in a wooden stall for years to depict cruelty in the veal industry. However, they have refused to identify the source of the picture or the photographer. The crate shown in the animal advocates' media campaigns is not used today and never was used extensively (L. Wilson 1992; Shurland 1990:11).

12. According to CEASE, no legislation specifically protected the welfare of farm animals. For example, the U.S. Animal Welfare Act, which is the legislation that protects animals in the United States, excludes farm animals used for food and fiber. The U.S. Humane Slaughter Act and federal and state transportation laws deal only with how animals are killed and transported, and they are outdated. For example, the laws were designed to regulate the transportation of animals by rail and do not apply to transportation by truck (AFBF 1991:8–9). The Massachusetts anticruelty statute had not been tested in court and did not define what is adequate housing and nutrition for farm animals.

13. They included Agway, Agrimark, county farm bureaus, the Wisconsin Farm Bureau Federation and farm bureaus in other states, the Midwest Livestock Producers Cooperative, Blue Seal, Massachusetts Poultry Association, Massachusetts Vegetable Growers' Association, the national and Massachusetts Grange, United Cooperative Farmers, United Egg Producers, Eifer Project International, Dekalb Poultry Research, Inc., the Massachusetts Department of Food and Agriculture, Massachusetts Veterinary Medical Association, American Feed Industry Association, the National Cattlemen's Association, National Pork Producers Association, American Farm Bureau Federation, American Veal Association, and veal packing companies such as Brown Packing ("Dutch Valley Veal"), Berliner and Marx ("Plume de Veal"), Provimi Veal, and Michigan Veal Company. Contributors also included the animal pharmaceutical companies: Monsanto, American Cyanamid, Pfizer, Hoffman-LaRoche, Merck, and Ceva Laboratories, Governor Dukakis, and the Massachusetts Senate and House (Slattery and Bragg 1989).

14. Those solidly in favor of the initiative tended to be women (many of whom did not work outside the home), have lower educational levels, be retired and older than sixty-five, clerical workers, Democrats, have annual incomes between $8,000 and $20,000, live in the northern urban part of the state, and not eat meat. Those solidly against the initiative tended to have a higher level of education (i.e., professionals), be aged forty-six to sixty-five, have an income in excess of $50,000, and be Republicans,

farmers, government workers, managers, and residents of the southern suburban and rural parts of the state (Cambridge Reports 1988, 1989).

15. BMc and Cambridge Reports had proposed conducting six polls from February to October. However, the campaign committee did not have the financial resources to do more than one baseline survey in February and one follow-up tracking poll in September (Cambridge Reports 1988, 1989).

# FOUR

# THE "BIG GREEN" CAMPAIGN
Hollywood and the Chemical Industry

## The Modern Environmental Movement

The modern environmental movement arose in amid the affluence that followed the end of World War II. Clean air, water, wilderness, better health, and recreation became, in effect, consumer products demanded by Americans who have economic security and leisure. Thus environmental quality became part of the American middle-class conception of a higher standard of living (Hays 1987:4–22).

The environmental movement has undergone three waves of evolution. In the 1960s public interest groups were dedicated to protecting natural resources. Major environmental SMOs, such as the Sierra Club under the leadership of David Brower, lobbied government to block dams in Dinosaur National Monument and the Grand Canyon and to save the redwood groves in California's Mineral King Valley. The Sierra Club, and other groups such as the Conservation Foundation, used the popular media to build public support for protecting the land, stopping pollution, and other ecological issues such as the effect of pesticides on the environment. Another significant force in the environmental movement during the 1960s was the influence of Supreme Court Justice William O. Douglas, an avid hiker and camper who championed "wilderness values" and successfully campaigned to preserve the Chesapeake and Ohio Canal, designated a national historical park in 1971 (Shabecoff 1993:102–103).

A major achievement during this stage of the movement was to bring environmental issues to public awareness. The movement framed environmentalism in terms of the fragility of the planet and the universal responsibility to protect it. This placed technological progress and growth in the context of societal responsibility to protect natural resources. Tesh and Williams (1996:286) point out that the movement used pictures of the Earth from outer space, wounded animals, and devastated forests and wilderness areas to create impetus.

During the 1960s litigation emerged as a political strategy for blocking projects that threaten the aesthetic values of the environment. A landmark case for the environmental movement during this period was a suit filed by the Scenic Hudson Preservation Conference against the Federal Power Commission to prevent Consolidated Edison from building a pumping station in the Hudson Valley. The U.S. Court of Appeals ruled in favor of Scenic Hudson, noting that it had standing for suit based on "aesthetic, conservational and recreational" interest in the area. The appellate ruling forced Con Ed to build a pumping station at an another site. This set the stage for a whole generation of litigation-oriented environmental SMOs such as the Environmental Defense Fund and the Natural Resources Defense Council (Shabecoff 1993:103).

In the second wave of the movement, which began during the late 1970s, the focus shifted from the human destruction of the environment to the effect of the polluted environment on humans. Environmental organizations mobilized citizen protests of the dire health consequences of chemical waste sites and the dangers of pesticides and industrial pollution. The accent was on the irresponsible application of science and technology, which threatened life. For example, Rachel Carson's book, *Silent Spring,* brought to public attention the danger of chemical pesticides such as DDT.

The first Earth Day in 1970 had signaled the emergence of environmentalism as a mass social movement and emphasized the dangers of pollution to human health. This and subsequent Earth Days involving millions of demonstrators and volunteers who pick up trash captured the public imagination and profoundly affected government policies, industry, education, and the physical world by preserving the natural environment and open space (Shabecoff 1993:114).

College students were especially energized by Earth Day. Young activists who joined the movement also tended to be involved in a broader set of social justice issues, including civil rights, protesting the war in Vietnam, the Native American rights movement, and feminism. Students perceived these issues as being related to the deterioration of the environment and quality of life. This spawned a new wave of radical environmental leaders and organizations. SMOs such as Greenpeace, Friends of the Earth, the Environmental Policy Institute, Earth First, and the California League of Conservation Voters emerged with a radical political agenda. Some of these organizations were dedicated to protecting the environment through direct action (such as protests and spiking trees), civil disobedience, and ecosabotage. Others established staffs of lawyers, lobbyists, economists, fund raisers, scientists, and public relations experts to influence government policy. These activists also joined mainstream environmental organizations and infused them with new aggressive political strategies and agendas (Shabecoff 1993).

The third wave of the environmental movement began in the late 1980s and was characterized by a more pragmatic and professional attitude. The leadership recognized that litigation, direct confrontation, and lobbying were no longer sufficient to realize their goals. They recognized that industry opponents had adopted a more aggressive strategy of challenging the environmental movement in Congress, statehouses, and the courts (Shabecoff 1993).

To meet this challenge the movement adopted the techniques of mass-marketing, public relations, fund-raising, large memberships, and media campaigns. Examples of the third wave approach to environmental activism are the Natural Resources Defense Council and the Environmental Defense Fund. They stress the importance of professionalism, using the mass media, conducting political campaigns, and negotiating with public officials to achieve their goals (Shabecoff 1993).

### Prelude to Big Green: Proposition 65

An expressive interest group called Campaign California waged a highly successful campaign in 1986 to ban chemicals known to pose a "significant risk" of causing cancer or birth defects. The initiative was called the Safe Drinking Water and Toxic Enforcement Act, or Proposition 65.[1] Campaign California led a coalition of environmental SMOs, including the Natural Resources Defense Council, Environmental Defense Fund, Sierra Club, and the California League of Conservation Voters. It had the support of leading Democratic politicians, including California Attorney General John Van de Kamp and key assemblymen Lloyd Connelly (Democrat of Sacramento) and Tom Hayden, the former 1960s radical who was now a Democratic assemblyman from Santa Monica. The campaign was supported by a coalition of consumer and labor groups, including the AFL-CIO and Ralph Nader's Public Interest Research Group.

The effort was led by Campaign California under the direction of Hayden and his then-wife, Jane Fonda. Hayden and Bob Mulholland, executive director of Campaign California, devised the strategy and tactics for the Proposition 65 campaign. Hayden and Fonda also contributed $800,000 to the campaign, and Fonda solicited large campaign contributions from Hollywood stars. Hollywood celebrities attracted attention for Proposition 65 from the powerful southern California entertainment establishment.

Cosponsors of the initiative were the major environmental SMOs—the Natural Resources Defense Council, Environmental Defense Fund, and the Sierra Club; their members helped gather the signatures necessary to place Proposition 65 on the ballot. Proposition 65, which voters approved, was the most ambitious safe drinking water legislation in the country at the time. It bans industry from discharging into the state's drinking water 260 carcinogens and reproductive toxins identified by federal and international agencies. Violators are liable for fines of as much as $2,500 a day, and citizens have the right to sue polluters and receive as much as 25 percent of any judgment.

The successes of the federal Toxic Substances Control Act and the Clean Air Act pale in comparison with the success of Proposition 65, also known as the California Safe Drinking Water and Toxic Enforcement Act of 1986. For example, the federal Clean Air Act of 1972 banned only thirteen contaminants. Twelve years after passage of the Toxic Substances Control Act in 1982, which was intended to determine which of the thirty thousand chemicals in commercial use need regulation, only fifteen chemicals had been identified as dangerous. By contrast, four months after Proposition 65 took effect, California listed twenty-nine chemicals as dangerous. Proposition 65 applies to workplace exposure, consumer products, and industrial pollutants in businesses that employ ten or more people. Almost every product for sale in California is now subject to the Proposition 65 warning requirement. Warning signs are prominently displayed in grocery stores, restaurants, bars, and banks. Because building materials contain carcinogens, contractors have even hung such warning signs in new houses to avoid lawsuits.

But passage of Proposition 65 was no sure thing; it faced strong political opposition. Industry and the state government regard Proposition 65 as an administrative nightmare to enforce. Most of Proposition 65 has yet to be implemented, although more than five hundred chemicals have been identified as dangerous. That list could be expanded to include an indeterminate number of chemicals, such as alcoholic beverages because alcohol may be both cancer causing and has been implicated in birth defects (Lyons and Zalom 1990:3–4). According to Jeffrey Nedelman, the vice president for public affairs for the Grocery Manufacturers of America, Proposition 65 made California's birth-defect standard ten times more stringent than anything endorsed by any scientific community in the world. A 1992 report by a review panel concluded that by federal standards Proposition 65 represented "100 years of progress in the areas of hazard identification, risk assessment, and exposure assessment" (Vig and Kraft 1997:39).

An industry coalition called the Environmental Working Group was originally organized to contest the referendum on Proposition 65. Its members included the California Chamber of Commerce, League of Food Processors, California Manufacturers' Association, and California Farm Bureau. The coalition spent $5 million in a losing effort to defeat Proposition 65, arguing that it was extreme and unnecessary. Various industries feared its effects on a multitude of products and said its standards were highly subjective and almost impossible to implement. For example, many of the listed chemicals are omnipresent.

Benzene, among the substances regulated by the measure, is found in minute amounts in many food products, comprises 2 percent of most gasoline, occurs in the formaldehyde widely used in the manufacture of mobile homes, and is present in most furniture and permanent-press clothing. Proposition 65 requires that all such substances be labeled as dangerous. George Deukmejian, the Republican governor at the time, supported the industry's position and sought to limit the number of chemicals listed under Proposition 65 as dangerous. Indeed, the supporters of Proposition 65 were forced to sue the governor to force him to implement the initiative.

Nevertheless, the environmental SMOs backing Proposition 65 saw it as the beginning of a more ambitious campaign. For example, when the initiative was first proposed in 1986, its backers wanted to make public agencies, such as municipal water and sewage systems, subject to its provisions. However, they decided not to include these agencies to avoid enforcement complications. After it passed in 1986 by a margin of 2 to 1, however, environmentalists recognized that this decision was a miscalculation and subsequently sought to expand the scope of Proposition 65 and take the campaign to other states. For example, the Sierra Club and Environmental Defense Fund planned grassroots campaigns similar to Proposition 65 in

New York, Massachusetts, Texas, Oregon, Tennessee, and Hawaii (Russell 1988:788).

## The Big Green Campaign

"Big Green" was the most ambitious environmental legislation ever proposed in the United States. The 1990 California initiative (Proposition 128) was so all encompassing that it was popularly known as Big Green.[2] The measure was designed to attack environmental degradation on all fronts. One observer described the bill as taking the U.S. Marine Corps approach on land, sea, and in the air.

The initiative's major elements would have

Phased out the use on California food of pesticides that are believed to cause cancer or birth defects.

Eliminated chlorofluorocarbons (CFCs) and reduced carbon dioxide emissions, which are linked to the thinning of the earth's ozone layer.

Banned the drilling of oil off the shore of California.

Strengthened laws controlling the treatment of sewage.

Banned the cutting of old-growth redwood forests.

Created an elected statewide political office of environmental czar that would supersede all other environmental agencies. The czar would have had the power to sue any polluter or government agency that failed to prevent pollution in the state.

The most controversial element of Big Green was the pesticide provision. Proponents of the bill targeted the petrochemical industry as the principal culprit in environmental destruction and principal threat to human health. They singled out the chemical companies because environmentalists had found a similar strategy successful in 1986 with the passage of Proposition 65.

The expressive group that led the campaign for Big Green in 1990 was also Campaign California. The principal SMOs supporting the campaign were the Natural Resources Defense Council, Sierra Club, National Toxics Campaign, Pesticide Watch, and the California League of Conservation Voters. Their chief nonmovement allies were Hollywood celebrities, and their political allies were members of the California Legislature and the state Democratic Party. Arrayed against them were the chemical industry, the California Farm Bureau, the California Chamber of Commerce, and the large timber companies. Industry defeated Big Green.

The California business community felt threatened by Big Green, fearing that the passage of Proposition 65 was a harbinger of an even more ambitious Big Green initiative. Businesses did not think they could defeat it. They worried that the underlying purpose of the bill was to destroy California's petrochemical industry and set a precedent for the entire country.

### Political Origins of Big Green

Big Green was part of a unique gubernatorial election campaign strategy. John Van de Kamp, the attorney general of California in 1989, was the leading Democratic candidate for governor when Deukmejian, the popular conservative Republican governor, announced that he would not seek a third term.[3] Van de Kamp's thirty years in politics and family background had made his a household name. He was related to the Van de Kamp family bakery chain that sold cookies, bread, and condiments in grocery stores throughout California under its name. Just before he announced his candidacy in January 1990, he had campaign funds of $2 million in the bank. Although he was a tedious campaigner, Van de Kamp had a reputation as a competent attorney general and was a rare law-and-order Democrat. Nevertheless, Van de Kamp had a major negative: his role in the highly publicized Hillside Strangler case of ten sex-related murders in 1981, while he was the Los Angles district attorney (see Lubenow 1991:39).

One suspect, Kenneth Bianchi, agreed to plead guilty to five counts of murder in a plea bargain to avoid the death penalty. In return, Bianchi agreed to testify against his accomplice, Angelo Buono. However, after the plea bargain Bianchi began to alter his testimony, which raised grave doubts among prosecutors about Bianchi's reliability as a witness. Prosecutors in Van de Kamp's office felt that Bianchi was so unreliable that they recommended dropping murder charges against Bianchi. Instead, they would prosecute Bianchi for lesser sex crimes against women who had survived attacks and could corroborate the charges (Lubenow 1991:39–40).

Van de Kamp approved this recommendation, which would have made Bianchi eligible for release on bail of only $50,000. However, Superior Court Judge Ronald George took the unprecedented step of rejecting Van de Kamp's motion to drop the murder charges against Bianchi and ordered the prosecution to proceed under the original indictment. The case was transferred to the state attorney general, then George Deukmejian.

Deukmejian successfully prosecuted Bianchi for murder, securing nine out of ten convictions.

Given the public concern about crime in California, it was virtually a certainty that both Republican and Democratic candidates in the 1990 gubernatorial race would use the so-called Buono affair against Van de Kamp. His campaign staff felt that a dramatic and unconventional campaign strategy was necessary to shift public attention away from the Hillside Strangler case. The key political consultant for Van de Kamp was Richie Ross, who had a reputation for being brash and unorthodox (Van de Kamp interview 1994).

Ross urged an ingenious high-risk, high-profile campaign strategy pegged to Big Green that would also give Van de Kamp instantaneous support and enable the campaign to get around campaign financing limits imposed by 1988's Proposition 73 (Van de Kamp interview 1994). Proposition 73 limited campaign contributions to $1,000 per person in a single fiscal year. This meant that to raise the large sums required to run a state election campaign in California, a candidate would have to have an extensive network of campaign contributors. This required a large organization and the time necessary to create it. However, Proposition 73 did not apply to campaign financing for initiatives on the ballot. Ross reasoned that if initiatives formed the core of Van de Kamp's election platform, the unrestricted financing for initiatives could circumvent Proposition 73's restrictions on Van de Kamp's campaign (Van de Kamp interview 1994).

Van de Kamp's polling data had identified three major issues of concern to California voters: the environment, crime, and campaign reform or term limits. Ross argued that Van de Kamp should link his gubernatorial campaign to the ballot initiatives (originally twelve, later narrowed to three) corresponding to the three areas of public concern. What was novel about this strategy was the hope that by making initiatives the core of Van de Kamp's platform, support for the initiatives would transfer to Van de Kamp himself.

One of his platform planks was the environment; the other two were crime and campaign reform. The crime plank was designed to deal with drug abuse by establishing an antidrug "superfund," speeding up trials, and strengthening enforcement and prosecution of criminals. The campaign reform or ethics plank was designed to drain the "ethical swamp" of special interests in Sacramento. Specific provisions included limiting campaign spending, limiting state officials and legislators to twelve years in office, providing taxpayer financing for candidates, and establishing a code of ethics for elected officials and office holders.[4]

Backing these three measures would also enable Van de Kamp to claim that, unlike other candidates, voters knew exactly what legislation Van de Kamp would support if elected. Furthermore, each issue had its own constituency, organization, and funding. Van de Kamp wanted to use their constituencies on behalf of his campaign. Indeed, his support for these measures contributed to an initial eighteen-point lead in the polls over his principal Democratic rival, Diane Feinstein (Lubenow 1991:18–29).

However, Van de Kamp's strategy ultimately proved to be his downfall. It divided his campaign staff into warring factions over its wisdom, and it undermined Van de Kamp's one proven political asset—he was an insider in California politics. In particular, his backing of the drain-the-swamp measure alienated the political establishment, including the speaker of the California House, Willie Brown (among the most adept politicians in the country), and other state legislators. Once a source of political support Van de Kamp had always been able to count on, the political establishment deserted him because of the initiative strategy and allied with Feinstein's camp (Van de Kamp interview 1994).

Van de Kamp's environmental plank was designed to establish an alliance between the candidate and major environmental groups—the California League of Conservation Voters, Campaign California, National Toxics Campaign, Natural Resources Defense Council, Pesticide Watch, and Sierra Club California. Van de Kamp and Hayden brought these organizations and Democratic legislators together in Sacramento in 1989 to draft a bill to be placed on the November 1990 ballot ("Van de Kamp, Ecologists" 1989; Van de Kamp interview 1994).

The environmental SMOs did not want politicians to hijack their issues, and they did not want to have the various elements of what turned out to be Big Green placed in a single omnibus initiative. However, they reluctantly went along with the Van de Kamp strategy of creating an environmental wish list in a single initiative because they knew that Van de Kamp and Hayden could get it on the ballot. In hindsight, the wisdom of the environmental groups' opposition to a single bill was confirmed by the outcome.

The principal weakness of Big Green was that it was so all embracing that it was too complex and technical for the voting public to understand. Its very ambitiousness became its Achilles heel. That is to say, the scope of Big Green was so broad that it was perceived as a potential threat to most industries and businesses in California. This perception fueled a formidable opposition to Big Green.

The key legislators in the Big Green campaign, as in that for Proposition 65, were Hayden and Connelly. Hayden was campaign chairman, and the campaign manager was Mulholland, the Democratic political consultant and executive director of Campaign California. Mulholland chaired the Environmental Protection Act Steering Committee, which directed the Big Green campaign. The composition of Big Green's campaign steering committee was determined in part by the size of financial contributions to the campaign. Anyone who contributed $100,000 or more and generated 100,000 signatures for the initiative petition (the campaign needed to gather at least 372,178 signatures to appear on the ballot) got a seat on the campaign steering committee. (The requirements for membership on the committee later became $100,000 *or* 100,000 signatures because the SMOs failed to reach their targets. Volunteers on college campuses and elsewhere lacked enthusiasm.)

Fonda worked closely with Patrick Lippert, the director of the Culver City–based political action committee known as the Entertainment Industry Support Coalition for the Environmental Protection Initiative. They coordinated their efforts to raise money from Hollywood celebrities for the Big Green campaign. Lippert had been soliciting campaign money from Hollywood celebrities for political issues for the last five years. Fonda personally contributed more than $100,000 to the Big Green campaign and generated more than $500,000 in contributions from the Hollywood community. Hayden, divorced from Fonda the year before, made a personal contribution of $1 million to the campaign.[5]

As the chief sources of financing, Hayden and Campaign California dominated the campaign. The environmental SMOs on the Big Green steering committee and the Van de Kamp campaign committee contributed money and gathered signatures. However, Hayden and Campaign California played the most important role. For example, Mulholland's deputy, David Cameron, coordinated the entire petition drive for signatures to qualify the initiative for the ballot. The petition-gathering operation included a professional signature-gathering company, Van de Kamp's campaign organization, twelve thousand volunteers, and more than forty environmental organizations. Indeed, the dominance of Hayden and Mulholland gave rise to tension between Mulholland and the environmental groups on the steering committee. They criticized Mulholland, who has been described as the James Carville of the California Democratic Party, for his failure to consult them and seek their participation in campaign policy decisions such as hiring and spending.[6]

Hayden, Fonda, and Van de Kamp had given money to the Proposition 65 campaign in 1986, and Van de Kamp was comfortable working with Hayden, Fonda, and the Hollywood establishment. Proponents as well as opponents saw Big Green as an expanded version of Proposition 65. Indeed, the drafters and promoters of Big Green were almost identical to those who had backed Proposition 65. Van de Kamp supported Hayden's Proposition 65 campaign in 1986, was wealthy, personally acquainted with Hollywood movie moguls, and was well connected to the powerful southern California media establishment. However, they had different priorities. Van de Kamp saw Big Green primarily as a political strategy for winning the governorship. However, environmental SMOs were not necessarily committed to Van de Kamp's candidacy. Instead, they wanted all the gubernatorial candidates to support Big Green. They resented the resistance of the Van de Kamp's staff to attempts to secure the endorsement of the initiative from the Republican candidate, Pete Wilson, and Democratic rival Diane Feinstein. Unbeknown to the environmental groups, Van de Kamp's staff did not even inform Wilson or Feinstein of the plans for the Big Green initiative, let alone ask them to endorse it. From Van de Kamp's perspective that would have undermined his entire campaign strategy (Van de Kamp interview 1994).

Van de Kamp touted Big Green as "a bill of rights" for all California residents that would place the right to clean beaches ahead of the right of oil companies to drill for oil and dump refuse along the coast, according to the *Sacramento Bee* (October 11, 1989). He claimed that by approving the initiative, "Californians can make a sweeping pronouncement on behalf of environmental protection that will help turn the tide, not only here but throughout the world," adding that "this is a moment in history when we are waking up to the reality that we are killing ourselves" ("Van de Kamp, Ecologists" 1989; *San Diego Union,* October 11, 1989:A3).

Hayden claimed that Big Green was the most significant proposal for protecting the environment ever placed before voters in the United States (*Los Angeles Times,* October 11, 1989:A20). He said that the point of the initiative was to "end a decade of environmental neglect and begin a decade of environmental action" (*Daily News,* October 11, 1989:4).

Environmental SMOs were no less enthusiastic about Big Green. For example, Lucy Blake of the California League of Conservation Voters said that "by supporting this initiative, California voters will be making a personal commitment to the planet" (*San Jose Mercury News,* October 11, 1989:8B). And the Sierra Club's state director, Michael Paparian, said,

"California voters will do something no voters have ever done anywhere in the world. In one single action, they will vote to change our environmental future," according to a press release from the Environmental Protection Act Steering Committee.

Hayden and Mulholland played a key role in the Big Green initiative, especially after Van de Kamp's loss to Feinstein in the Democratic primary in June 1990. Ironically, Van de Kamp's initiative strategy backfired insofar as it alienated the Democratic rank-and-file. Democratic Party elites opposed Van de Kamp's term limit initiative and restrictions on campaign financing. In effect, after the primary Hayden, Mulholland, and the Campaign California staff carried the Big Green initiative by themselves. Passage of the initiative had the potential for serving Hayden's long-term political ambitions for higher government office. To Hayden, Big Green represented not only the next step of his highly successful Proposition 65 initiative but career advancement if he were to become the first elected environmental advocate in the country.[7] It would also provide Hayden with an opportunity to remake his tarnished left-wing anti–Vietnam War image and allow him to become a mainstream politician.

### Nonmovement Allies

Hollywood celebrities were the principal nonmovement allies of the Big Green campaign. They provided most of the campaign financing and helped drum up a significant amount of publicity for Big Green. Prindle and Endersby have described Hollywood as a "gigantic potential propaganda machine" (1993:136). The average adult watches three hours of TV a day, and Americans purchase about one billion movie tickets each year. The authors underscore the consensus that the industry constitutes a powerful vehicle for mass learning.

On the basis of survey research conducted on the Hollywood elite from 1989 to 1990, Prindle and Endersby concluded that as a group, they are significantly more liberal than the general population and they strongly support the Democratic party.[8] They identify with the label "environmentalist" and think there should be increased government control of business, and increased spending, to protect the environment.

Fonda and Hayden have been credited with awakening the political interests of younger celebrities in the movie industry. Indeed, Mulholland was convinced that the role of Hollywood luminaries would ensure the passage of Big Green. He declared that Hollywood personalities "are our

No. 1 asset for raising money and getting our message across" (*Outlook*, November 14, 1993:A3). He said he assumed that the Hollywood community reflected the California public. He reasoned that celebrities attract the media, which in turn carries the message to the voting public, which would approve Big Green because the celebrities had endorsed the measure (*Outlook*, November 14, 1989:A3). Mulholland assumed too that Big Green would pass because voters had approved Proposition 65 and because Van de Kamp's early opinion polls showed overwhelming public support for it.

In September 1986 about forty Hollywood stars, including Robin Williams, Chevy Chase, Whoopi Goldberg, and Cher, had toured California in buses to promote Proposition 65. Fonda organized an even larger Hollywood campaign for Big Green in 1989. Fonda said at the time that while "we the environmentalists" cannot raise as much money as the "polluters," the Hollywood community could create a public awareness of the cause by participating in the Big Green campaign (*Outlook*, November 14, 1989:A3).

Mulholland elaborated by saying that Big Green would be even bigger for "stargazers" than Proposition 65. Because Big Green was so much broader in scope, he reasoned that it would attract much wider support in the movie community. He said that the environment was among the top two political issues for Hollywood. It would be one of the most important issues on the November 1990 ballot. Mulholland said that since 1987 several "issue-oriented groups" had emerged to express Hollywood's political interests. He was referring to a younger group of Hollywood celebrities who were environmentalists and were prepared to campaign for causes like Big Green (*Outlook*, November 14, 1989:A3).

### Earth Day Media Event

The twentieth anniversary of Earth Day on April 22, 1990, was an opportunity to generate public support and gather momentum for environmental issues, and the Big Green initiative undoubtedly was a beneficiary of the attention paid to the anniversary. For example, network and cable TV programs promoted the Big Green campaign by saturating programs with "saving the Earth's environment" themes. The Hollywood community did this without any cost to the campaign. Among the most environmentally conscious TV networks was the Turner Broadcasting System (TBS) of Ted

Turner, Fonda's companion at the time and future husband, and contributor of $100,000 to Big Green. TBS produced an animated cartoon series for children called *Captain Planet.* TBS consulted Campaign California for the program, which featured cartoon characters battling environmental threats such as oil spills, drift nets, the ozone hole, the destruction of forests, and "smog monsters."

TBS also produced a weekly program called *Earthbeat* that began on October 15, 1989, and was designed to show how individuals, companies, and countries can help save the planet. Turner also hired environmentalist Barbara Pyle to make environmental documentaries for TBS, and he cofounded the Better World Society, which produced or acquired more than forty documentaries on the environment.

CBS aired sixty-second "Earth Quest" spots, which replaced the network's "Presidential Portraits," and planned five one-hour specials on the environment in April 1990. ABC's series *Head of the Class* produced six new episodes with an environmental theme. In a November 1989 episode of *Murphy Brown,* Candice Bergen accepted a bet that she could make her lifestyle more "environmentally responsible." Puppeteer Jim Henson developed a children's show about nature called *W.I.L.D.* Olivia Newton-John was named the first United Nations goodwill ambassador for the environment and planned an environmental holiday special called *A Very Green Christmas.*

Barbara Streisand, Kevin Costner, and other stars hosted a two-hour special on Earth Day called *A Practical Guide to How You Can Save the Planet.* And *Time* named "endangered Earth" its "man of the year" in January 1989. Thus it was no surprise that Earth Day was the most successful day the Big Green campaign had in gathering signatures to place the initiative on the ballot.

Fonda and a group of Hollywood environmental groups called the Entertainment Industry Coalition organized numerous fund-raising events. They included a family picnic hosted by Meyera and Jay Gordon, both pediatricians used by Hollywood celebrities, and Philip Trask, a dentist to the stars. The picnic was cochaired by Mothers and Others for Pesticide Limits, an environmental SMO chaired by Meryl Streep, and its purpose was to introduce the doctors' Hollywood patients to the Big Green initiative. Representatives of environmental groups on the Big Green steering committee attended and explained to the stars the importance of giving financial support to the campaign (Sanders and Lippert 1990).

On the evening before the Academy Awards, the Entertainment Industry Coalition organized a celebrity briefing on Big Green. Invitations to it went out over the names of coalition members, who included Chevy Chase, Ted Danson, Don Henley, Meryl Streep, and Fonda. At the gathering Hayden and the environmental groups briefed the celebrities on the importance of supporting Big Green (Sanders and Lippert 1990).

The Entertainment Industry Coalition also sponsored a "viewing party" for the *ABC Earth Day Viewing Special* to be held at the t-Maple Drive Restaurant in Beverly Hills. Those attending were asked to contribute $500 to $1,000 per person to Big Green. Another fund-raising event for Big Green featured the Go Go's, a disbanded but highly successful all-female rock 'n' roll group that held a reunion concert and a party afterward. This too was sponsored by the Entertainment Industry Coalition, as well as MCA Records, Hard Rock Cafe, KIIS-FM, Danny Goldberg, and Gold Mountain Records. They sold six thousand general admission tickets at $21 each and four hundred sponsor tickets at $250 each.

High-dollar "kick-off" events to launch the Big Green campaign included a cocktail party hosted by Browne Greene, a wealthy Hollywood trial attorney, and his wife, Iva, with special guest Morgan Fairchild. They invited other trial attorneys and asked them to contribute at least $5,000 each. Other fund-raising cocktail parties included those hosted by Bristol and Richard Ogner of Malibu and chaired by Lisa and Kris Kristofferson, Burgess Meredith, Jayni and Chevy Chase, and cohosted by Susan and Jeff Bridges, John Candy, Rita Wilson and Tom Hanks, Victoria Tennant and Steve Martin, and Nancy and Martin Short. Eva and Kenny Loggins also held fund-raising cocktail parties.

A variety of other events also served as fund-raisers, including river rafting, and a roller-skating party with special guest Ed Begley Jr. In September 1990 Bette Midler and Friends held a fund-raising concert for Big Green at the Hollywood Bowl, and in November another major concert–fund-raiser at the Santa Monica Civil Auditorium featured musicians Bonnie Raitt and Ry Cooder and comedian Bobcat Goldthwait. A reception was held after the concert for people willing to pay an additional $250. There were also numerous raffles to which artists donated their work to raise money for Big Green.

In July 1990 the campaign produced a unique thirty-minute commercial narrated by some of the biggest names in the entertainment industry, including Jeff Bridges, Chevy Chase, Jamie Lee Curtis, Robert Downey Jr., Michael Landon, Jack Lemmon, Demi Moore, Gregory Peck, Susan Sarandon, Cybill Shepherd, Jimmy Smits, Oliver Stone, Bruce Willis, Alfre Woodard, Fonda, and Raitt. Hayden served as executive producer for the ad, which cost $100,000 to produce. Big Green initially purchased $100,000 in TV time, mostly on cable channels such as VH-1 and TBS. It aired seventy-four times on broadcast and cable TV stations in the Los Angeles, San Diego, and San Francisco Bay areas. The video featured a 900 number that viewers could call to make a $5 contribution to the campaign. The video was also widely distributed to supporters of Big Green, who were asked to host house parties to show it to their friends and solicit from them contributions of $500 to $10,000 to support Big Green.[9]

The theme of the ad was that the petrochemical industry was hooked on pollution and did not want to spend money to kick the habit. According to the commercial, this was why the big oil, chemical, agribusiness, and timber companies opposed Big Green. The ad claimed that these companies were responsible for filling the air with smog, the food with deadly pesticides, the ocean with oil, and "shooting the ozone layer full of holes." The ad said that companies were spending $16 million to oppose the Big Green initiative. Thus it was vital for viewers to contribute to the campaign in order to ensure a clean California. In the ad Demi Moore denounced a "slow motion" killer pesticide called Captan. She said it is a known cancer-causing agent and that pesticides like Captan cause three thousand deaths a year. Jeff Bridges stated that twenty thousand Americans would develop cancer in 1990 because of pesticide exposure.

A common theme of the Big Green ad campaign was that chemical companies were intentionally spreading death with their pesticides for profit and that pesticides were not monitored or tested. This theme was repeated in a sixty-second radio ad in September 1990 that featured Michael Landon in which he said that the chemical companies would say anything to kill Big Green because the initiative would stop them from marketing twenty cancer-causing chemicals that threatened children's health. The campaign spent $300,000 to air the ad, according to a September 12, 1990, press release from the Environmental Protection Act Steering Committee.

### Role of SMOs in the Campaign

The chief author of the pesticides section of Big Green was a leading environmental SMO, the Natural Resources Defense Council (NRDC). NRDC's senior attorney, Al Meyerhoff, scientist Lawrie Mott, and others at NRDC had drafted the measure's pesticides provision. The NRDC was founded in 1967 and functioned as the litigation arm of the environmental movement. As a rule, it did not do its own scientific research.

The NRDC had a national membership of 100,000, including 20,000 in

California. It was well funded and in 1985 was rated by the Environmental Protection Agency and congressional staff members as the most influential environmental lobbying organization. The NRDC has even been referred to as the "shadow EPA." NRDC had a reputation for being highly critical of virtually everything government and industry did regarding food safety. However, at the FDA the NRDC had the reputation for being careless with scientific data and exaggerating the danger of chemicals in food production.[10] Indeed, the NRDC had a tendency to appeal to public fear of chemicals in its campaign. The organization saw its role as a watchdog of the petrochemical industry. Its mission was to expose the chemical industry's contamination of the country's food and water supply.

The NRDC was also the author of Proposition 65. Assemblyman Lloyd Connelly, who cosponsored Proposition 65 and Big Green, was a strong supporter of Al Meyerhoff's and the NRDC. Meyerhoff also worked closely with Hayden on earlier environmental campaigns. In addition, the NRDC had formed one of the principal campaign fund-raising and lobbying organizations in Hollywood, Mothers and Others for Pesticide Limits.

NRDC was committed to eliminating the use of pesticides in food production, taking the position that the government should follow a "zero risk approach" to pesticides. In other words, any substance that might cause cancer or birth defects in humans should be banned, no matter how small the dose. The public's failure to understand the fundamentals of toxicology gave the NRDC great influence on public food policy.

### Zero-Risk Approach in Big Green

Big Green adopted the NRDC's zero risk approach to regulating pesticides. That is to say, if a pesticide increased the statistical probability, however small, of causing cancer or producing birth defects in laboratory mice or rats, the pesticide should be banned. The standard laboratory testing procedure is to expose mice and rats to chemicals at a high dose, just below lethality, for short periods. These results are used to predict the effects of chemicals on humans who are exposed to minute doses of chemicals over a lifetime (National Academy 1993:127–57).

For example, for humans to absorb the amount of Alar that produced cancer in rats, they would have to eat the equivalent of 861 pounds of apples a day (Rosen n.d.:9, 11). Because this is clearly absurd, Big Green's proponents argued for the vulnerability of children to any level of pesticide exposure in an effort to justify their claims about the danger of pesticides. For example, Harvey Karp, a pediatrician used by Hollywood stars and supporter of Big Green, said that "when a 2-year-old eats an apple, it's like an adult eating five apples—pound for pound. Over the life-time of the child there is cause for concern" (*Sacramento Union,* September 30, 1990).

However, no scientific consensus supports Karp's contention about the vulnerability of children to pesticide residues in food. In the most comprehensive study of the danger of pesticides to infants and children the National Research Council of the National Academy of Science stated that the research was insufficient for drawing solid conclusions. For some pesticides, infants and children were at greater risk than adults, and for other pesticides, they were not at any greater risk (National Academy 1993:359).

Several problematic assumptions underlie the NRDC's approach. The first is that we know what causes cancer; no one does.[11] Indeed, the NRDC acknowledged that fact. Nevertheless, the NRDC argued that since 1950 the incidence of cancer in the United States, including cancer of the liver, bladder, thyroid, and the brain, has increased by more than 22.6 percent (Meyerhoff, Mott, and Hayden 1990:45).

If lung cancer is added to this figure, the incidence of cancer has increased 36.6 percent. According to the NRDC, this adds up to one million Americans each year, about half of whom die from cancer. The NRDC claims that pesticides cause cancer and other health problems in lab animals and have the same consequences for humans. This leads to the NRDC's conclusion that no level of exposure to cancer-causing pesticides is safe for humans and therefore all pesticides must be banned (Meyerhoff, Mott, and Hayden 1990:45).

The problem with NRDC's zero risk approach to pesticides is that naturally occurring cancer-causing agents are far more significant than pesticides. Dr. Bruce Ames, a biochemist at the University of California at Berkeley and one of the world's top cancer researchers, said, "We are making a big fuss about tiny traces of pesticides and other synthetic chemicals while 99.9 percent of the chemicals we are exposed to are natural and we pay no attention to that" (*New York Times,* March 5, 1989:24E).

Ames says that Americans consume fifteen hundred times as many natural carcinogens in food as they do pesticides and other synthetic chemicals and do so without harm. Most cancers come from natural causes such as sunlight, plant poisons, tobacco, food, and other things that people encounter every day. Natural toxics or cancer-causing agents are found in virtually all foods, including beans, tomatoes, potatoes, lettuce, carrots, and corn. They are part of nature's defense mechanism to ward off pests, and the human body is armed to cope with these toxins.

Ames argues that pesticides and other artificial substances constitute only a tiny proportion of cancers. Thus the government is wasting its time trying to reassure the public that banning pesticides protects society. In other words, the NRDC's preoccupation with pesticides is out of proportion to the real health hazards. For example, Dr. Robert Scheuplein, the U.S. Food and Drug Administration's leading food safety microbiologist, claims that pesticide residues pose a cancer risk of only 0.0000076. That is to say, they are believed to cause less than five-hundredths of 1 percent of all cancers per year nationwide (*Sacramento Union,* July 13, 1990).

Despite the scientific consensus that pesticides do not threaten the food supply, the proponents of Big Green insisted that pesticides were a threat and called for a higher or "no risk" standard for pesticides rather than the "negligible risk" standard that guides FDA policy.[12] For example, Big Green's advocates cited the work of Dr. Richard Jackson, chairman of the American Academy of Pediatrics' environmental hazards committee, who estimated that 25 percent of preschoolers will contract cancer during their lifetime. That worked out to about 4.5 million cases in 1989. Based on this probability, Jackson estimated that pesticides may cause five thousand of these cancers (Begley, Hager, and Howard 1989:74).

The NRDC and other food safety groups use comparable projections, which tend to alarm the public and create citizen support for legislation to ban pesticides. The organization argues that despite the admittedly low number of deaths resulting from pesticide use, "your child may be one of the 5,000 victims of dangerous cancer-causing chemicals" (Begley, Hager, and Howard 1989:74–75).

The California Departments of Food and Agriculture (CDFA) and Health Services as well as the EPA use the negligible risk approach to regulating pesticides. In their view a pesticide may be used if it does not exceed the cancer risk of one in a million over and above the average cancer risk without the pesticide. Statistically, one in four people, or 25 percent of the entire population, can be expected to get cancer during their lifetime. These agencies reason that if a pesticide does not increase that probability to more than 25.0001 percent, which is statistically insignificant, it may be used in food production (Begley, Hager, and Howard 1989:74–75).

Actually, this overstates the danger because it assumes that every pesticide is used on every crop to the maximum legal limit. A study by Dr. Sandra Archibald of the Stanford University Food Research Institute and Dr. Carl Winter of the University of California at Riverside showed that EPA risk assumptions significantly overstate the actual risk by 2,600 times for tomatoes, 21,000 times for apples, and 300 times for lettuce. Indeed, Dr. Sanford Miller, the dean of the Graduate School of Biomedical Science at the University of Texas Health Science Center at San Antonio, said that "the risk of pesticide residues to consumers is effectively zero" (Brookes 1991:28).

At least fourteen scientific societies representing 100,000 microbiologists, toxicologists, and food scientists said the same thing during the Alar scare in 1989. And a study by the National Academy of Science in 1989, by nineteen scientists surveying about six thousand studies, concluded that there was "no evidence that pesticides or natural toxins in food contribute significantly to cancer risk in the United States" (p. 15). The National Academy recommended that people eat five or more servings of vegetables and fruits every day, especially green and yellow vegetables and citrus fruits, concluding that this would significantly reduce the risk of cancer, not increase it.

### Industry Reaction to the Campaign

The California business community's first reaction to Big Green was alarm and resignation. Business elites did not believe that they could defeat an environmental initiative in California. The passage of Proposition 65 had created a powerful myth that environmental causes were invincible. Industry had spent more than $5 million to try to defeat Proposition 65, only to lose badly. Business believed that the only way to combat a popular environmental initiative was to sponsor a counterinitiative that would have even greater popular appeal. The California Constitution provides that if voters approve two competing initiatives on a ballot, the initiative that receives the greatest number of votes prevails and the losing initiative fails.

However, the business community was divided on what to do about Big Green. Various sectors perceived the threat differently. Business elites formed three factions based upon their differing perceptions.[13] The factions were represented by the Western Agricultural Chemical Association (WACA), representing agrochemical companies; the California Farm Bureau and Western Growers Association, which led the agricultural community; and oil, aerospace, automobile, utility, and industrial chemical companies. Each group adopted a different approach to Big Green.

WACA was an agrochemical lobbying organization representing companies such as Monsanto, Du Pont, Dow Elanco, Ciba-Geigy, American

Cyanamid, and Rhone-Poulenc. It was based in Sacramento and was led by Elin Miller, the executive director of Dow Elanco. WACA constituted the core of industry opposition to Big Green because the chemical industry was the measure's principal target. Based on the Proposition 65 campaign, WACA knew that Big Green would single out the chemical companies as the state's principal polluter and threat to food safety. If Big Green got on the November 1990 ballot, WACA would be forced to fight it openly.

By contrast, other sectors, such as the agricultural producers, had a positive public image and felt they could protect themselves by publicly disassociating themselves from the chemical industry. The timber industry followed the same strategy as the growers, and both groups sponsored counterinitiatives to neutralize the effects of Big Green upon them.[14]

Thus WACA was left to lead the political opposition to Big Green, and it carefully monitored the initiative as soon as it surfaced. Above all, the chemical industry wanted to avoid a repeat of the Proposition 65 campaign. The industry had been slow to respond to that campaign and did not have reliable information about the effect the proposition would actually have on it. The industry panicked and exaggerated the proposition's adverse effects. For example, it claimed that Proposition 65 would double the price of agricultural and manufactured products and would devastate whole sectors of the state's economy, throwing thousands of people out of work. However, none of these dire predictions materialized after voters approved the initiative. The industry recognized that if it used the same strategy, it would have no chance of defeating Big Green.

Getting an initiative on the California ballot takes a year. If WACA wanted to sponsor a counterinitiative, it would have to start early. The chemical industry also wanted to avoid being placed on the defensive, as it was with Proposition 65.

WACA created a political action committee, Californians for Food Safety, to finance the campaign. And WACA adopted a two-pronged strategy. The first phase lasted from August to October 1989 and involved an assessment of Big Green's economic effect on the industry, polling voters, getting a legal opinion of Big Green's compliance with state law, and hiring a campaign management firm to coordinate the campaign. WACA hired the prestigious San Francisco–based Republican firm of Woodward and McDowell, which had never lost an initiative campaign. Dick Woodward, the company's president, directed the campaign and hired several research firms to examine Big Green (Woodward interview 1994). These reports would form the basis of Woodward's campaign strategy.[15]

At an October meeting of campaign contributors Woodward outlined what he thought were Big Green's most important elements. He said that the pesticide section would reduce California's gross state product by $10 billion a year, roughly equal to the damage caused by the October 1989 earthquake in San Francisco. He also said that Big Green would lead to the loss of more than 220,000 jobs. It would ban half of WACA's chemical products and would seriously curtail the use of others (Spectrum Economics 1990).

According to Woodward, California farmers would lose $1.2 billion annually, or 20 percent of net farm income, if Big Green were approved. California's canned fruit and vegetable processors would lose $140 million more, and agricultural chemical manufacturers would lose $175 million, or 75 percent of their annual net income (Spectrum Economics 1990).

NRDC got hold of Woodward's cost estimates and argued that they were fundamentally flawed. They claimed the estimates were based on false assumptions, faulty legal analysis, and cooked statistics. NRDC argued that the report was deliberately biased to support the industry's exaggerated claims of impending disaster (NRDC 1990).

According to NRDC, Woodward's figures ignored the economic benefits of Big Green and focused only on the costs. For example, the benefits included reductions in urban smog, acid rain, oil imports, oil spills, crop and forest damage, building and bridge weathering, pollution-related deaths and illnesses, and a reduced risk of global climate change. NRDC set the value of these benefits at $28 billion a year. NRDC argued that, even if one agreed with Woodward's Big Green cost estimate of $10 billion a year, the losses would be outweighed by substantial net gains for California (NRDC 1990).

What is important to note about both the industry and NRDC analyses of Big Green is that both exaggerated the cost-benefit estimates. No one could really provide accurate estimates of such unprecedented and far-reaching legislation. The data on both sides were designed to support each camp's conclusions about Big Green. For example, the nonpartisan California Legislative Analyst Office in Sacramento estimated the direct costs of Big Green as in excess of $2.6 billion over twenty years. The office added that there were sizable but unknown state and local costs. For example, revenues lost as a result of Big Green's ban on offshore oil drilling might be as much as $3 billion (McCarley 1990).

Big Green would also ban all pesticides "known to cause cancer or reproductive harm" by the end of 1995. This included pesticides listed by the EPA as known (Group A) cancer-causing chemicals and probable (Group B) carcinogenic chemicals. In addition, even innocuous pesticides would be banned if, after they were transformed into metabolites (degraded), they contained toxins or cancer-causing contaminants. Harmless pesticides that are metabolized would be banned if the new chemical compound contained toxins. Thus, if a safe chemical pesticide became toxic after being absorbed by the soil or after bacteria, mammals, birds, fish, or fungi had eaten and excreted the pesticide, it would be banned. This was without regard for the dose or level of concentration of the toxin or poison in the new transformed chemical (Eliason interview 1995).

Big Green would further ban pesticide chemicals degraded by the effects of nonliving organisms such as sunlight or water. If a pesticide developed cancer-causing toxins, regardless of the concentration of the toxin or danger to humans, it would be banned. Further, if minute toxic contaminants such as copper, lead, sand, or benzene entered a chemical pesticide inadvertently through the normal manufacturing process, the pesticide would also be banned. For example, if the production process introduced infinitesimal traces of benzene (in parts per billion or trillion) to a pesticide, which is almost inevitable when producing any petroleum-based product, the pesticide would be banned. The ban would apply even if the pesticide itself was harmless to humans and would not turn up as a residue in food. The ban would also apply to sand, which is on the Proposition 65 list of banned chemicals. Any pesticide with traces of sand, regardless of how small, would be banned (Woodward interview 1994).

Woodward claimed that the passage of Big Green meant the immediate banning of thirty-six pesticides, increasing in subsequent years to include 50 to 70 percent of all pesticides. This would reduce the availability of many foods and push up California consumer prices for fruits and vegetables by 50 percent or more. He estimated that within six years of Big Green's passage, most chemicals used in agriculture would be eliminated. Such a short period of time would not allow growers to develop alternatives to the banned pesticides (Woodward interview 1994).

Supporters of Big Green dismissed these concerns by saying that only nineteen, not thirty-six, pesticides would be banned immediately, and alternatives were available for most of them. The chemical industry did have a history of exaggerating the dire consequences of eliminating cancer-causing chemicals. That was the industry's tactic when the EPA banned the use of DDT, when nitrofen, a carcinogenic herbicide, was banned in 1980, and when Proposition 65 was proposed in 1986 (Spectrum Economics 1990).

When California banned DBCP, a pesticide designed to reduce fruit crop losses (after it was found to cause infertility in workers and cancer in animals) in 1977, the agricultural and chemical industries predicted that California peach producers would lose $39 million annually within three years and that nationwide losses would reach $80 million a year. They also predicted that grape growers would suffer annual losses of $65 million nationwide. However, the yields of these crops continued to rise or remained the same, and no measurable losses or price rises linked to the chemical ban were recorded. Therefore, NRDC concluded, it was feasible to phase out cancer-causing pesticides (NRDC 1990).

*The Strategy to Defeat Big Green*

Woodward commissioned opinion polls to test the popularity of Big Green and to determine whether WACA could defeat it with a counterinitiative. He also wanted to know whether the chemical industry's image would hurt any campaign WACA might launch. The results of the September and December 1989 polls formed the basis of the industry's strategy.[16] They showed that Californians regarded environmental issues as the third most important, after drugs and crime. Fifty-seven percent of respondents felt that the environment was in "bad" shape, and 17 percent said it was in "very bad" shape. Asked about specific environmental problems addressed by Big Green, respondents selected global warming and the use of pesticides as their top concerns. This reflected national publicity at the time regarding the "greenhouse effect," the hole in the earth's ozone layer, and the 1989 Alar apple scare (Charlton Research 1989).

The polls also sought to determine whom respondents believed was best at solving environmental problems. A surprising 33 percent chose the initiative on the California ballot as the best way to solve the problem, and only 24 percent thought the EPA was the best problem solver. Fewer than 10 percent thought that business should handle the problem, whereas 20 percent thought that government could deal with it (Charlton Research 1989). This was bad news indeed for the industry. The public's faith in initiatives on environmental issues was undoubtedly connected with the success of Proposition 65.

The pollsters showed respondents three mock ballots and asked how they would vote. The first round of balloting confirmed the industry's worst fears. They found that an overwhelming 78 percent of voters favored the initiative; 61 percent favored it strongly, and only 14 percent opposed it. When asked why they voted for the initiative, respondents said that Big Green was necessary to protect the environment. They also were asked to rank parts of the initiative they thought were most important. The top two responses were that Big Green would help with the ozone problem and all pesticides known to cause cancer should be banned. The second ballot gave respondents the industry's scientific arguments against Big Green. Nevertheless, 77 percent still favored the initiative, and 18 percent opposed it—hardly any shift at all (Charlton Research 1989).

On the third ballot, however, voters were told that Big Green would cost the California economy $10 billion annually, it would lead to a 40 percent reduction in the availability of fruits and vegetables, and food prices would jump 50 percent. When told this, voters began to shift away from Big Green. Those favoring Big Green dropped to 58 percent, and those opposing it rose to 36 percent (Charlton Research 1989).

Another argument that changed respondents' minds about Big Green was the suggestion that Hayden's political ambitions were behind it. Although this finding gave the industry some hope, the polls still showed that if the election were held then, Big Green would pass. Woodward felt that WACA had no choice but to emphasize the economic effects and Hayden's ambitions in the campaign against Big Green (Charlton Research 1989).

The industry took its next step at a meeting of about 150 leaders of the aerospace, oil, chemical, and banking industries called by the California Manufacturers' Association in May 1990. Woodward, his team of advisers, and Kirk West, president of the California Chamber of Commerce, briefed the business leaders on the strategy they were recommending to defeat Big Green.

They decided to call the campaign, the "anti-Hayden initiative" in response to the high negatives associated with Tom Hayden in the polls. A popular slogan floated at the meeting was "environmental Ayatollah," a reference to Hayden and Big Green.

Woodward formed a political action committee, the California Coordinating Council, to solicit campaign donations to defeat Big Green. It was nominally cochaired by West and William Campbell, the chief lobbyist and president of the California Manufacturers' Association. However, it was actually directed by Woodward, working closely with Miller of WACA.

The California Coordinating Council was an umbrella PAC that brought together all segments of California's business community to fight Big Green. It incorporated other industry PACs that were formed to respond to Big Green before an overall industry strategy was worked out. All industry groups claimed they were environmentalist. However, they said they differed from the advocates of Big Green in that they were "rational" as opposed to "radical." This meant that they preferred incremental or minimal changes in policy to deal with environmental problems. They said they opposed sweeping changes that would damage California's economy (i.e., disrupt their business operations) and make no real improvement in the environment.

Woodward's message was that the industry could defeat Big Green if it was organized, raised enough campaign money, and waged an effective campaign. The campaign would not discuss ethics, morality, or the governments' role in society—just Big Green's economic costs. They obviously did not want to try to prove they were true environmentalists. Instead, they were going to emphasize the price tag of Big Green. Woodward's polls showed that the arguments that moved voter opinion against Big Green were (listed by order of importance).

1. Tom Hayden's sponsorship of Big Green and his potential role as environmental advocate.
2. The $12 billion cost of the initiative.
3. Reduction in the availability of food.
4. A 40 percent increase in food prices.
5. Initiative's reliance on politics not science.
6. The ban on chlorine, which is needed to prevent hepatitis and guarantee a safe water supply.

Woodard was confident that industry could win an outright victory over Big Green but believed it would be a close election. He anticipated that Big Green would get plenty of news coverage but that the editorial boards of major newspapers would oppose the measure (Woodward interview 1994). Indeed, Big Green was heavily covered in the news columns, but the editorial pages of the seven biggest daily newspapers advised voters to reject it (Beall and Hays 1991).[17]

Woodward laid out a list of requirements for the campaign. Foremost among them was money—lots of it and right away. In "Campaign Plan to Defeat the Hayden Initiative," a document that Woodward prepared and presented to the PAC, he gave the rationale for the campaign and fundraising targets for each industry (see table 4.1). He quoted Hayden's declaration that "we will do whatever it takes" to win. Well aware that the vast resources of the Hollywood community were behind Big Green, Woodward argued that industry had to come up with more than $10 million to defeat it. Expecting that industry would give less than he sought, Woodward pegged the cost of the campaign at $17 million (Woodward and McDowell 1990).

Indeed, industry's actual campaign contributions came to about $15 million. The agrochemical (WACA) and petroleum industries contributed the most, meeting their targets of $3 and $2 million, respectively. WACA's contribution to the campaign was much greater than what the dollar figure reflects. WACA was the most important industry group opposing Big Green; it was the first to provide money and contributed on a matching basis as an incentive for other industries to pony up (Woodward interview 1994).

TABLE 4.1 **Industry's Fund-raising Targets for Campaign Against Big Green**

| Industry | Contributions |
|---|---|
| Agrichemical | $ 3,000,000 |
| Petroleum | 2,000,000 |
| Food processing/food | 1,500,000 |
| Manufacturing/agriculture | 1,500,000 |
| Construction | 1,000,000 |
| Timber/paper | 1,000,000 |
| Aerospace | 1,000,000 |
| Nonagrichemical/plastics | 1,000,000 |
| Refrigeration/air-conditioning | 1,000,000 |
| Mining/metals | 1,000,000 |
| Restaurants | 750,000 |
| Food retailers | 500,000 |
| Other retailers | 500,000 |
| Insulation | 500,000 |
| Transportation-trucking/rails | 500,000 |
| Motor vehicles | 250,000 |
| Financial Institutions | 250,000 |
| Electronics | 250,000 |
| Utilities | 250,000 |
| | $17,250,000 |

*Source*: *Woodward and McDowell*

Miller worked with Woodward on a daily basis. She stayed in close touch the agrochemical companies based on the East Coast or overseas and persuaded them of the urgency of opposing Big Green. Skepticism that Big Green could be defeated made fund-raising difficult for Woodward. It is no exaggeration to say that without the backing of WACA and the dogged determination of Miller, the campaign never would have gotten off the ground (Woodward interview 1994).

The utility companies contributed more than requested, but the timber, aerospace, mining, and metals industries contributed far less than requested. The timber industry gave less than $1 million because it was financing its own counterinitiative campaign to block the timber provisions in Big Green. Likewise, agriculture did not contribute because it was pushing its initiative called CAREFUL (Proposition 135), which was designed to nullify the pesticides provision of Big Green.[18] This created tension between agriculture and the industry groups backing the Woodward campaign. Woodward badly needed financial support, especially early on. He felt that agriculture's expenditure of $5 million on its initiative to defeat Big Green's pesticides provision was a waste of money that weakened the overall campaign (Woodward interview 1994).

Woodward's efforts to create a large coalition to campaign against Big Green clearly encountered a free-rider problem. According to Mancur Olson (1965:51), the larger the group, the more members prefer to ride free on the efforts of those pursing the "collective goods" of an organization. In the case of the campaign against Big Green, both timber and agriculture recognized they would benefit from Woodward's campaign, but they had no special incentives to join it. Instead, they felt they could protect their special interests by launching independent campaigns against Big Green (Woodward interview 1994).

West, chairman of the California Coordinating Council, tried to put the best face on the decisions of agriculture and timber, appealing for unity in the campaign against Big Green. He told business leaders, "Imagine Tom Hayden as the chairman of your board." Big Green was so carefully crafted that, if it passed, it would take at least ten to twelve years of litigation to water it down, West told them. He also promised that the California Coordinating Council would work closely with the agricultural and timber initiatives. This meant that Woodward would coordinate both the overall campaign against Big Green and coordinate it with the agricultural and timber initiatives designed to neutralize or cancel particular provisions of Big Green (Woodward interview 1994).

Despite their commitment to their counterinitiatives, agriculture and timber were indirectly involved in the overall campaign against Big Green. For example, the Agricultural Council of California contributed to both the industry's Big Green campaign and to the farmers' CAREFUL initiative. Lee Ruth was the president of the Agricultural Council and chaired the finance committee of the CAREFUL campaign. Lee Stitzenberger, president of the Dolfin Group, a Republican campaign organization in Los Angeles, was hired to carry out the campaign.

Furthermore, a representative of the California Chamber of Commerce, which cochaired the California Coordinating Committee, was a member of the steering committee that directed the CAREFUL campaign. The overall strategy was that industry in general would directly oppose Big Green, while timber and agriculture would drain off support for the measure by "giving the voters something positive to vote for" (California Manufacturers' Association 1990).

In other words, the agricultural and timber initiatives were designed to bleed support from Big Green and make it easier for the campaign against Big Green to succeed. All three campaigns shared polling data and economic impact studies, and Woodward directed the timber industry initiative. Although the farmers used a different consulting firm for their CAREFUL initiative, they shared data and coordinated their strategies with Woodard.

### The CAREFUL Initiative

Agricultural producers had heated discussions about the wisdom of joining the campaign against Big Green. In mid-1989 agricultural producers formed the Agricultural Food Study Group to consider how to deal with Big Green. It was organized by the Western Growers Association, the California Grape and Tree Fruit League, and the California Farm Bureau.[19] The study group commissioned polls to answer three questions:

Does Big Green have a high probability of passage?

What are the themes or messages that move voters against the initiative?

Is a stand-alone pesticide initiative that would block the pesticide provision of Big Green likely to pass?[20]

The results of the survey were similar to what the Woodward polls showed. For example, the survey found that the public supported Big Green by a margin of 4 to 1. But when voters were asked whether the "pesticide banning issue" should be considered separately from the rest of Big Green, half would rather it was separate (Charlton Research 1989).

The majority of voters felt that the food supply was safe, although a sizable number felt that pesticide residues in food were not. More worrisome to the farmers was that 57 percent of voters felt pesticide standards were lax. Based on these findings, the farmers concluded that agriculture should not defend the status quo but instead should press for higher standards and increased monitoring of pesticide use in order to offset the bans in Big Green. Agriculture also tried to determine whether economic arguments would neutralize public support for banning pesticides. The industry found that support for Big Green eroded somewhat when voters were told that banning pesticides could lead to significantly higher food prices. Nevertheless, a majority of voters still favored banning pesticides (Charlton Research 1989).

Respondents were given three choices on the issue of food safety and pesticides: status quo, increased monitoring and testing, and banning pesticides. Fifty-one percent preferred a policy of increased monitoring. This led the pollsters to recommend that the farmers back a "stand-alone" pesticide initiative that would encourage change but not the radical solution of banning pesticides altogether. They concluded that because Big Green was likely to pass, the best way to counter it would be to sponsor an alternative initiative and get it approved by a larger margin than the one for Big Green, which would cancel out Big Green's pesticide provisions (Charlton Research 1989).

In a follow-up poll the farmers tested the popularity of the CAREFUL initiative compared to Big Green. They found that both initiatives would pass by a large margin but that CAREFUL, which emphasized monitoring pesticides, not banning them, would beat Big Green. They also found that any identification or association of the CAREFUL initiative with the chemical industry produced a strong negative voter reaction (Charlton Research 1989).

The implications were clear. If agriculture sponsored the CAREFUL initiative, which reassured the public that pesticides would be monitored more carefully and tested rather than banned, CAREFUL would pass. And if CAREFUL received more votes than Big Green, it would neutralize or defeat the pesticides provisions of Big Green.

So the farmers saw CAREFUL as an insurance policy in the event that the industry campaign failed to defeat Big Green outright. At a meeting with Woodward the farmers specifically asked him if he would bet the farm on defeating Big Green. He said that he felt they could bet their farms, although he would not bet on an outright victory. He also acknowledged that anything could happen. For example, a major oil spill or serious food poisoning case two weeks before the election could change everything.

The farmers decided that they needed more than a hope and a prayer and that they had better run their own initiative to counteract Big Green in case it passed. But they continued to work informally with Woodward in support of his campaign against Big Green.

### Expressive Group and SMO Reaction

The reaction of Campaign California and SMOs to CAREFUL was predictable. They called it "Big Brown" and said it was a fraud. Van de Kamp said it was designed by the pesticide industry to protect its profits rather than public health. Michael Paparian of the Sierra Club said Big Brown was a Trojan horse, but instead of soldiers it was full of poisonous pesticides to be sprayed on food supplies (Environmental Protection Act Steering Committee press release, May 25, 1990).

Hayden called CAREFUL one of the greatest cases of voter deception in recent California history (Environmental Protection Act Steering Committee press release, May 25, 1990). In fact, CAREFUL was based largely on California Assembly Bill No. 2161, which the legislature approved overwhelmingly and the governor signed in 1989. This law gave California the most restrictive pesticide control and food safety regulatory program in the country.[21]

The key area of difference between Big Green and CAREFUL was that Big Green followed the "zero-risk" approach to pesticide regulation while CAREFUL followed the "no significant risk" approach. Hence, Big Green would immediately ban cancer-causing pesticides, whereas CAREFUL called for more monitoring and testing of pesticides to determine if they were a significant risk to human health.

SMOs dismissed CAREFUL as a public relations stunt to weaken citizen support for real reform that would guarantee a safe food supply. For instance, instead of banning all cancer-causing pesticides, CAREFUL would allow such chemicals to remain in the food supply indefinitely. Under CAREFUL the basic power over pesticides remained with what the Big Green advocates derisively labeled the "old boy network" of the state Department of Food and Agriculture instead of transferring the power to ban and regulate pesticides to the California Department of Health Services.

CAREFUL also did not give the power to regulate pesticides to an elected environmental advocate as called for in Big Green. Instead of eliminating carcinogenic pesticides and establishing a higher health standard for exposure of children to dangerous chemicals, CAREFUL merely called for more studies. Critics argued that pesticide testing was already inadequate and that CAREFUL carried no authorization to increase resources or personnel in order to improve safety standards.

The advocates of Big Green and CAREFUL engaged in a bitter and acrimonious public debate that had little to do with the real issues. The debate was about four propositions on the ballot (Propositions 128, 130, 135, and 138), and it pitted an expressive group, SMOs, and Hollywood celebrities against farmers, chemical manufacturers, loggers, and timber companies.

## The Expressive Group Campaign

After qualifying the initiative for the November 1990 ballot, Campaign California and the SMOs launched the Big Green campaign in July 1990. At a news conference Michael Picker of the National Toxics Campaign stood behind barrels painted black and labeled with the names of chemical companies and declared, "It's Californians versus the chemical industry." Industry responded by portraying Big Green as a radical left-wing measure designed to promote Hayden's political career by creating a new elected office of environmental czar (*Sacramento Bee*, July 20, 1990).

Each side spent more than $1 million during the last ten days of the campaign on high-profile TV ads. The focus of attention was the so-called dueling pesticides initiatives—Big Green versus CAREFUL. In a TV spot that began running in October 1990 *Twin Peaks* stars Kyle MacLachlan and Michael Ontkean attacked CAREFUL by saying that it was designed by the pesticide industry to mislead the voters, that it did not protect the public from cancer-causing pesticides, and that taxpayers would have to pay for chemical clean-ups if CAREFUL were approved. MacLachlan and Ontkean erroneously claimed that Republican gubernatorial candidate Pete Wilson opposed CAREFUL and said that it weakened drinking water protection.

Mulholland called CAREFUL "a big fraud" and claimed that "most voters know that the agricultural industry and the pesticide industry are the same." He pointed out that the people who were opposing Big Green were backing CAREFUL. Mulholland also said that proponents of Big Green wanted to take the "cigarettes of the pesticide industry off the market" (*Sacramento Union*, September 30, 1990).

Vilification became so intense that each side sued the other for distorting the facts. A Sacramento County Superior Court judge ruled that opponents of CAREFUL could not say that it was backed by the chemical industry because financial records showed the chemical industry had not contributed to the CAREFUL campaign. And Woodward's campaign against Big Green was forced to withdraw a TV ad because it violated campaign finance reporting laws by not mentioning that chemical companies had sponsored it (*Sacramento Union*, August 15, 1990).

But the sensational attacks continued. For example, *OILscoop*, an industry newsletter, said that Big Green was "sponsored by Vietnam's representative to our Assembly, Tom Hayden" and that the measure promised voters an environment with zero risk from pesticide residues and an environmental czar to monitor society. The article suggested that Meryl Streep might become environmental czar. *OILscoop* claimed that zero risk would mean zero crops and zero jobs, California would eventually become a big parking lot, and that "Jane Fonda and Ted Turner will keep us happy watching the boob tube all day while eating our rice bran-fortified imitation crab legs."

One of Woodward's anti–Big Green ads prominently featured former surgeon general C. Everett Koop, who said that Big Green was based more on emotion than science. He said that the study of pesticide exposure is an inexact science and that no technology existed that could establish a link between pesticides and health. Koop went on to say Big Green would not solve problems with pesticides and water and air pollution (*Sacramento Bee*, September 7, 1990). "Big Green is a scare tactic not based on sound science," Koop intoned. "If I thought this proposition would protect the health of mothers and children, as its proponents claim, I'd be with them. I'm not. Proposition 128 would not protect Californians' health" (*Fresno Bee*, August 7, 1990).

### Outcome of the Election

Throughout the Big Green and CAREFUL campaigns the polls showed that both would pass. So the key issue became which proposition would receive the greatest number of votes and would therefore prevail. The proponents of Big Green were dismayed that the public was unable to discern the difference between Big Green and CAREFUL. In a poll of likely voters carried out just two weeks before election by Marttila and Kiley on behalf of Campaign California, voters supported CAREFUL by 49 to 34 percent. The Field Institute poll taken in mid-October confirmed the Marttila and Kiley poll. Field found that when voters were read the ballot wording for Big Green and CAREFUL, 62 percent said they would vote for Big Green and 61 percent said they would vote for CAREFUL (Solis 1994).[22]

## The Defeat of Big Green

In the end 64 percent of voters rejected Big Green; they also rejected CAREFUL and the timber initiative. Several factors explain their defeat. Campaign California and the SMOs believed that Big Green simply was too ambitious and tried to do too much. Indeed, the industry campaign against Big Green capitalized on this reasoning. Kirk West had called Big Green a catchall environmental wish list with twelve highly technical sections; it was thirty-nine pages and sixteen hundred words long, the equivalent of fifteen major legislative bills (West interview 1994).

The sheer size and complexity of the initiative made it vulnerable to the charge that it cost too much, tried to do too much, and would create more problems than it solved. The effect of the campaign against Big Green, plus the CAREFUL and timber industry initiatives, was to clutter the message of Campaign California with bewildering complexity and contradictions. The voters' response was to reject them all.

Industry disputes this interpretation. Business attributes Big Green's defeat to a change in the political climate from the measure's introduction in June 1989 to the general election in November 1990. Industry credited both the Gulf War and the decline in California's economy for the change (Charlton Research 1990).

A postelection analysis conducted by the industry's pollsters argues that the vote on Big Green had little to do with Californians' interest, or lack of interest, in environmental issues. For example, the public's interest in the environment was high in June 1990, before the Big Green campaign was mounted, and it remained high after the November 1990 election (Charlton Research 1990).

What changed was the public's perception of the economy. In June 1990, 35 percent of voters cited the environment as the number one problem facing the state, whereas 18 percent listed economics as the most important issue. Overall, economics was the third most important issue to voters. But by November 1990 the public's priorities had shifted. Only 28 percent of voters put environmental concerns at the top of their list, whereas 30 percent cited economic issues as most important to them (Charlton Research 1990). This made economics the number one issue.

The higher priority given by California voters to economic issues stemmed from the imminent threat of the Gulf War and its anticipated effect on the price of gas in California. Voters attached a higher economic cost to Big Green in November 1990 during the Gulf crisis than in 1989, before Saddam Hussein invaded Kuwait. Combined with the already high unemployment rate and economic recession in California at the time, a new environmental law with potentially great economic cost worried voters sufficiently that they rejected it (Charlton Research 1990).

### Conclusion

For the Big Green campaign, the expressive group Campaign California coordinated SMOs in the environmental and toxics movement such as the Natural Resources Defense Council, Sierra Club, and National Toxics Campaign. Campaign California also had the support of political elites in the state legislature and state Democratic Party. The campaign had the strong support of nonmovement allies, Hollywood celebrities. Hollywood contributed heavily to the campaign, and stars waived their usual fees to appear in campaign ads.

There were two reasons that Campaign California lost despite this support. The first was a flawed framing process, and the second was a free-rider problem. Big Green was far too ambitious. The scope and complexity of the initiative made it difficult to frame the campaign in a way that mobilized citizens. If Big Green's backers had focused on one issue, such as safe water, air, *or* food, they would have found mobilizing collective action on behalf of the campaign far easier. With such a large and varied number of issues, ranging from oil spills to sewage treatment to preserving forests, the SMOs and their constituencies were fragmented and difficult to mobilize.

By contrast, the industry opponents of Big Green were more effective in reframing the issue. They dubbed Big Green the Hayden initiative, after Tom Hayden, the 1970s antiwar protester and state assemblyman. Hayden was the founder and director of Campaign California, the expressive group that directed the Big Green campaign. The industry characterized the initiative as a thinly veiled vehicle for advancing Hayden's political career. Hayden and his wife, Jane Fonda, were widely known for their anti–Vietnam war protests during the 1970s, and this was a negative to mainstream voters. The industry knew that by reframing Big Green in this way it would put the expressive campaign on the defensive.

As for the free-rider problem, the SMOs had supported the Democratic gubernatorial candidacy of John Van de Kamp, who was committed to the Big Green initiative. But after Van de Kamp lost the Democratic nomination, the SMOs came under the leadership of Campaign California and the Democratic Party. That's when SMO support for Big Green flagged. Environmental groups felt they did not have real influence in the campaign and therefore did not feel they had a direct stake in it. They also feared that the campaign was being used to advance the political agenda of political elites. So they allowed Campaign California and the Democratic Party to run the campaign. As a result, Big Green did not have the grassroots social movement support necessary to win the election.

## NOTES

1. The California initiative process was created in 1911 by Governor Hiram Johnson, a member of the progressive wing of the Republican Party. It was established as a defense against the domination of the legislature by railroad interests. From 1911 through February 1990, 680 proposed initiatives had appeared on the California ballot, 40 percent of them during the 1980s (twenty-five initiatives, a record, were proposed for the November 1990 ballot). Initiatives allow California voters to make law directly, thereby circumventing the legislature. From 1978 to 1989 Californians used the ballot to try to lower insurance rates, limit state and local government spending, cut property taxes, limit campaign contributions, and deny public services to illegal aliens.

2. The official name of Proposition 128 was the Natural Environment, Public Health, Bonds, Initiative Statute. "Big Green" was coined by journalist Bill Bradley and came to be used extensively in the media.

3. Deukmejian was popular for his opposition to tax increases, his appointment of tough law-and-order judges to the state Supreme Court, and his having overcome a large budget deficit inherited when he was first elected governor in 1983. Deukmejian's dull plodding style was a marked and comforting contrast to the previous sixteen years of colorful and flamboyant governors, Ronald Reagan and Jerry Brown.

4. This initiative was copied from an initiative backed by Pete Wilson's crime victims' groups and district attorneys in the state. The campaign reform or ethics initiative was also drafted in consultation with expressive groups such as Common Cause.

5. In 1989 Hayden, who was not wealthy in his own right, reportedly agreed to a divorce settlement of a lump sum payment of $10 million from Jane Fonda.

6. Mulholland enjoyed an almost mythical reputation as a brilliant campaign adviser. Until the loss of Big Green, he had never lost a campaign. His appointment as manager of Proposition 65 and later Big Green was particularly astute because he was stricken with cancer, which he claimed was caused by his exposure to Agent Orange in Vietnam.

7. Hayden had expressed interest in winning statewide elected office since his failed bid for the U.S. Senate in 1982. He talked about running for state insurance commissioner in 1990 but had a falling out with Voter Revolt, the organization that sponsored the initiative that created an elected office. Instead, Voter Revolt backed Conway Collis, chairman of the state Board of Equalization for the position.

8. The research was based upon open-ended interviews with thirty-five top "opinion leaders" in Hollywood, including studio and network executives, journalists, and actors. Forty percent of the sample was Jewish. Two-thirds of the group earned in excess of $100,000 per year and one-third earned more than $500,000 annually. Social liberalism was defined as being prochoice on abortion, supporting gay rights, favoring the women's movement, spending more government money on the homeless, health care, public schools; spending less for defense, and opposing prayer in public schools. Economic liberalism was defined as favoring government intervention to equalize wealth and power, favoring labor over management, supporting government regulation of business, and being more concerned than the general public about environmental damage caused by industrial growth.

9. Big Green lost money on the project. The targeted audience was young viewers of VH-1. They watched the video but did not contribute, nor did they become involved or even vote in large numbers in the election.

10. In the case of the Alar scare, in 1989 the Natural Resources Defense Council released a study called "Intolerable Risk: Pesticides in Our Children's Food" (Sewell and Whyatt 1989), which purported to demonstrate the toxic threat posed by the use of Alar. This is the trade name for daminozide, which regulates growth to promote the uniform ripening of red apples and to enhance the appearance of the fruit. The report was the basis of numerous media reports that the NRDC orchestrated to force the company producing the chemical, the Uniroyal Chemical Company, to withdraw Alar from the market. However, the NRDC never submitted its report to the scientific community for evaluation (which was not based on any research the NRDC conducted). Indeed, Frank Young, then the commissioner of the Food and Drug Administration, criticized media reports based upon the NRDC study as "one of the worst instances of where statements were made without the benefit of scientific review" (Gladwell 1989:A12).

11. The scientific consensus is that damage to chromosomes and improper cell division are at the heart of cancer. However, beyond that no one is certain why that breakdown occurs.

12. The Delaney clause, which is part of the Federal Food Additives Amendment passed by Congress in 1958, nominally guides FDA policy concerning the safety of pes-

ticides. According to the Delaney clause, no food additive may be used if it is found to cause cancer. In other words, the provision calls for a zero or "no-risk" standard for food safety. However, this applies only to processed food and not to fresh fruits and vegetables. In the case of fresh produce, the FDA uses an "action level" or "negligible risk" level of no more than one part per million. The NRDC argues that the Delaney clause should be fully implemented and applied to both processed food and fresh produce. A related problem with the Delaney clause is that the technology for measuring chemical residues has been vastly improved. Therefore, in 1958 when the Delaney clause was passed, zero or no risk was measured as 50 parts or less per million. Now, however, technology is so much more powerful that it can measure parts per quintrillion. If the Delaney clause were to be literally enforced today, just about everything would be banned because everything is to some degree contaminated.

13. Another reason for the factions was that when Big Green was first proposed, they did not know exactly what it would say. Would there be a few major elements affecting a few industries, or would it be an omnibus bill affecting all industries?

14. Four environmental organizations—the Environmental Protection Information Center, NRDC, the Sierra Club, and the Planning and Conservation League—sponsored a separate initiative, Proposition 130, to place a moratorium on the clear-cutting of forests and authorize the sale of $742 million in bonds to buy forest land. The Western Timber Association, representing companies such as Pacific Lumber, Sierra Pacific, Georgia Pacific, Louisiana Pacific, Simpson Timber, and Fiberboard, responded with a counterinitiative, Proposition 138, designed to neutralize some of the adverse effects. Proposition 138 banned clear-cutting of ancient redwood stands and reduced clear-cutting of other forests by 50 percent for five years. It also set aside $300 million for tree planting in urban areas and authorized the purchase of sixteen hundred acres of new redwood parks.

15. WACA hired the law firm of Kahn, Soares, and Conway to analyze the initiative. GRC Economics, a division of the Republican public policy firm Hill and Knowlton, and Spectrum Economics, another public policy firm in San Francisco, analyzed the potential effect of Big Green on the agrochemical industry. WACA's pollster, the San Francisco–based Charlton Research Company, assembled four focus groups and conducted a statewide poll on Big Green in late September 1989 (Charlton Research 1990).

16. The September poll (Charlton Research 1989) was statewide and included interviews of 1,200 likely voters. Charlton used open-ended questions with the four focus groups. The December poll included 1,000 interviews with registered voters in California (Charlton 1989).

17. The newspapers included in the study were the *Sacramento Bee, San Francisco Chronicle, San Jose Mercury News, Los Angeles Times, Los Angeles Daily News, Orange County Register,* and *San Diego Union* (Beall and Hayes 1991).

18. The official title of Proposition 135 was the Consumer Pesticide Enforcement Act for Food, Water, and Worker Safety.

19. The executive committee for the farming initiative campaign formed a PAC called CAREFUL (Californians for Responsible Food Laws) to finance the initiative campaign named Proposition 135 in the 1990 election. They choose the name CAREFUL to reflect the initiative's emphasis on food safety and not pesticides. The committee was comprised of Bob Vice, president of the California Farm Bureau; Dave Moore, president of the Western Growers Association; Lee Ruth, president of the Agricultural Council of California representing farmer co-ops; Mike Durando, president of the Grape and Tree Fruit League; and Joel Nelson, president of the California Citrus Mutual.

20. The survey consisted of 750 randomly selected California voters and was conducted from September 30 to October 3, 1989.

21. CAREFUL required the California Department of Food and Agriculture (CDFA) to conduct a statewide survey of food consumption among children to determine whether pesticide residues had a unique dietary and physiological effect on them. It also required the strengthening of pesticide residue detection and registration and designated both the CDFA and the California Health Service to evaluate pesticide risk assessment. In addition, it called for research for alternatives to aerial spraying of malathion to combat the medfly.

22. However, when voters were read the fiscal impact statements for Big Green and CAREFUL, only 37 percent said they would vote for for Big Green and 40 percent for CAREFUL (Solis 1994).

# FIVE

# THE SECONDHAND SMOKE CAMPAIGN

Antismoking Groups and the Philip Morris Company

## The Modern Health Movement

Medical research during World War II led to the production of penicillin, sulfanamides, and improved vaccines. These "miracle drugs" severely reduced the incidence of typhus, tetanus, yellow fever, pneumonia, and meningitis. Malaria was controlled, and great progress was made in surgery because of the availability of plasma and blood for transfusions. After the war the American public associated the idea of progress in science and medicine with the national interest.

Postwar economic prosperity made possible increased medical research and improved national health. For example, from 1950 to 1970 the number of medical workers increased from 1.2 million to 3.9 million, and all medical expenditures for research and health care increased from $12.7 to $71.6 billion—an increase from 4.5 percent of the gross national product to 7.3 percent (Starr 1982:335).

Among the many movements spawned by the civil rights movement was health rights, which emerged during the 1970s. The health movement demanded legal rights for patients, including the handicapped, developmentally disabled, and mentally ill (Starr 1982:388). This included the right to see one's medical records, the right to determine appropriate treatment, and the right to due process of law in committing people to mental institutions. The health movement also made demands for equal treatment of rich and poor patients and equal representation of women in the medical profession (Starr 1982:391).

The public conception of health problems also changed. Concerns about health shifted away from infectious diseases, which were effectively treated by antibiotics, toward chronic diseases such as cancer, heart disease, and Alzheimer's. Health problems associated with an affluent society, such as obesity, smoking, and psychological disorders, as well as aberrant behavior such as juvenile delinquency, sexual deviancy, and narcotics addiction also became matters of public concern (Starr 1982:337).

The health "lifestyles" campaigns of the 1980s and 1990s represent an extension of the health rights movement. Nonprofit charitable health associations such as the American Cancer Society, American Heart Association, the American Lung Association, and thousands of other health-related organizations engaged in public education programs. The National Health Council, a private nonprofit clearinghouse for voluntary health agencies, estimated that in 1990, thirty-nine health agencies spent $3 billion, 66 percent of which went for educational programs and community services (NHC 1991:1–2).

For example, the American Heart Association spent $37.5 million on its public education program in 1988, describing it as follows:

> The endeavor focuses on providing health information at the workplace, schools, grocery stores and eating places, and health care sites. Public and professional education and community service programs emphasize the prime risk factors that can lead to heart attacks and strokes—poor nutrition, smoking and high blood pressure. *(AHA 1988:2)*

Its 1991 fund-raising brochure offered the following advice: (1) If you smoke, stop now; (2) check your blood pressure and cholesterol; (3) reduce fat, cholesterol, and salt intake; and (4) take regular aerobic exercise. The American Cancer Society, American Lung Association, and other nonprofit health charities offer similar lifestyle advice.

This educational and community service network constitutes a formidable infrastructure for the health movement. For example, the American Cancer Society has fifty state organizations; four regional affiliates in New York, Puerto Rico, Philadelphia, and the District of Columbia; and thirty-five hundred community-based agencies (Bennett and DiLorenzo 1994:73). The organization also claims to have 2.5 million volunteers participating in its programs, largely by going door to door to collect donations and disseminate educational information. The American Heart Association claims to have about 2.4 million volunteers and the American Lung Association 3.5 million.

In addition, in 1997 an estimated 59 percent of all hospitals were non-profit and 25 percent were operated by local or state governments (American Hospital Association 1998:8). The health charities work closely with non-profit and public hospitals, clinics, schools, and community centers to solicit donations, distribute information, and recruit volunteers.

## Origins of the Antismoking Movement

The antismoking movement in the United States has a long history.[1] It marks the ebb and flow of the movement's social, moral, and political successes, its failures, and the cycles of growth and decline in the smoking population of the country. The contemporary antismoking movement and earlier attempts to ban smoking have many parallels.

Efforts to abolish smoking in America began in the 1630s when the Massachusetts Bay Colony adopted a law banning smoking, and Connecticut banned public smoking in the 1640s. However, the laws were not enforced and ultimately failed when religious ministers adopted the habit and tobacco became an important cash crop in the southern colonies. Indeed, tobacco achieved the status of an alternative medium of currency in Virginia.

The first organized antismoking movement in the country emerged in the 1840s and 1850s when the temperance movement included smoking in its crusade against alcohol. Adherents argued that smoking "dried out" the mouth, a condition that could be ameliorated only by drinking whiskey or brandy. One antitobacco tract illustrated the connection between smoking and alcohol with the metaphor "Prime Minister Tobacco assisted King Alcohol in evil deeds" (Tate 1989:108). Health advocates such as Joel Shew, a hydrologist and the inventor of the water cure, argued that smoking was responsible for eighty-seven ailments, including heart disease, cancer, constipation, insanity, acne, and tooth decay. Smoking was also associated with a long list of negative personal traits such as licentiousness, being unclean, rudeness, criminality, baldness, impotence, profanity, moral degeneracy, and poverty.

The campaign to ban smoking legislatively began in the United States in the 1890s. By 1893 fourteen states had outlawed the sale, advertisement, possession, and use of cigarettes, and twenty-one other states and territories were considering similar laws. Congress considered stamping cigarette packages with a skull and crossbones and marking them "Poison." Employers refused to hire smokers, and nonsmokers claimed that secondhand smoke threatened their health. As Tate notes, when Surgeon General C. Everett Koop stated in May 1988 that cigarettes were as addictive as heroin and cocaine, he was following in the tradition of the antismoking movement that had begun more than one hundred years earlier (Tate 1989:107–108).

Moral outrage and indignation that children were being targeted as customers by the tobacco industry also has a long tradition in the antismoking movement. In the 1890s the Women's Christian Temperance Union (WCTU), under the leadership of Lucy Page Gaston, formed hundreds of anticigarette leagues throughout the Midwest and led a crusade against smoking and drinking alcohol. Gaston founded the Anti-Cigarette League of America, which claimed a membership of 300,000. WCTU groups asserted that cigarettes caused "insanity and death" to American youth, and they demanded federal laws to abolish the cigarette industry altogether (Dillow 1981:10). Indeed, by 1890 the movement had succeeded in securing legislation that prohibited the sale of cigarettes to minors in twenty-six states and territories (Tate 1989:114).

Despite the best efforts of the early antismoking movement, however, smoking became a widespread practice. Table 5.1 shows the growth of U.S. cigarette consumption from 1900 to 1994. At various periods in history the antismoking movement lost its momentum, eclipsed by such public issues as the Civil War, both world wars, and the Great Depression of the 1930s. Indeed, Table 5.1 clearly shows that the depression and the world wars coincided with major expansions in the smoking population. During World War I, for example, consumption increased from 16.5 million cigarettes in 1914 to 44.6 million in 1920.

At the time smoking was equated with bravery and masculinity. American soldiers were given a daily K-ration of cigarettes, and military commanders regarded smoking as essential for the fighting man. In the 1920s smoking ads associated smoking with the women's suffrage movement and the emancipation of women. And during the depression smoking was a symbol of economic democracy and the success of the common person. This removed much of the social stigma associated with smoking.

### The Modern Antismoking Movement

According to John Banzhaf III, a lawyer and founder of Action on Smoking and Health (ASH), one of the most important litigation-minded antismoking organizations in the country, the modern antismoking movement has had two phases. He dates the first phase from 1964 to 1973, when tobacco critics targeted smokers, and dates the second phase from the mid-1970s, when the movement began to focus on nonsmokers.

TABLE 5.1 U.S. Cigarette Consumption, 1990 – 1994

| Year | Billions Sold | Cigarettes per Capita |
|------|---------------|------------------------|
| 1994 | 488.6* | 2,514* |
| 1990 | 523.2 | 2,826 |
| 1980 | 631.5 | 3,849 |
| 1970 | 536.5 | 3,985 |
| 1960 | 484.4 | 4,171 |
| 1950 | 369.8 | 3,552 |
| 1940 | 181.9 | 1,976 |
| 1930 | 119.3 | 1,485 |
| 1920 | 44.6 | 665 |
| 1910 | 8.6 | 151 |
| 1900 | 2.5 | 54 |

*Estimates.

Source: Economic Research Service, Field and Specialty Crops Branch U.S. Department of Agriculture, 1995.

The first phase of the movement was designed to persuade smokers to quit. It began with the surgeon general's 1964 report on the health dangers of smoking. This was followed by health education campaigns, a 1968 ruling by the Federal Communication Commission (FCC) that entitled antismoking advocates to free television time, Congress's ban on cigarette ads on television in 1971, the placement of health warnings on cigarette packs, and the requirement that the tobacco companies publicly disclose the amounts of tar and nicotine in cigarettes.

In 1964 Luther L. Terry, the surgeon general, issued the first government report that concluded that smoking was a primary cause of lung cancer and contributed to emphysema, chronic bronchitis, cardiovascular disease, and premature death. Although antismoking activists, who were largely scientists and physicians at the time, felt vindicated by the report, there was no organized effort to campaign against smoking. It was one thing for the government to conclude that smoking was a health hazard but quite another to persuade smokers to quit. The former is in the realm of science, and the latter is in the area of social and political reform.

However, the surgeon general's report was followed by a major change in public opinion. For example, a Gallup poll of adults conducted in the late 1950s found that only 44 percent believed that smoking caused cancer. By contrast, in 1968, four years after the report was published, those who believed smoking caused cancer had increased to 71 percent. And a Louis Harris poll carried out in 1968 found that the percentage of Americans older than twenty-one who smoked had fallen 5 percent in the four years since the report (Kluger 1996:325–26).

Much to the chagrin of antismoking activists, however, the "Big Three" health charities—the American Cancer Society, American Heart Association, and American Lung Association—and the American Medical Association (AMA) were not willing to carry out any public relations campaign against smoking. In fact, they even stood in the way of implementing the surgeon general's 1964 report. For example, just two months after the report was released the executive vice president of the American Medical Association testified before the Federal Trade Commission that placing health warning labels on cigarette packs would "not necessarily serve the public interest"—on the disingenuous ground that the dangers of smoking were already well known (Kenny 1986a).[2] The refusal of the AMA and health charities to run antitobacco campaigns did not change until well after public opinion shifted against smoking in the 1980s.

The next significant development during the first phase of the movement occurred in 1968. Banzhaf single-handedly altered the course of the movement by winning an FCC ruling against the tobacco companies. Under the terms of the Fairness Doctrine, the FCC ordered TV and radio stations to provide free air time equal to the air time used by ads sponsored by the tobacco companies, or about $200 million in antitobacco ads. Ultimately, the FCC decision forced the tobacco industry to cease broadcasting to avoid being countered by free antismoking ads. It also led Congress to ban all broadcast smoking ads in January 1972. This deprived the tobacco industry of a powerful marketing tool, and antismoking ads started to undermine the legitimacy of smoking in the public mind.

Banzhaf and his organization continued to litigate to advance their antismoking agenda. For example, ASH sued United Airlines in 1971 to establish nonsmoking sections on its flights, pressed for the first state nonsmokers' rights law (enacted in 1973), was instrumental in the Civil Aeronautics Board's ban on cigar and pipe smoking on aircraft in 1979, and urged the Interstate Commerce Commission to ban smoking on interstate buses, which it did in 1990. ASH expanded the scope of its litigation by suing chain restaurants for failing to protect patrons from the health risks created by secondhand smoke. The organization also encouraged legal complaints against the owners of apartments and condominiums where smoking occurred and argued that smoking constituted child abuse in child custody cases.[3] ASH's successes were consistent with the continuing shift in public opinion against smoking. For example, in 1975 the U.S. Public Health Service conducted a large opinion survey that found that 77 percent of nonsmokers were annoyed to be near someone who was smoking (Kluger 1996:469).

## Nonsmokers Unite

The backdrop for the second stage of the antismoking movement was a report issued in 1971 by Surgeon General Jesse Steinfield. It declared that secondhand or ambient smoke is dangerous to the health of nonsmokers. This was precisely the kind of health warning the movement needed to mobilize nonsmokers in the antismoking campaign. It also enabled antismoking groups to adopt the strategy of early crusaders, who had focused on children as the most vulnerable victims of smoking. The argument was that secondhand smoke was responsible for the deaths of and diseases suffered by thousands of children who are exposed to smoke.

According to Banzhaf, antismoking groups understood that in order to destroy the tobacco industry, they had to get away from scientific findings and into the world of politics. The movement had won the medical argument. However, just like Lucy Page Gaston and the WCTU a hundred years before them, the next logical front in the war against tobacco was Congress, the state legislatures, and local governments throughout the country. Antismoking groups referred to this phase as the "nonsmokers' rights" movement. It has proved to be the most critical stage and constitutes a genuine grassroots movement, which explains much of its political success.

In 1989 few state governments had laws that controlled tobacco. Only twelve state health agencies had comprehensive antismoking regulations. However, increasing public concern about the health risk of secondhand smoke aroused nonsmokers throughout the country.

Two years after the U.S. Surgeon General's 1986 report, "The Health Consequences of Involuntary Smoking," nineteen states had four hundred local ordinances limiting smoking. In 1990 the U.S. Environmental Protection Agency published the draft of a report entitled "Environmental Tobacco Smoke Risk Assessment," which designated secondhand smoke as a cancer-causing carcinogen and linked secondhand smoke to lung cancer. This stimulated additional local laws and was supported by public opinion. For example, in 1987 an AMA survey revealed that 87 percent of nonsmokers and about half of all smokers believed that nonsmokers had the right to a smoke-free environment. A 1987 survey by the Centers for Disease Control showed that 75 percent of the public believed that secondhand smoke was harmful to nonsmokers. And a 1987 Gallup poll disclosed that 84 percent of the adult population favored either a total ban on smoking in public areas or separate smoking areas (Kluger 1996:678–79).

Initially, local smoking ordinances required separate smoking and nonsmoking areas. However, as reports of the linkage between secondhand smoke and cancer grew more numerous, antismoking laws became increasingly restrictive. Localities began to ban smoking in restaurants and workplaces. By September 1994 more than seven hundred local antismoking laws were on the books in the United States (California Wellness Foundation 1995:5).

By mid-1994 more than 130 local laws had completely eliminated smoking in public places and workplaces. For example, Andover, Massachusetts, and Pitkin County, Colorado, adopted laws mandating 100 percent smoke-free public environments, and Omaha made it illegal to hand out free samples of tobacco and to sell individual cigarettes. Localities reduced the sections in which smoking was permissible in public buildings from 75 percent of their total area to as little as 20 percent. Baltimore and Cincinnati banned tobacco billboards (California Wellness Foundation 1995:5).

### Antismoking Campaigns: Focus on Lifestyle
The key element of the contemporary grassroots antismoking campaign is that the major health charities and AMA work with antismoking groups such as the Americans for Nonsmokers' Rights. The American Lung Association, American Heart Association, and American Cancer Society all became involved in the antismoking movement during the mid-1980s as part of their educational programs.

The three charities embarked on campaigns to discourage the public from bad lifestyle choices. They ran expensive ad campaigns that encouraged people to change their diets, engage in exercise, and stop smoking. To this end, the Big Three spent hundreds of millions of dollars each year on public education campaigns to warn of the dangers of various foods, smoking, and lack of exercise. In 1985 they formed two political coalitions to promote the antismoking agenda, Tobacco Free America (TFA) and the Coalition for Smoking OR Health.[4]

TFA was created to run the grassroots campaign against tobacco. According to Holt and Pambianco (1994), the organization had three objectives: to form state coalitions of the American Medical Association, American Lung Association, American Cancer Society, and American Heart Association to lobby for antismoking legislation; make smoking socially unacceptable by tarnishing its public image; and achieve a "smoke-free" America by the year 2000. To this end, the TFA produced a 1990 report entitled "Blueprint for Success: Countdown 2000—Ten Years to a Tobacco-Free America." The report contained a plan of action that was widely circulated in all states and localities.

TFA joined forces with other antismoking groups, such as Americans for Nonsmokers' Rights (ANR), to create a formidable grassroots political movement. ANR is a nonprofit antismoking organization based in Berkeley, California, and is influential on the West Coast. It was founded by Dr. Stanton Glantz, an associate professor of medicine and chairman of the graduate program in bioengineering at the University of California at San Francisco.[5]

The ANR was organized primarily to lobby for local and state anti-smoking ordinances. According to Kevin Goebel, its legislative program manager, in the 1970s "secondhand smoke was considered merely a nuisance. That's all changed. It's a health issue now." Goebel said that the ANR wants to completely protect nonsmokers, which can be achieved only by eliminating smoking (Holt and Pambianco 1994:5–6). Glantz has expressed the objectives of ANR in less diplomatic language. In a 1990 address to the Seventh World Conference on Tobacco and Health in Perth, Australia, Glantz said,

> The main thing the science has done on the issue of ETS [environmental tobacco smoke] in addition to help people like me pay my mortgage, is it has legitimized the concern that people have that they don't like cigarette smoke. And that is a strong emotional force that needs to be harnessed and used. We're on a roll, and the bastards are on the run. *(Holt and Pambianco 1994:5–6).*

Glantz's strategy was to encourage nonsmokers to assert their political rights to be protected from the danger posed by smokers. One way to do that was to turn smokers into social outcasts. By 1994 California had 330 local ordinances and nationally there were more than eight hundred that restricted or banned smoking altogether.

Not only was Glantz successful in helping to create a grassroots anti-smoking constituency but he also prepared antitobacco reports for the EPA that were widely publicized. In 1994 Glantz received a $484,233 grant from the state of California to carry out his antismoking campaign. The ANR also received a grant from the National Cancer Institute to campaign against smoking.[6]

## Grassroots Antismoking Campaigns

According to Samuels and Glantz (1991:2110), the grassroots movement for nonsmokers' rights began in the 1970s. The strategy was to enact local anti-smoking laws on the assumption that local officials were more responsive to voters than were state and national politicians. Activists felt that the southern "out-of-town" tobacco companies would have less influence at the local level than in state legislatures and Congress. Antismoking groups used this approach to offset the tobacco industry's huge lobbying resources.

The grassroots strategy had two major assets. The first was the strong network of antismoking health advocates in local communities. The second was that those people had a close working relationship with their local elected officials. That made the antismoking forces more than a match for the tobacco companies.

In 1978 the Tobacco Institute, the chief Washington, D.C.–based lob-bying organization for the cigarette industry, had commissioned a Roper poll and accompanying report that reflects its awareness of the grassroots strategy. The report accurately assessed the threat posed by the grassroots antismoking campaign. The survey, which included smokers and non-smokers, revealed a highly negative public attitude toward smoking and the tobacco industry (Roper Organization 1978:A-7).

Among other things, the survey found that 9 in 10 Americans believed that smoking was a health hazard. The majority felt that being around smokers was dangerous even to those who did not smoke, and they favored separate smoking places in public buildings. A majority also believed that the tobacco industry knew that the health arguments against smoking were true. Favorable attitudes toward the tobacco companies was at an all-time low. Respondents even said they would vote for, rather than against, a can-didate who favored a ban on smoking in public places (Roper Organization 1978).

The report warned that if nonsmokers were convinced that smokers posed a danger to their health, the industry was facing two threats. The first was that nonsmokers would insist on separate indoor public facilities for smokers. But if inconvenience and the social stigma connected with it did not convince smokers to quit, antismoking groups were likely to demand a ban on smoking altogether. To the industry the most troubling aspect of the report was that it confirmed that the tobacco industry had no credibil-ity with the public. This is a fatal weakness for any industry, especially when it is under political attack (Roper Organization 1978).

The report outlined a broad strategy, including short-term and long-term plans, for coping with the antismoking movement. The long-term strategy was to come up with credible medical evidence that smoking was not harmful to nonsmokers and to publicize this widely (Roper Organization 1978). The industry obviously wanted to do that but could find no credible scientific proof that secondhand smoke is benign.

The short-term strategy was to slow down the grassroots antismoking movement and buy time to produce scientific evidence refuting the danger of secondhand smoke (Roper Organization 1978). The industry advised owners and operators of restaurants, bars, taxis, and other public places confronted with the prospect of an outright ban on smoking to argue for the right to establish their own smoking policy, so long as it was clearly posted (Roper Organization 1978).

The Roper report also recommended that businesses formally complain to the Federal Trade Commission (FTC) about public service advertising by antismoking organizations that misquoted the facts about smoking and health. They should insist, the report said, that "corrective" ads be broadcast. Roper had found that although a majority of the public favored government programs that discouraged smoking, they did not favor the use of tax money to support such programs. Therefore, Roper said, businesses should remind the public about the costs of antismoking programs sponsored by government. Although the study found that the public favored government action against smoking, a majority of respondents opposed intrusions into other areas of life, such as prohibiting alcohol, unhealthy food, or dangerous sporting activities. The report recommended that the industry try to exploit that public concern by warning that antismoking regulations constituted the first step toward overregulation and intrusion into citizens' private lives. The report said that the tobacco companies should try to divide the antismoking movement into "zealots" who had an unreasonable fear of smoking and those who were less concerned about the health effects of secondhand smoke (Roper Organization 1978).

*Popular Epidemiology and Secondhand Smoke*
A key factor in the grassroots nonsmokers' rights campaigns is the use of "popular epidemiology" as a political strategy against the tobacco industry. According to health writer Phil Brown, "Popular epidemiology is the process by which laypersons gather scientific data and other information, and also direct and marshal the knowledge and resources of experts in order to understand the epidemiology of disease" (1991:269).

Brown says that poplar epidemiology is actually good science, for four reasons:

Citizen involvement exposes cases of "bad science," by which he means flawed studies, secret data, and failure to inform health officials.

It underscores that the demanding standards of proof required by "normal science" often are unobtainable.

It leads citizens to use nonscientific modes of communication to express their concerns about health dangers.

It provides valuable data on an environmental danger that might otherwise be ignored. (1991:269–70)

The canons of conventional science and industry reject popular epidemiology. Critics argue that it encourages conspiracy theories about the corruption and malfeasance of industry and government. They say it stimulates citizen anger against public authorities without illuminating the causes or effects of environmental dangers. Finally, it undermines sound scientific procedures, which are necessary to understand the real environmental dangers to health, critics say (Wildavsky 1995:400–402).

The impetus for popular epidemiology is a widespread public belief that industry and government misuse science to defend or conceal pollution of the environment. Indeed, opinion polls reveal the public's belief that environmental health risks have increased. "Quality of employment" surveys carried out by the University of Michigan's Institute for Social Research in 1969, 1972, and 1977 show this trend (Brown and Mikkelson 1990:164–65). From 1969 to 1977 workers who said they were exposed to workplace hazards increased from 38 to 78 percent. The surveys found that people polled in 1977 were more concerned than those polled in 1969 and 1972 about technological health risks, including contaminated drinking water, accidents at nuclear power plants, toxic wastes, and cancer-causing chemicals.

Advocates for smoking bans rely heavily on popular epidemiology to justify bans on smoking. To understand how grassroots political campaigns use science, it is necessary to briefly examine the scientific basis for the claim that environmental tobacco smoke is a major public health hazard.

The antismoking groups frequently cite three government reports, "The Health Consequences of Involuntary Smoking" from the surgeon general and *Environmental Tobacco Smoke: Measuring Exposures and Assessing Health Effects* from the National Research Council of the National

Academy of Science, both released in 1986, and the EPA's "Respiratory Health Effects of Passive Smoking: Lung Cancer and Other Disorders," released in 1993.

The 1986 reports arrived at two conclusions concerning secondhand smoke. The first was that the exposure of nonsmokers to secondhand smoke increased their risk of lung cancer. The second was that the children of smokers had more symptoms of respiratory disease than the children of nonsmokers. However, the reports said that given the low risks associated with secondhand smoke and that other factors contribute to lung cancer and respiratory diseases, it was impossible to reliably estimate the danger of secondhand smoke to public health. In other words, it contributed to lung cancer and respiratory disease, but neither study could determine the extent of its contribution to these diseases.

### Scientific Skepticism

Indeed, the connection between secondhand smoke and lung cancer was challenged in a British study directed by P. N. Lee of the Institute for Cancer Research, published in the July 1986 issue of the *British Journal of Cancer*. The Lee study screened twelve thousand hospital patients for smoking-related diseases and flatly contradicted the conclusions of the surgeon general and of the National Research Council. Lee found that the risk of harm from smoke in the air was "at most small, if it exists at all." He also concluded that it was difficult to determine statistically whether secondhand smoke causes lung cancer because so few nonsmokers get lung cancer.

The 1993 EPA study went far beyond the 1986 reports, however, in estimating the health risks of secondhand smoke. That study concluded that about three thousand nonsmokers die each year of lung cancer resulting from secondhand smoke. It claimed that each year children younger than eighteen months account for 150,000 to 300,000 cases of lower respiratory illness, including pneumonia, bronchitis, and bronchiolitis, resulting in 7,500 to 15,000 hospitalizations. The report also stated that secondhand smoke causes asthma symptoms in 400,000 to 1 million children and increases coughing, sputum, and wheezing in children and adults. It also increases middle-ear infections and the incidence of limited lung capacity in children and adults, the study said.

This alarming EPA report gave the antismoking movement a powerful political argument for banning smoking. However, its scientific validity has been questioned. For example, Dr. M. R. Guerin, coauthor of a book on the chemistry and composition of secondhand smoke, testified in 1993 before the House Subcommittee on Health and the Environment that the EPA had overestimated the risk of secondhand smoke (U.S. House 1993b:92–93). Henry Waxman (D-Calif.), subcommittee chairman, noted that the EPA listed secondhand smoke as a "class A carcinogen," along with benzene, arsenic, asbestos, and radon, because of its similarities with "mainstream smoke." He asked Guerin to distinguish between mainstream smoke and environmental tobacco smoke.

Guerin said that the critical difference is how the smoke is inhaled. In the case of active or mainstream smoke, it is drawn directly into one's mouth, normally by inhaling deeply and forcefully exhaling the smoke. In the case of passive "sidestream smoke," on the other hand, it is inhaled under normal breathing conditions. Another difference is the level of concentration. Mainstream smoke is far more concentrated than secondhand smoke. The chemicals in mainstream smoke are a hundred thousand to a million times higher than in secondhand smoke. Finally, mainstream smoke contains short-term chemical agents called "free radicals," such as tar, which might contribute to lung cancer but are not present in secondhand smoke.

Given the relatively low level of chemical concentration in secondhand smoke, Guerin raised a question regarding the health risk it poses: "What exactly is secondhand smoke?" Ironically, despite the EPA claims that it is a cancer-causing agent, the agency acknowledges that it is difficult to even determine when it is present. For example, secondhand smoke is clearly present in a smoke-filled room. However, is it also present in a room hours, days, or months after smoking has ended? As secondhand smoke moves throughout a building, it changes in concentration and composition. In this situation it is difficult to determine when secondhand smoke ceases to be tobacco smoke.

Among the questions raised by Guerin was level of exposure to secondhand smoke. There is a huge difference in health risk for a person exposed to high concentrations of secondhand smoke—such as a nonsmoking spouse who has lived with a smoker for years—and that for a person exposed to low levels of secondhand smoke for short periods, such as a few hours in a restaurant where smoking is allowed. According to Guerin, unless secondhand smoke includes smoking cigarettes in private residences, where nonsmoking spouses are exposed to high concentrations of smoke for prolonged periods, secondhand smoke cannot be classified as causing cancer. And even this assumes that a scientific basis exists for concluding that the exposure of spouses to secondhand smoke significantly increases their cancer risks (U.S. House 1993b).

The problem of detecting the level of exposure to secondhand smoke was also discussed in the congressional hearings. The most common measure of exposure to secondhand smoke is the presence of airborne nicotine or cotinine in urine. However, this test does not detect short-term exposure to secondhand smoke. Guerin concluded that at some level of exposure secondhand smoke causes cancer. However, exactly what that level is is unclear, and the EPA study did not establish the level at which it is dangerous. Guerin concluded that it was not yet possible to classify secondhand smoke as a known human carcinogen.

Dr. Alvan Feinstein, a clinical epidemiologist at Yale University Medical School and editor of *Clinical Epidemiology,* also had problems with the FDA's scientific evidence for declaring secondhand smoke a cancer-causing agent (U.S. House 1993b:75–110; Feinstein 1992). He pointed out that in the surgeon general's 1964 report, which declared a corollary between active smoking and lung cancer and coronary diseases, established two criteria for the scientific reliability of evidence. (He was referring to the Bradford Hill criteria, named after a scientist who served on the surgeon general's committee that prepared the 1964 report.) The first criterion had to do with the "consistency of the association," which means that there should be few, if any, contradictions in the scientific studies.

The second criterion was a high-risk ratio. The 1964 report found that the statistical probability of getting lung cancer is about ten times greater for average smokers than nonsmokers and twenty times greater for heavy smokers. Therefore, for a risk ratio to be statistically significant, it must be greater than two times and preferably more than three times the average.

The reason for this is that statisticians, like lawyers, try to put the best spin on their findings. Feinstein illustrated this with a hypothetical clinical trial in which death rates were found to drop 1 percent (from 3 percent to 2 percent). The *New England Journal of Medicine* and the front page of the *New York Times* might report the result of such a study to be a 33 percent reduction in the death rate. Strictly speaking, that would be true. However, such a finding does not have a high confidence level because the difference is so small—only 1 percent. If the study were repeated, the probability of achieving the same result would also be low. In other words, the statistical relationship could disappear altogether.

Feinstein further illustrated the subjectivity surrounding any statistical analysis. He said that when he taught a seminar at Yale, he asked students to consult the *United States Statistical Abstract* and find the best statistical relationship they could between any two variables. In 1993 the winner of the best statistical relationship was that of the sale of videocassette recorders and the incidence of AIDS. He said that it is even possible to give this silly relationship meaning by suggesting that AIDS is contracted while watching videos (U.S. House 1993b:99). Statistics can be helpful, but they must be interpreted sensibly by those with a knowledge of the subject.

But Feinstein said that the EPA's 1993 report on secondhand smoke had not used the criterion of consistency of association (U.S. House 1993b). This introduced a potential bias in the findings. For example, the failure to consider the consistency of association of the evidence of a relationship between secondhand smoke and cancer risk resulted in conflicting studies. In other words, the studies cited by the EPA went in opposite directions—some confirmed secondhand smoke as a cancer risk and others rejected it. Of the thirty-five studies in the report, six studies had cancer risks below 1 (no increased risk), which suggests that exposure to secondhand smoke actually lowers the risk of cancer. Fourteen of the studies revealed a low relative risk of between 1 and 1.49. Eight studies put the risk at 1.5 to 1.99, and seven studies found an increased risk of 2 to 2.1 (U.S. House 1993b:79–80).

These are clearly inconsistent results and, by the Bradford Hill criteria, should have been thrown out. Instead, the EPA pooled all the studies as if they went in the same direction and concluded that secondhand smoke significantly increases the risk of cancer. Another problem with the EPA report is the use of a controversial procedure called "meta-analysis." Meta-analysis is a research method in which the results from a number of studies are pooled or combined. Some scientists regard it as alchemy or witchcraft, whereas others believe it is a significant contribution to modern science.

Feinstein said he had no problem with meta-analysis, provided that all the studies are "randomized." That is to say, did all the studies in the EPA report select test groups in the same way? For example, did all the studies select groups of nonsmoking spouses for the secondhand smoke-exposed group that had never smoked, and were they exposed to their smoking spouses for the same period of time? Did all the studies consider incidences of asthma, heart disease, and other ailments? However, none of the test groups in the EPA study were randomized. This means that some groups were more susceptible to contracting cancer than others before their exposure to secondhand smoke. This was particularly troublesome to some scientists because the EPA did not conduct any of the research for the report. It merely processed, interpreted, or editorialized the results of other studies.

Feinstein observed that the EPA data on secondhand smoke for Greece, Hong Kong, Japan, the United States, Western Europe, and China also moved in opposite directions. The studies in Europe and China were below 1 (exposure to secondhand smoke lowers the risk of cancer) and none was above 2, which is below the standard minimum level of significance in epidemiological studies of 2 or 3. The polled level of risk for these studies was 104 to 119 (100 is no additional risk), which is about as marginal a risk as one can have. This is perhaps why the EPA excluded the international studies from the report.

Feinstein pointed out additional problems with the EPA report. For example, the U.S. studies ignored the different kinds of cell types in lung cancer (epidermoid, adenose, and small cell and large cell) that would be associated with secondhand smoke if it causes cancer. The Scientific Advisory Board, an eighteen-member panel of eminent scientists in the field appointed by the administrator of the EPA to ensure that the agency followed accepted scientific procedures, warned the agency not to claim that secondhand smoke causes three thousand cancer deaths a year (U.S. House 1993b:88).

However, the EPA ignored the Scientific Advisory Board's admonition and included the estimate of three thousand deaths in the report. The EPA also excluded the largest secondhand smoke research ever conducted, the Brownson study, on the ground that it arrived too late to be included (Brownson 1992). The EPA refused to include the Brownson study, although it was published in a major scientific journal, which meant that the study was known to scientists in the field before the EPA study was released. Furthermore, the EPA accepted another study in its report that arrived late and had not been considered by a research journal. Inclusion of the Brownson study might have eliminated the significance level of the findings on secondhand smoke. As it was, the EPA took the unusual step of lowering the 95 percent confidence interval to 90 percent to get a marginally positive cancer risk for secondhand smoke.[7] Indeed, in order to reach the conclusion that secondhand smoke causes cancer, the EPA, using meta-analysis, pooled eleven studies of nonsmoking spouses exposed to smoking spouses. However, ten of the studies showed no statistically significant increase in cancer among nonsmokers.

Feinstein concluded his testimony by saying that if for social reasons Congress wanted to ban smoking, it should do so as a matter of policy. However, Congress should not misuse science to justify a policy objective. But, he said, neither science nor public policy is served when science is sacrificed to meet the goals of policy. Feinstein speculated that the reason EPA declared secondhand smoke to be a cancer-causing agent was that top EPA officials had set a policy and said, in effect, "We would like to get the evidence to prove this point." And as any loyal government staff members would do, scientists in the agency tried to assemble evidence to support that policy. Government research funding agencies and foundations are also unlikely to fund research that challenges the antismoking doctrines currently in vogue in the country (U.S. House 1993b:103, 14).

However, Feinstein's criticism ignores a fundamental premise of popular epidemiology: the reliance on nonscientific, often anecdotal, reports of those suffering from the hazards of secondhand smoke. Those gathering this data (reports from those who believe they are suffering from an environmental health hazard) often are scientifically trained. However, they do not rely on standard scientific statistical probability to determine whether a health hazard exists. For example, the final three-volume EPA study of the Love Canal chemical hazard concluded that the incidence of cancer and birth defects was not significantly higher in that community than in the general population. However, those who believe in the value of popular epidemiology reject those conclusions and say, essentially, ask the former residents of Love Canal.

### The Role of Antismoking Scientists

The influence of antismoking advocates during the debate about whether to ban smoking in the workplace is a clear illustration of the success of the antismoking expressive group with federal regulatory agencies. It is also an example of an expressive group's effectively advancing its agenda from within a government bureaucracy.

Anti-smoking scientists played a key role in drafting and publicizing the government reports that warned of the dangers of smoking and secondhand smoke. Although all government hearings are advertised as "fair, accurate, and objective," several well-known antismoking activists participated in the deliberations by the Occupational Safety and Health Administration (OSHA) on whether to ban smoking in the workplace.[8] Two, James Repace and Stanton Glantz, not only testified at the hearings but functioned as OSHA staff members.

Repace was a physicist, and Glantz was trained in mechanical engineering. Neither had a background in medicine. However, both had long and well-known histories of antitobacco activity. Repace, who was in charge of the EPA's indoor air program, was temporarily assigned to OSHA during the hearings. And Glantz was an official OSHA witness, a member of the OSHA staff, and cross-examined tobacco industry witnesses during the November 1994 hearings. Despite public assurances that OSHA's hearings on secondhand smoke would not start with a fixed and predetermined position, these two antismoking activists played a key role as part of the OSHA staff at the hearings.

For example, in 1980 Repace was coauthor of an article that claimed that indoor air pollution from tobacco smoke constitutes a serious danger to the health of nonsmokers and demands as much attention as outdoor air pollution (Lowrey and Repace 1980). In 1985 Repace again helped write a controversial article that claimed that secondhand smoke was a greater health risk than all industrial pollutants combined (Repace and Lowrey 1985). He also stated publicly that as many as five thousand Americans die each year from exposure to secondhand smoke.

Repace also worked with antismoking groups such as the Group Against Smoking Pollution (GASP) and ASH. He appeared as an expert witness before various legislative bodies and in foreign countries to argue for smoking bans. And he worked closely with Glantz in preparing antismoking films about secondhand smoke.

Glantz was also well known for his antitobacco activity. Like Repace's, Glantz's views on secondhand smoke were widely known long before the OSHA hearing in 1994. For example, at the antismoking conference in Perth, Australia, in 1990, Glantz said that "it's very nice to see that the same ideas that a few of us were advocating in 1983 which were viewed as so strange, radical and hopeless, have now really become very mainstream" (Holt and Pambianco 1994:6). And in a 1987 article for the *Western Journal of Medicine* Glantz stated that "the biomedical community [was in agreement] that involuntary smoking (secondhand smoke) is a significant health hazard and that scientific common sense suggests that toxins in (secondhand smoke) affect nonsmokers who breathe them" (Glantz 1987:636–37). Glantz also was the founder and president of Americans for Nonsmokers' Rights and president of the American Nonsmokers' Rights Foundation.

Repace and Glantz, as well as other movement opponents of smoking, have written reports for the EPA, produced antismoking films used by the antismoking movement, and served on the staffs of and have been consultants to government regulatory agencies. As director of the indoor air quality division of the EPA, Repace functioned as an in-house government representative of the antismoking movement. He also collaborated with Glantz and other antismoking advocates, such as A. H. Lowrey and Judson

Wells, experts on indoor air quality, in testifying against secondhand smoke at EPA and OSHA hearings and in state legislatures throughout the country.

Glantz collaborated with Richard Daynard, a Northeastern University professor of law who chaired the antismoking Tobacco Products Liability Project, which sues tobacco companies. In 1991, two years before the EPA's secondhand smoke study, Glantz and Daynard claimed that lung cancer caused by secondhand smoke kills about 3,700 Americans a year and that heart disease caused by secondhand smoke kills about 37,000 each year (Glantz and Daynard 1991).

The influence of antismoking advocates during the OSHA secondhand smoke hearings clearly illustrates the success of the antismoking expressive group in federal regulatory agencies. It is an example of an expressive group's effectively advancing its agenda in a government bureaucracy. In the case of the 1994 OSHA hearings on secondhand smoke, the government promoted the litigation and antitobacco objectives of the nonsmokers' rights movement.

### The California Campaign

The acid test of the effectiveness of the campaign against secondhand smoke occurred in California in 1994. The tobacco companies were sponsoring an initiative, Proposition 188, designed to override the state's Smokefree Workplace Act of 1994 (also known as AB13), scheduled to take effect in January 1995.[9] The act, which was driven by the 1993 EPA report that concluded secondhand smoke caused lung cancer, would have banned smoking in nearly all California workplaces. It was one of the strongest antismoking laws in the country and was certain to become a model for antitobacco groups in other states.

Taking on the tobacco companies, which were led by Philip Morris, was an expressive group, the Coalition for Healthy California. The SMOs supporting the campaign included the American Cancer Society, American Heart Association, American Lung Association, California Nurses Association, California Association of Hospitals, Americans for Nonsmokers' Rights, and the Sierra Club. The principal nonmovement allies were the Parent-Teacher Association (PTA) and the California Wellness Foundation. The secondhand smoke campaign's political allies were the California

Legislature, the governor, and city and county councils. The Coalition for Healthy California won.

## The Tobacco Industry's Campaign

Five major tobacco companies—Philip Morris, R. J. Reynolds, Brown and Williamson, American Tobacco, and Lorrillard—put up about $18 million (mostly Philip Morris's money) in their attempt to nullify the Smokefree Workplace Act.[10] Philip Morris, the largest tobacco company in the world with 45 percent of the U.S. market, took the lead in sponsoring Proposition 188. The other tobacco companies entered the campaign late and only after a great deal of hesitation. They feared that the initiative would be defeated and that the companies would receive negative publicity if they campaigned against a popular smoking control law.

Except for R. J. Reynolds, which contributed almost $3.4 million, the tobacco companies did not make significant financial contributions to the campaign. Philip Morris alone spent about $12.5 million. In effect, Philip Morris was the originator and principal sponsor of the initiative, which opponents promptly dubbed the "Philip Morris initiative."[11]

Proposition 188 was also designed to eliminate stiff local antismoking ordinances. For example, 287 of California's 470 cities, as well as seventeen of the state's thirty-six counties, had smoking restriction ordinances. Of these local ordinances, at least 120 communities had smoking provisions more restrictive than what was called for in Proposition 188 (*Redding (California) Record Searchlight*, October 15, 1994:A1). Table 5.2 compares Proposition 188, AB13, and local laws.

The tobacco industry took its stand in California for two reasons. California was the biggest cigarette market in the country, and the non-smokers' rights movement was sweeping the state. If this trend continued, the antismoking groups would have succeeded in its intermediate goal of making it difficult to smoke in public, thereby stigmatizing smokers. To the industry the grassroots antismoking strategy was death by a thousand cuts. It not only threatened the cigarette market but local ordinances were beyond the control of the state and federal governments, where the tobacco companies had traditionally been able to block antismoking legislation. And since 1981 the tobacco companies had seen serious erosion in cigarette consumption in California (see figure 5.1).

**TABLE 5.2  Comparison of Smoking Laws**
AB13, Proposition 188, and Local Laws

| Workplaces | AB13 | Proposition 188 | Local Laws |
|---|---|---|---|
| Exemptions | Businesses with no more than 5 workers; ware-houses | Private Offices | None |
| Conference rooms | Prohibited | Allowed with consent w/ ASHRAE vent** | Prohibited |
| Cafeterias | Prohibited | Smoking Allowed in 25% of seating with ASHRE vent** | Prohibited |
| Restaurants | Prohibited | Smoking allowed in 25% of seating w/ASHRAE vent** | Prohibited |
| Bars | Prohibited by Jan 1, 1997 | Smoking allowed | None |
| Hotel Rooms | Smoking in 65% of rooms | No restrictions | 30%–75% smoke free |
| **Method of Sale** | | | |
| Vending machines | No provision | Banned if not super-vised | Only in bars |
| Billboards | No provision | Prohibited within 500ft of schools | None |
| **Enforcement** | | | |
| Workplace | State Health & Safety Dept. | Only Cal-OSHA | Local |
| Public places | State Health & Safety Dept. | Police Dept. | Local |

*Local restrictions in force in 21 counties and cities in southern California. (Mayes 1994).
**American Society of Heating, Refrigerating, and Air Conditioning Engineer's standards. Written in 1989 before the 1993 EPA report on secondhand smoke. Antismoking advocates reject this standard on the ground that it is to reduce smoke odor and not to remove harnful chemicals.

## State Support for Antismoking Programs

The antismoking groups and the tobacco industry agreed on one point: the decline in cigarette sales in California was directly attributable to passage of Proposition 99, the Tobacco Tax and Health Promotion Act of 1988. Proposition 99 increased the state's tobacco tax from ten to thirty-five cents per pack, and it required that these tax revenues be put into the newly established Tobacco Tax Surtax Fund. This fund, like the federal Highway

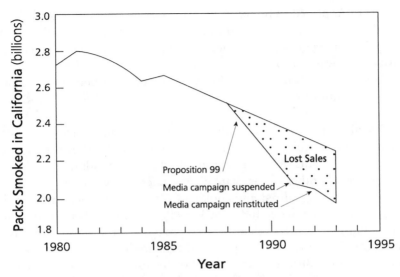

**FIGURE 5.1 Total Cigarette Consumption in California**
Proposition 99, which took effect in 1988, cut consumption by 1.1 billion packs
SOURCE: BEGAY, TRAYNOR AND GLANTZ (1994:5)

Trust Fund, was not part of the state's general fund. It could be used only to finance antismoking programs. For example, the health education account was to receive 20 percent of total cigarette tax revenues for school and community tobacco education and prevention programs.[12] The account also authorized funds for antismoking media programs.

These antismoking programs were unprecedented in several respects. The state had never before financed a media campaign to counter the tobacco industry. The campaign was designed to "delegitimize" the tobacco industry and "denormalize" tobacco use (California Wellness Foundation 1993:11). The message was that the tobacco companies were plotting to take control of childrens' bodies by addicting them to nicotine. The programs also emphasized the health dangers of secondhand smoke to children.

Revenues from Proposition 99's provisions funded sixty-one local lead agencies (LLAs), which were under the jurisdiction of county or city health departments. The LLAs planned, organized, and coordinated community antismoking activities, including the formation of coalitions of health advocates, civic leaders, county offices of education, and others to implement Proposition 99. That law mandated a 75 percent reduction in cigarette consumption in California by the year 2000. It also required that schools become "tobacco free" by 1996.

The LLAs played an important role in creating smoke-free workplaces, and they were effective in training and organizing local antismoking groups to campaign for antitobacco ordinances. For example, when Proposition 99 was approved in 1988, only one city in California banned smoking in public buildings and in workplaces and restaurants. By 1993 about 130 communities had done so (California Wellness Foundation 1994).

One of the ironies of the California antismoking movement is that one of its most successful grassroots antismoking organizations, Ameri-cans for Nonsmokers' Rights (ANR), has received substantial funding from the sale of cigarettes. In other words, state tax revenues derived from the tobacco companies has subsidized antismoking SMOs that are dedicated to the destruction of the tobacco industry. Thus Proposition 99 helped create the largest and most aggressive antitobacco program in the world. From 1989 through 1994 Proposition 99 provided $455 million for the antitobacco movement in California. According to the annual California Tobacco Survey reports, required by Proposition 99, state-financed antismoking programs were highly effective in accelerating the decline of smoking in the state (Pierce 1994). Indeed, antismoking groups such as ANR and the Big Three health charities say that Proposition 99 is responsible for one million fewer smokers in California. They also claim the measure saved the state more than $386 million in medical costs to treat smoking-related diseases in 1993 alone. They estimate that the tobacco companies sold more than a billion fewer packs of cigarettes than they would have without Proposition 99 (Begay, Traynor, and Glantz 1994:6–7).

The basic political challenge to the industry was the formation of local antitobacco groups lobbying for local ordinances to ban and restrict smoking. The revenues generated by Proposition 99 had promoted the formation of such groups. For example, the Long Beach Tobacco Control Coalition, which received funding under Proposition 99 and had the support of the Long Beach City Council, was created in 1991.

The Long Beach Tobacco Control Coalition recommended that the city adopt an antismoking ordinance. The city council agreed that such legislation was desirable and held public hearings on the proposed ban on smoking. At the hearings antismoking advocates, including physicians representing the American Lung Association, American Heart Association, and American Cancer Society as well as the coalition, testified in favor of an antismoking law. They relied heavily on the reports from the surgeon general, EPA, and OSHA that condemned secondhand smoke as a cancer-causing agent (Traynor, Begay, and Glantz 1993:481–82; Samuels and Glantz 1991). Despite strong opposition from the tobacco industry, the city of Long Beach adopted a strong antismoking ordinance.

### The Philip Morris Strategy

Dismayed by the effects of Proposition 99 on their business, Philip Morris executives met with the powerful speaker of the California Assembly, Willie Brown, in November 1990 to solicit support for legislation that would stop the spread of local antitobacco ordinances. Brown was the industry's strongest supporter and the top recipient of tobacco industry campaign contributions. For example, in 1994 Brown received $152,975 in campaign contributions from the tobacco companies and had gotten $659,492 from the industry since 1980 (Aguinaga et al. 1995:3).

Brown suggested that the tobacco executives adopt a two-pronged strategy. The first was to write a preemptive smokers' rights bill that would override local antismoking laws. The second was that the bill would have to be a comprehensive "antismoking bill" in order to gain the public support needed for passage (Macdonald, Traynor, Glantz 1994:8). The idea was to sponsor a nominally tough statewide antismoking law that also would stop the spread of local antismoking ordinances.

To that end, tobacco industry supporters sponsored Senate Bill 376 in 1991; the measure was the preemptive strike that Brown had suggested. But the bill was killed when a confidential memorandum about the meeting between Brown and the tobacco executives was leaked to the press (Lucas 1991; Richardson 1991; Walters 1991; and Webb 1991). Undaunted, the tobacco industry persevered and got the Assembly to sponsor similar legislation. This legislation survived the lower house but was killed in the senate by members of the state Senate Health Committee, including Tom Hayden.

The industry was frustrated. Its traditional source of political support, the state legislature and the governor's office, had failed it. As a last resort Philip Morris decided to press ahead with the ingenious preemptive strategy suggested by Brown, this time through the initiative process.

And so it came to pass that the tobacco companies sponsored Proposition 188.[13] It was almost identical to the Assembly bill that Hayden had helped kill in the state senate. However, unlike the legislature, all Philip Morris had to do was persuade the voting public to support the measure.

*Public Support for the Philip Morris Initiative*

Philip Morris commissioned a public opinion poll in July 1994 to assess the strengths and weaknesses of its initiative and develop a campaign strategy. Based on the survey, the company decided to use two themes in its campaign. The first was that antismoking groups were overzealous in trying to control tobacco use; the second was that California would benefit from a single, uniform state law on smoking. The poll uncovered a public perception that antismoking groups were unreasonable in trying to impose their standards on others. The public also felt that there were too many local antismoking ordinances, which often overlapped and conflicted (Stitzenberger interview 1994).

A critical factor in the industry campaign was credibility. The poll found that 82 percent of California voters had heard of Philip Morris and identified it as a tobacco company. This raised a red flag for Philip Morris. If the voters did not trust the company and associated Philip Morris with Proposition 188, the initiative was in trouble. Indeed, this proved to be the company's most serious problem. When respondents were asked about their trust in what Philip Morris said about government tobacco policy, only 10 percent said they trusted the company. Trust of the tobacco industry in general dropped to only 8 percent (Stitzenberger interview 1994).

However, when voters were asked about the two political front groups Philip Morris had created to carry its campaign, Californians for Statewide Smoking Restrictions and the California Business and Restaurant Alliance, trust for these groups rose to 28 percent. By contrast, the antismoking groups had a public trust rating of 30 percent. In other words, the political groups for and against the Philip Morris proposition had low but roughly comparable public trust ratings (Stitzenberger interview 1994).

The poll's critical finding in terms of public confidence on antismoking issues involved the health charities, including the Big Three. All had high credibility ratings, as did C. Everett Koop, the former U.S. surgeon general.

Sixty-four percent of respondents said that they would probably or definitely support the position taken by the health charities on tobacco issues in the November 1994 election. By contrast, only 13 percent of voters said they would probably or definitely support the tobacco industry's position. Voters regarded Koop and the health charities as being nonpartisan, although they were outspoken in condemning the use of tobacco (Stitzenberger interview 1994).

Still, the poll found a glimmer of hope for Philip Morris: strong support for certain elements of the industry's initiative. When respondents were first read a description of the Philip Morris proposition, 50 percent said they would support it; 43 percent said they would not. The public favored many of the specific antismoking provisions in the initiative. Voters found the idea of a uniform statewide antismoking law appealing. For example, respondents supported the proposal that cigarette billboards not be allowed within five hundred feet of a school and that smoking should be allowed in all hotel rooms except those designated as nonsmoking by the management. They also favored the provision that smoking be permitted in 25 percent of a restaurant's seating, provided it was ventilated. Further, respondents felt that, with proper ventilation, smoking should be allowed in bars and taverns and private offices. What voters apparently did not understand about the Philip Morris initiative was that about 70 percent of existing antismoking ordinances in the state were already more restrictive (see table 5.2).

Another factor determining the nature of public support for the Philip Morris initiative was that 20 percent of respondents thought that Proposition 188 was sponsored by the health charities or the government. They did not understand that it was sponsored by the tobacco companies. For example, only 37 percent of women and voters older than sixty-five understood that Philip Morris was sponsoring the proposition (Marttila and Kiley 1994).

These two groups were particularly important for antismoking groups —once they understood that Proposition 188 was sponsored by the tobacco industry, they switched from supporting the initiative to opposing it. The antismoking groups targeted these groups, especially women, in their campaign to defeat the initiative (Marttila and Kiley 1994).

### Stigmatizing Proposition 188
When voters became aware of Philip Morris's sponsorship of the proposition, the 10 percent margin that had supported the initiative became a margin of 12 percent against it. In other words, after hearing that Philip Morris sponsored the initiative, 52 percent of voters said they opposed it.

Opponents of the proposition attributed the shift to a gender gap. Women were more inclined to oppose the initiative than men. Men were divided on the proposition, whereas women turned dramatically against it by a margin of 23 percent. Among nonsmokers the gender gap was even greater, with 36 percent more nonsmoking women than men opposing the proposition. Antismoking groups identified nonsmokers in general, and nonsmoking women in particular, as their base of opposition to the initiative.

The Philip Morris poll revealed that the most convincing argument in favor of its initiative was that it imposed tough new regulations on smoking. Some voters also supported the initiative because it would "level the playing field for all California businesses." The poll also found undecided voters tended to support the initiative because they believed that "antismoking zealots" had gone too far in California (Marttila and Kiley 1994).

Antismoking SMOs interpreted these polling results (which the newspapers reported) as suggesting that they should avoid the business implications of the initiative and should not respond to the argument that antismoking zealots had gone too far. Instead, they decided to discredit the idea that the initiative was an antismoking proposal. The best way to do that was to publicize Philip Morris's sponsorship. The theme would be that the tobacco industry was trying to fool the public (Nicholl and Knepprath 1994).

However, antismoking factions were concerned that Philip Morris could still manage to somehow use its vast resources to mislead voters into believing that the measure was a genuine antismoking proposition. They concluded that Philip Morris's image as a tobacco company was the strongest argument against the initiative. In other words, opponents could simply argue that a tobacco company was spending millions of dollars in a political campaign to protect its corporate profits. A related argument was that if the initiative passed, more people would smoke and breathe secondhand smoke, which would result in more deaths from cancer and other diseases.

### Philip Morris's Campaign

Philip Morris explained the purpose of its campaign in a letter to its stockholders in 1994. The company said that the initiative was of paramount importance to its customers, employees, and stockholders because it would prevent the statewide ban on smoking from taking effect.

The company hired Lee Stitzenberger, and his political consulting firm, the Dolfin Group, to run its campaign. The Dolfin Group is a well-known Republican firm based in Los Angeles. In 1986 Stitzenberger ran the successful campaign to unseat the chief justice of the California Supreme Court, Rose Bird, and two other justices. In 1988 he produced the Republicans' Willie Horton video in George Bush's presidential campaign against Democrat Michael Dukakis. Stitzenberger also conducted the CAREFUL campaign to defeat Big Green in 1990 (Stitzenberger interview 1994).

Stitzenberger's ingenious campaign strategy copied a strategy used by antismoking groups. He devised an anti-smoking theme and made the campaign grassroots in orientation.

Stitzenberger said he felt that antismoking sentiment in California was so strong that the tobacco industry could not run a smokers' rights campaign and hope to win. Indeed, the industry called its political action committee the Californians for Statewide Smoking Restrictions Committee.

In newspaper ads and mass mailings the "Yes on 188" campaign argued that the initiative was a tough antismoking measure. For example, in April 1994 Stitzenberger said that Proposition 188 was "tougher than 90 percent of the initiatives already on the books. Arguably, this is the toughest smoking control law in the country" (*San Francisco Examiner*, April 18, 1994:A-5).

The tobacco industry spent about $1.8 million to get 607,000 voters' signatures to qualify the initiative for the November 1994 ballot. Stitzenberger started the signature-gathering process in early March 1994, hiring a Sacramento company to collect the signatures. The company was paid $1.50 per signature, more than twice the going rate at the time (Stitzenberger interview 1994).

The Sacramento company circulated petitions in restaurants, bars, and gaming-entertainment businesses and sent millions of glossy packets by express mail to "supporters of tobacco control." It set up phone banks that called voters throughout California to ask whether they supported tough statewide antismoking legislation and, if so, to please sign a petition to place Proposition 188 on the ballot. The following day those voters got a packet by express mail that contained a brief explanation of the petition along with the complete text of the initiative. The phone bank followed up the next day by calling the voter with an urgent request to sign the petition and return it in the enclosed stamped envelope—after getting the signature of any other voter who lived at that address.

The three-page summary in the tobacco industry's packet emphasized the strict antismoking provisions. It pointed out that the initiative doubled the fine for selling tobacco to minors, severely limited minors' access to cigarette vending machines, prohibited smoking in restaurants and workplaces unless strict ventilation standards were met, banned billboard ads of tobacco products within five hundred feet of primary and secondary schools, required retailers to post signs that the sale of tobacco to minors was illegal, and required that 75 percent of all restaurant space be designated as nonsmoking.

The summary also stated that the initiative would impose tough smoking restrictions in more than two hundred localities that had no regulations. It would replace the "crazy patchwork quilt" of 270 local antismoking ordinances with a single, tough, uniform statewide law.

## Expressive Group Reaction

The antismoking brigade was caught off guard by the tobacco companies' strategy. Opponents were outraged but had no plan or strategy to combat it. For example, it was not until after the initiative qualified for the ballot that opponents even met to discuss a plan of action. They were overly confident that they had the public's support. Jack Nicholl, a veteran of the 1988 Proposition 99 campaign, experienced Democratic strategist, and former director of Hayden's Campaign California, was directing the campaign against the Philip Morris initiative. He called an emergency meeting to reassemble the committee that had led the Proposition 99 campaign.

The new committee was called the Coalition for a Healthy California and included the American Cancer Society, American Heart Association, American Lung Association, Americans for Nonsmokers' Rights, California Association of Hospitals and Health Systems, California Dental Association, and the Planning and Conservation League, which is a state environmental organization based in Sacramento.

The role of the Planning and Conservation League in the Proposition 99 campaign is a good example of the coalition strategy that expressive interest groups follow. Gerald Meral, the league's executive director, had proposed the measure that became Proposition 99. He set in motion the creation of a political coalition that backed an increase in the tobacco tax to raise money for environmental programs. In 1986 Meral broached the idea to Curt Mekemson, the state legislative director of the American Lung Association in Sacramento. Mekemson was the former executive director of the American Lung Association of Alaska, where in 1985 he had successfully organized a legislative initiative to double Alaska's cigarette tax from eight to sixteen cents. Meral proposed a five-cent per pack California tax increase, to be earmarked for environmental programs. But Mekemson thought the tax should be bigger. It was ultimately raised from ten cents to thirty-five cents per pack, and Mekemson thought that the bulk of that revenue should go for antismoking education and prevention programs (Traynor and Glantz 1995:4–5).

Meral and the Planning and Conservation League continued to play a key role during the Proposition 99 campaign. Wary of jeopardizing their nonprofit status, the health charities had traditionally avoided assuming an expressive role in political campaigns. Indeed, political campaigning was new and largely unknown to health professionals. By contrast, the environmental movement had experience in politics and thus initially helped to organize and lead the antismoking coalition in support of Proposition 99. However, the environmentalists were also self-motivated. Proposition 99 contained a provision that environmental programs would receive 5 percent of the tobacco tax revenues. As was the case with Big Green, Assemblymen Lloyd Connelly (Democrat of Sacramento) and Tom Hayden (Democrat of Santa Monica) and Hayden's former wife, Jane Fonda, took the lead in organizing the antismoking coalition's campaign for Proposition 99. Indeed, Hayden's Campaign California was a member of the executive committee of the Coalition for a Healthy California, and Jack Nicholl, executive director of Campaign California, directed the 1988 campaign.

Eight years later, however, they were not campaigning for tobacco-control legislation. They were confronted by a clever antismoking initiative sponsored by the tobacco industry. The coalition was not only surprised by Proposition 188 but underestimated it. For example, in February 1994, one month before Stitzenberger gathered 600,000 signatures to qualify Proposition 188 for the November 1994 ballot, Jack Nicholl declared that the coalition would mount a "quick three-month" campaign to demonstrate to Philip Morris the futility of wasting its money on a losing proposition (Nicholl and Knepprath 1994).

In a memo Nicholl asked supporters to urge their city councils and boards of supervisors to pass resolutions against Proposition 188 and suggested that coalition backers hold press conferences demanding that Philip Morris stop attacking their local autonomy and the public's health. Nicholl also asked coalition members to solicit editorials in local newspapers and on radio and TV demanding that Philip Morris withdraw Proposition 188 from the ballot. Nicholl asked educational organizations such as the PTA and boards of education and other community organizations to pass resolutions and speak out against the initiative.

The coalition used the 1993 EPA report on secondhand smoke as the principal authority for local resolutions condemning Proposition 188. For example, antismoking advocates cited the EPA's claim that secondhand smoke was responsible for three thousand lung cancer deaths a year in the United States. Indeed, they embellished the claim by saying that secondhand smoke was responsible for thirty-five thousand deaths a year (American Cancer Society of California 1994).

However, none of these actions discouraged Philip Morris or slowed the Proposition 188 campaign. The coalition was on the defensive and forced to appeal to the California secretary of state to invalidate Proposition 188 on the ground that many signatures were obtained fraudulently. The coalition charged that the phone calls to voters as well as the express mail packet forwarded for their signature deceived voters into believing that Proposition 188 was a genuine antismoking initiative.

The reality was that Proposition 188 was both weak and tough in relation to antismoking laws. It was a tough antismoking law in cities and counties that had no antismoking ordinances. However, it was weak in relation to local laws that banned smoking altogether, and it was weaker than the Smokefree Workplace Act (AB13). So the secretary of state could not legally invalidate the initiative. Proposition 188 may have been unethical, but it was not illegal.

This forced the coalition to rely on volunteers to generate media attention that would expose Proposition 188's "cloud of deception," as the coalition referred to the measure in a May 1994 press release. Only after Proposition 188 was officially qualified for the ballot in June 1994 did the coalition fully reactivate and devise a strategy to defeat it. In late July Nicholl and the press director, Paul Knepprath, drafted a campaign plan to defeat Proposition 188 (Nicholl and Knepprath 1994). The plan noted that, unlike Proposition 99, coalition members had nothing to gain financially by defeating Proposition 188, so they were unlikely to dig deep in their pockets to fund a war chest. Indeed, campaign contributions were low.

The coalition campaign did not even reach its modest goal of $1 million. Campaign contributions amounted to only $667,547, compared to the tobacco industry's $18 million. As was the case with the Big Green campaign, the coalition set a minimum contribution (but in this case, $25,000) for membership on the executive committee of the campaign. The organizations that came up with $25,000 and therefore qualified for the executive committee were the American Cancer Society, American Lung Association, Americans for Nonsmokers' Rights, California Dental Association, and the California Medical Association.

The health SMOs that supported the campaign but did not contribute $25,000 were the American Heart Association, California Association of Hospitals and Health Systems, California Nurses Association, California state PTA, Common Cause, and the Planning and Conservation League. Hayden's Campaign California also joined the executive committee. As in the 1990 Big Green campaign, the image of Hayden and his ex-wife, Jane Fonda, as leftist radicals was regarded as a political liability. Initially, executive committee members opposed giving Campaign California a seat on the committee. However, as the campaign progressed, and the threat of Proposition 188 increased, they relented and accepted Campaign California on the committee. Essentially, the coalition was a union of liberal political groups, environmental organizations, and health charities. The political groups provided the leadership for the coalition, and the health charities provided the grassroots base of support for the campaign.

The coalition commissioned a poll in July 1994 that formed the basis of its campaign (Solis 1994). Its campaign strategy had three elements. The first was to emphasize the association of Philip Morris with Proposition 188 in the minds of voters. The coalition saw this as essential to defeating Proposition 188. Since the tobacco companies had low public credibility, the coalition felt that associating the initiative and the tobacco industry would undermine the initiative. The coalition also decided to warn voters that if the initiative passed, more people would smoke and one million people, many of whom would be children, would be exposed to deadly secondhand smoke. The second element was to target "swing voters"—nonsmokers, women, and voters older than fifty—against Proposition 188. The third element of the campaign was for health SMOs, such as members of the American Cancer Society, local health departments, hospitals, and doctors, to take a prominent role in the campaign.

The coalition tried to reframe Proposition 188 as an election issue between health groups and the tobacco industry instead of a contest between antismoking groups and smokers. They wanted to avoid provoking a public backlash against "antismoking zealots." Their own polls showed, for example, that the majority of voters felt antismoking groups tried to impose their standards on everyone else in an unreasonable way. Many even felt that smokers were discriminated against too much.

Despite the coalition's best efforts, however, the Philip Morris initiative continued to lead in the polls. For example, a statewide Field poll showed that only 41 percent of voters had ever heard of Proposition 188. And of those who had heard of the initiative, 52 percent of voters supported it, while 38 percent were opposed. This meant that 59 percent of voters had never even heard of Proposition 188. Coalition members feared that uninformed voters would vote for the initiative in the mistaken belief that it was an antismoking law (Nicholl and Knepprath 1994).

## The Antismoking Coalition Changes Strategy

The Philip Morris campaign continued to rely on low-profile direct-mail and newspaper "education" ads until two weeks before the November election. Since September 1994 millions of Californians had received four separate glossy mailings urging them to support Proposition 188 (*Santa Cruz Sentinel* October 25, 1994). The direct mailings and newspaper ad strategy alone cost the tobacco companies about $8 million. By September, however, the pro-188 lead had almost disappeared. For example, in another Field poll in September 1994 the sides on the Philip Morris initiative were in a virtual dead heat (Solis 1994).

Nevertheless, fewer than 47 percent of all voters were aware of Proposition 188. And among those who had heard of it, 40 percent favored it, and 36 percent opposed it. Table 5.3 compares the Field poll results for July and September 1994.

The coalition was slightly encouraged by the poll results but was nevertheless worried that the initiative might pass (Knepprath 1994). Antismoking supporters were encouraged that the Field poll recorded a 10 percent drop in support for Proposition 188 among all respondents from July to September 1994 (Solis 1994). They felt that this showed that support for Proposition 188 had peaked and was now in decline. Furthermore, the decline occurred despite Philip Morris's full-page ads in major newspapers and its mailing of two slick direct-mail campaign pieces to four million Californians during this period. The decline confirmed the antismoking belief that once voters discovered that Philip Morris was behind Proposition 188, they would withdraw their support. However, the coalition cautioned supporters that

TABLE 5.3 **Voters' Awareness of Proposition 188**

|                      | July | September |
|----------------------|------|-----------|
| Have not seen/heard  | 59%  | 53%       |
| Have seen/heard      | 41%  | 47%       |
| Inclined to vote yes | 18%  | 19%       |
| Inclined to vote no  | 17%  | 17%       |
| Undecided            | 6%   | 11%       |

*Phone survey conducted July 12–17, 1994, among a representative statewide sample of 609 registered voters with a margin of error of ±5.6 percentage points. Second survey of 855 Californians conducted September 13–18, 1994, including 754 registered voters and a margin of error of ±4.3 percentage points.

*Source*: Solis Suzanne Espinosa. 1994. "Poll Finds Few Voters Know About Fall Initiatives" *San Francisco Chronicle*, July 28: A17.

Proposition 188 was still doing well in the polls and that Stitzenberger was likely to pump up the campaign to compensate for the decline (Nicholl and Knepprath 1994).

The tobacco industry disputed the coalition's contention that the initiative was losing in the polls. Stitzenberger cited a Times Mirror poll conducted from October 8 to 11, 1994, that showed that when a description of the initiative was read to voters, 47 percent supported it, and 45 percent were against it (Feldman 1994). Indeed, he argued that the margin of support for Proposition 188 had increased, not decreased, as the coalition believed. Thus, with less than a month to go in the campaign, voters were about evenly divided on Proposition 188.

The coalition panicked. If the tobacco industry's strategy worked, it would put California's antismoking movement back ten years. It would also encourage the industry to undertake similar campaigns throughout the country and would threaten the entire antismoking movement, the coalition believed. This fear prompted the health expressive group to alter its strategy. The coalition believed that raising the public profile of the issue was essential so that voters would clearly understand that Philip Morris was behind the initiative. However, the coalition did not have the financial resources to undertake an expensive media campaign (Nicholl and Knepprath 1994).

In late October 1994 the coalition unveiled broadcast ads featuring the respected former surgeon general C. Everett Koop, who claimed that Proposition 188 could lead to smoking in museums, libraries, and theaters and would expose millions of children to deadly secondhand smoke (*Santa Cruz Sentinel*, October 26, 1994). The California Health and Safety Department also stepped up the number of ads it ran during October and November as part of its $12.5 million annual antismoking campaign. However, the media campaigns did not shift public support away from the initiative.

At this critical stage the coalition persuaded a nonmovement ally, the California Wellness Foundation, to provide most of a $4 million grant for a media campaign. The foundation, originally chartered in 1992, focuses on community health issues (California Wellness Foundation 1996).[14] The foundation worked closely with Americans for Nonsmokers' Rights, the health charities, environmental organizations, and groups such as Common Cause.

The foundation hired the Public Media Center to conduct an expensive high-profile advertising blitz against Proposition 188. The media center was a San Francisco–based nonprofit ad agency created in 1974 to champion the

FCC's Fairness Doctrine. The center had a staff of twenty-eight, an annual budget of $2 million, and spent more than $1 million each each year on advertising time and space. The center was committed to correcting the lack of social accountability for corporations and believed that the Reagan administration had been responsible for the suffering of millions in the 1980s (Public Media Center 1995).

The center's ad campaign against the initiative during the last three weeks was highly effective. The purpose of the ads was to make voters understand Philip Morris's sponsorship of Proposition 188. The ads listed the top five financial supporters of the initiative and its five leading opponents. To protect their nonprofit status, however, the California Wellness Foundation and the center claimed their ads were educational and not political (*Public Media Center v. Californians* [1994], Colvin 1995).

The first ads ran in major California newspapers on October 17, 1994; the Koop ads had begun to appear in early October. Their effect was almost immediate. A Field poll conducted from October 21 to 30, 1994, found that 53 percent of likely voters were against Proposition 188, while 39 percent supported it (*Sacramento Bee* November 3, 1994). This showed a reversal of the July 1994 field opinion poll in which 52 percent of the voters supported the initiative (see table 5.3).

The tobacco industry's tracking polls during the final stages of the campaign showed support for Proposition 188 declined from 47 percent in September 1994 to only 33 percent in November. By contrast, opposition to Proposition 188 had increased from 32 percent in September to 52 percent in November (Stitzenberger interview 1994). In the November 8 election Proposition 188 lost by an even wider margin—42 percent to 29 percent.

## Conclusion

The expressive group that campaigned to defeat the Philip Morris initiative was the Coalition for Healthy California. The coalition had the support of SMOs from the health and environmental movements, including the American Cancer Society, the American Heart Association, American Lung Association, Americans for Nonsmokers' Rights, Sierra Club, and Planning and Conservation League. It also had the backing of nonmovement allies, including the Parent-Teacher Association, the California Wellness Foundation, and Campaign California. The foundation provided millions of dollars for the massive last-minute ad campaign that led to the defeat of the Philip Morris initiative.

The expressive group's campaign had the benefit of a well-organized antismoking infrastructure that brought together parents, teachers, local health professionals, and county and city governments dedicated to banning smoking. The success of the antismoking movement had in fact forced the tobacco companies to sponsor the initiative to slow down or stop the spread of antismoking bans.

Philip Morris tried to frame its initiative as an antismoking proposal, its deception was exposed by the coalition's media blitz, which reframed the initiative as a prosmoking rather than an antismoking measure. The coalition did this by publicizing who was sponsoring the initiative—the tobacco companies. Indeed, the coalition dubbed it the "Philip Morris initiative," after the largest, and best known, tobacco company, and the measure's principal sponsor.

The coalition's campaign did not have a free-rider problem because the SMOs were deeply committed to the cause and they carried the burden of mobilizing citizen protest action through their antismoking infrastructure. Through their last-minute ad campaign they galvanized opposition to the Philip Morris initiative in the public schools, hospitals, clinics, doctors' offices, and in hundreds of county and city governments.

### NOTES

1. See J. Meyer 1992; Tate 1989; Dillow 1981; Ecenbarger 1991; and Kenny 1986a, 1986b.

2. Several reasons have been offered to explain the reluctance of the AMA to campaign against smoking. It had substantial stock in the tobacco companies, received research grants from them, and recognized the need for political support in its fight against "socialized medicine" from members of Congress representing southern tobacco states. See Miles 1982 and Whelan 1984.

3. A number of other legal advocacy groups champion the antismoking cause, including the Group Against Smoking Pollution (GASP), founded in Boston in 1972 and led by Richard Daynard. GASP pursues product liability damage suits. It advances the proposition that the tobacco companies are responsible for the health damage caused by their products. The companies have long been aware that cigarettes are dangerous, but they failed to warn consumers (before Congress mandated warning labels), who became sick and died, GASP reasons. In March 1995 four states—Florida, Mississippi, Minnesota, and West Virginia—formed the National Coalition of States for Tobacco Liability. These states shared depositions and legal resources in class-action

suits designed to force the tobacco companies to reimburse the states for smoking-related medical costs for welfare recipients. In 1997 Congress began to consider a settlement with the tobacco industry. The major elements of the proposed federal settlement are that the tobacco industry would pay billions to fund health care as a punishment for past actions and would place new warning labels on each pack. The industry would disclose ingredients in cigarette brands to the FDA and submit safety testing results of each ingredient within five years. In return, the tobacco companies would be exempt from class-action or other lawsuits but could face suits brought by individuals. Payments under the settlement would be treated as business expenses for tax purposes. The industry would pay for the enforcement of state laws barring sales to minors, and all outdoor advertising and other promotional material would be banned. Finally, government could not ban nicotine until at least 2009.

4. The Coalition for Smoking OR Health worked closely with the Washington, D.C.–based Advocacy Institute in filing briefs and lobbying the federal regulatory agencies to get them to push Congress for an increase in the excise tax on cigarettes and to set restrictions on tobacco ads.

5. Despite Glantz's role as a leading national health expert on the dangers of smoking, his professional training is in mechanical engineering, not medicine. He was the principal author of a 1991 EPA study that claimed that secondhand smoke kills fifty-three thousand nonsmokers every year. Although the EPA did not officially endorse the report, it received widespread coverage, and the ANR and TFA used it in promoting local antismoking ordinances.

6. The ANR received financing from a special state fund authorized by an antismoking initiative (Proposition 99) that the ANR sponsored and voters approved in 1988. The ANR was also involved in litigation to gain control of $165 million in Proposition 99 revenue that was diverted by Governor Pete Wilson, a supporter of the tobacco industry, to other state programs. The suit remained unresolved as this book went to press.

7. The significance of this is that extreme results—in this case, negative secondhand smoke cancer risk studies—were discarded from the pooled results. The suspicion is that if the EPA had retained its standard 95 percent confidence interval level, the agency would not have come up with even a marginally increased secondhand smoke cancer risk.

8. Joseph A. Dear, assistant secretary of labor; Dr. Michael Silverstein, OSHA's director of policy; and Robert Reich, the secretary of labor, said at a press conference that the 1994 hearings on OSHA's rules for indoor air quality and indoor smoking would be held without any "rigid preconceptions or fixed positions." Silverstein said that they would keep an open mind and would develop a fair, accurate, objective, and complete administrative record regarding the indoor air rule-making process (Andrade and Tyson 1994:2–3).

9. The official title of the initiative, also known as Proposition 188, was the Smoking and Tobacco Products, Local Preemption, Statewide Regulation Initiative.

The Smokefree Workplace Act was popularly known as the Friedman Bill after its sponsor, Terry Friedman, a Democratic California assemblyman representing San Francisco.

10. According to their annual reports for 1993, R. J. Reynolds contributed about $3.4 million, Brown and Williamson $1.3 million, American Tobacco $756,000, and Lorrillard $414,000. Nontobacco contributions to the Proposition 188 campaign came mostly from restaurant associations and did not exceed $11,000 from all of them combined (Macdonald, Traynor and Glantz 1994:9).

11. Philip Morris, producer of Marlboro, Benson and Hedges, Merit, Virginia Slims, Parliament, Cambridge, Basic, Alpine, Players, Bucks, and Bristol cigarettes, had 1993 revenues of $60.5 billion; its net income was $3.1 billion. Tobacco accounted for 43 percent of Philip Morris's revenue and 62 percent of its operating profit. The second-largest tobacco company, R. J. Reynolds, producer of Winston, Salem, Camel, Doral, Vantage, More, NOW, Magna, Century, Monarch, and Sterling cigarettes, had 1993 revenues of $15.1 billion but a net loss of $464 million. Reynolds had about 30 percent of the U.S. market, and tobacco sales accounted for 56 percent of its revenue and 65 percent of its operating profit.

12. Five percent of Proposition 99 funds were authorized for basic research into the causes and treatment of tobacco-related diseases; 45 percent went to the Hospital Account and Physicians Services Accounts to reimburse the cost of uncompensated health care; and 5 percent went into the Public Resources Account for environmental work. The balance went into an Unallocated Account, which the legislature could spend as it saw fit.

13. Proposition 188 had eight elements: it would have banned cigarette billboards within five hundred feet of schools; permitted smoking in all hotel rooms except those designated by the management as nonsmoking, in 25 percent of restaurant seating provided it was properly ventilated, in all bars and taverns, and smoking by employers in private offices with proper ventilation; barred local cities and counties from passing smoking laws tougher than the state law; replaced all local smoking laws with a single state law; and designated that smoking laws be enforced by police departments and the state worker safety agency, not health departments.

14. The California Wellness Foundation was formed in response to the privatization of Health Net, one of the largest HMOs in California. Health Net agreed to transfer about $800 million to finance the foundation, which has five areas of primary concern and must spend 5 percent of its resources each year to retain its tax-exempt status. Its primary areas of concern are preventing teenage pregnancy; preventing violence; promoting community health through such programs as good diet and nonsmoking education; promoting population health, including family planning; and promoting work and health antipoverty programs in urban areas, for example.

# SIX

# THE ENDANGERED SPECIES CAMPAIGN

Property Rights Advocates and Environmental Groups

The position of the property rights movement is that private property rights are sacred. Proponents believe as founder John Adams did, that private property is the foundation of human liberty. In this regard they cite Adams's often quoted statement: "Property is surely a right of mankind as really as Liberty. The moment that idea is admitted into society that property is not as sacred as the Laws of God, and that there is not a force of law and public justice to protect it, anarchy and tyranny commence. Property must be sacred or liberty cannot exist" (Adams 1851:9).

Activists note that most of the thirteen colonies adopted constitutions that included Adams's natural rights concept of property. Every state constitution embraces this right, and it is in the Bill of Rights. The Fifth Amendment protects private property rights by requiring due process and just compensation for the taking of private property for public use. Property rights activists argue that this fundamental guarantee is the cornerstone of American prosperity and democracy.

The movement believes that this fundamental right is under attack by the government in response to pressure from the environmental movement. Proponents view the common law doctrine known as the public trust, which environmental SMOs have used in litigation, as a surreptitious way of taking away private property rights without compensation. According to this doctrine, some public interests are deemed to be so important that they cannot be protected by constitutions or legislatures. The public trust doctrine holds that the government can grant private ownership only for land that is not essential for the public interest. For example, navigable waters are necessary for the public use and therefore cannot be privately owned. By implication, any private land-ownership that threatens the public trust can be revoked without compensation, because no right to harm the public trust exists.

The property rights movement sees the public trust doctrine as a thinly veiled rationalization for a "regulatory taking" of property without just compensation as required under the Fifth Amendment. For example, the rules for protecting wetlands are so strict that many landowners cannot use their land as they wish. They also cannot sell their land because the wetlands restrictions frighten away buyers.

Similarly, the property rights movement sees the Endangered Species Act (ESA) as having a potentially devastating effect on property owners. If a plant or animal species that is classified by the U.S. Fish and Wildlife Service as endangered or threatened is found on private property, the habitat of that species cannot be "harmed." Therefore, one effect of the ESA may be to restrict privately owned land from residential, agricultural, or commercial use.

Thousands of property rights organizations purport to represent four million citizens. They are supported by what is called the "wise-use" movement, which represents another ten million people (Cushman interview 1995). The latter campaign against what they regard as excessive government regulation of public property and the country's natural resources, including national parks. They argue for a balanced environmental policy that protects both the ecology and the economy.

The goals of the property rights and wise-use movements include protecting private property rights, reducing the federal deficit through the development of federal lands, developing the petroleum resources of the Arctic National Wildlife Refuge in Alaska, and opening wilderness and national parks to cattle grazing, oil exploration, mining, and energy production. They take the position that citizens are harmed when onerous restrictions are placed on private property and the wise use of the country's natural resources (Cushman interview 1995).

## The Endangered Species Act

The Endangered Species Act is arguably the most powerful environmental law of the United States. It requires the secretary of the interior to list rare species of animals and plants that are endangered or threatened with extinction. Once species are listed as endangered, private landowners can be prosecuted if they harm such species on their property. The ESA also prevents any landowner from damaging or altering the habitat of endangered species. The ESA has become one of the country's most controversial environmental issues.

Two federal agencies are responsible for administering the ESA, the Fish and Wildlife Service (under the Interior Department), which is responsible for animals and plants on land and in freshwater, and the National Marine Fisheries Service (under the Commerce Department), which is responsible for marine animals and plants. The heart of the act is the listing by these agencies of endangered and threatened species in the *Federal Register*. Listing a species as endangered or threatened, as set forth in Section 4 of the act, automatically triggers the government's enforcement powers to help species recover. The decision to list a species is supposed to be based on biology and ignore social and economic considerations.

Two other important sections of the act are sections 9 and 7. Section 9 outlaws the sale or transport of listed species across state lines as well as "taking" them (the act defines *take* as to "harass, harm, pursue, hunt, shoot, wound, kill, trap, capture or collect") and bars the destruction of their habitat. Section 7 directs all federal agencies to avoid taking any action that results in the destruction of or damage to habitat. Most conflicts between government actions and the owners of private land that contains listed species emerge at this stage.

Any public or private project or development can be stopped or altered if it is found to damage the habitat of a listed species. However, Congress amended the act to provide for an appeal to a special committee (comprised of federal officials and a representative of the affected state) in the event of hardships to property owners. In May 1992 a dispute involving the protection of the northern spotted owl and the logging of old-growth forests in the Pacific Northwest was referred to just such a committee.

As a result of the controversy surrounding the spotted owl dispute, the new Clinton administration created a cabinet-level committee to avoid what Interior Secretary Bruce Babbitt called "train wrecks." The committee came to be called the "God squad." After listing a species, and defining its critical habitat, the appropriate secretary (of the interior or commerce) prepares a plan designed to allow a species to recover to the point where it can be removed from the list. From 1983 to 1992, during the Reagan and Bush administrations, the two agencies prepared fifteen habitat conservation plans (HCPs). By 1995 under the Clinton administration they had completed thirty more, and one hundred were in progress across the country.

## The Compensation Issue

If the government takes ownership of private property to construct a highway, dam, or airport, the Constitution requires payment for the land at a fair price. However, if the government does not take physical possession of private property but merely regulates it, the question of compensation becomes cloudy. The Fifth Amendment forbids the government from taking private property for public purposes without just compensation. However, the courts have traditionally granted compensation to private landowners only when they suffer a total economic loss. The courts have tended to deny compensation to private owners for the partial loss of property value resulting from government regulation.

Supporters of the ESA endorse this judicial philosophy and argue that when the government regulates the use of private land to protect public welfare, it is under no obligation to compensate private landowners for any loss of land value. In this regard, they cite President Theodore Roosevelt's 1910 statement that "every man holds his property subject to the general right of the community to regulate its use to whatever degree the public welfare may require" (League of Conservation Voters 1994:5).

Environmental SMOs interpret this to mean that city zoning codes that prevent heavy industry from locating in residential areas; the Clean Water Act, which forbids a factory from discharging polluted water; the protection of wetlands for water filtration; flood protection; and wildlife protection are all in the public interest and therefore do not require government compensation. They argue that if the government had to compensate private property owners for economic loses resulting from regulation, such a requirement would break the federal budget and gut vital environmental, safety, and health laws (League of Conservation Voters 1994:5).

Because landowners usually can make more money by selling property to industrial developers than developers of private housing, a city council that zones land would have to make up the difference between industrial and residential sales. In the case of the Clean Water Act, the government would have to pay industries not to pollute. And in the case of wetlands and endangered species protection, a handful of private landowners would be paid not to destroy wetlands and endangered species. Indeed, environmentalists maintain that government regulation generally guarantees rather than undermines property rights. Everyone is potentially downstream or downwind from pollution or dangerous activity. Therefore, property rights are strengthened, not weakened, by government regulation of land use (Endangered Species Coalition 1993).

The opponents of the ESA take a very different position. They argue that the courts are heavily biased against property owners and that this violates the just compensation clause of the Fifth amendment. Property rights advocates reject the argument that compensation for regulatory takings will prevent the government from protecting land. To the contrary, they say, property rights legislation will ensure that owners are protected from government intervention that destroys the value of their property. In other words, compensation is a safeguard against arbitrary government action. It forces the government to carefully weigh the costs and benefits to society of regulatory schemes (Lambert and Smith 1994).

They also reject the claim that property owners should pay for the benefits of government regulation of their land. They argue that the so-called benefits from regulation are already paid by property owners. For example, property owners pay special assessments when sewer lines are installed and a tax for mosquito abatement. Property owners do not get a free ride. Property rights advocates say they are not asking for a government windfall but simply want their constitutionally guaranteed rights of protection from a government taking of their property (Adler 1995).

Critics of the ESA also reject the contention that private property rights legislation will result in economic chaos by bankrupting the U.S. Treasury. However, they say that even if that were so, the economic chaos argument does not justify the imposition of regulatory burdens on individual property owners in order to achieve a social objective. They contend that instead of bankrupting the federal government, property rights legislation will have the opposite result. It will force the federal government to be more careful before imposing regulatory burdens on property owners (Adler 1995, NESARC 1995b).

Requiring government to carry out a "takings impact analysis" before imposing regulations would keep costs down, they say, by forcing the government to carefully assess the costs. Private property rights legislation also would save the government expensive and lengthy litigation. Either the government would automatically pay compensation for a regulatory taking, or it would avoid the taking through careful planning. In either case, the burden on the taxpayer would be lightened (Adler 1995, NESARC 1995b).

Proponents of property rights legislation also reject environmentalists' contention that such legislation threatens clean air and water, health, and even civil rights. They note that the government has always had the power to prevent harmful or noxious uses of land without compensating owners. The Fifth Amendment does not interfere with the government's efforts to prevent harm to the public safety or health or its ability to eliminate a public nuisance. Property rights legislation would not require payment to property owners when a government acts to protect public welfare, they say (Adler 1995, NESARC 1995b).

### Property Rights Legislation

On December 21, 1995, the Senate Judiciary Committee approved an omnibus property rights bill (S.R. 605). The bill required that government compensation be paid to landowners whose property values declined as a result of government action. Under the bill property owners would receive compensation if the value of their property declined by 33 percent or more of the total value. Landowners would be compensated for the difference between the fair market value of their property before government action and the value after that action. Compensation would be paid out of the budget of the federal agency responsible for the taking. Earlier in 1995 the House approved a similar property owner compensation bill (H.R. 9), which would have made landowners eligible for compensation if the value of their property declined by 20 percent or more because of government regulation. The House bill specified that "regulation" included wetlands protection and the Endangered Species Act. President Bill Clinton threatened to veto S.R. 605 or any similar bill because it "creates a system of rewards for the least responsible and potentially most dangerous uses of property" and it "would effectively block implementation and enforcement of existing laws protecting public health, safety, and the environment" (Broderick 1995:A-2).

The critics of the ESA believe that property rights legislation is needed to provide clarity and predictability in the takings controversy. Without such legislation no clear definition of taking exists. Government decisions are made on a case-by-case basis. This situation is unsatisfactory because it fails to provide a clear guideline for federal agencies and Congress. Therefore, government agencies cannot avoid takings, these critics reason (Defenders of Property Rights 1995).

They believe that either of two approaches would be a reasonable way to resolve the problem. One is based upon the relative loss of the economic value of property, and the other asks whether government has taken a recognizable property interest.

Finally, property rights proponents argue that legislation should provide fair and prompt compensation to private landowners when a taking occurs. They say that government agencies tend to circumvent the takings issue altogether by relying on procedural confusion. For example, when sued, the government relies on technicalities such as the statute of limitations, lack of jurisdiction, and mootness or lack of ripeness to avoid the issue of compensation for a regulatory taking. Therefore, critics believe, the United States needs property rights legislation to bring government practices into conformity with the Fifth Amendment (Defenders of Property Rights 1995).

## Backlash Against the ESA

In 1988 the Reagan administration issued Executive Order 12630, "Governmental Actions and Interference with Constitutionally Protected Property Rights." The order required every federal agency to carry out a takings impact assessment before taking any action to regulate private property for the protection of public health and safety. It also required that the attorney general develop guidelines for all federal agencies to follow in implementing the executive order. However, federal agencies and the courts largely ignored the executive order. As a result, property rights proponents turned to Congress to get legislation authorizing compensation for regulatory takings.

Senator Kay Baily Hutchison (R-Tex.) was among the leading advocates of property rights in Congress. She and Senator Pete Domenici (R-N.M) introduced a bill in September 1994 to amend the Endangered Species Act. The amendment was designed to compensate private property owners for economic losses resulting from ESA regulation (*Cong. Rec.* 1994). Property rights proponents also convinced members of Congress, such as representatives Billy Tauzin (D-La.) and Jack Fields (R-Tex.), to attach a moratorium to "prevent monies from being spent on new listings of threatened or endangered species and on new designations of critical habitat" through fiscal 1995 to two continuing resolutions of Congress that provided government funding on a short-term basis. One of the continuing resolutions, which took effect in April 1995, chopped funding for Fish and Wildlife Service listings to zero. In effect, this shut down the ESA listing program (Miller 1996; Silverman 1996).

In introducing the amendment to the ESA, Hutchison stressed that Congress and the Washington bureaucracy had been negligent in failing to protect the constitutional rights of property owners. The senator and other property rights proponents effectively framed the ESA issue by singling out heartrending cases of poor families or impoverished widows whose livelihood or well-being was threatened by the ESA. This is similar to the animal rights movement's success in framing its campaign issue around the inhumane treatment of veal calves in the Massachusetts campaign.

Hutchison noted, for example, that the Fish and Wildlife Service was preparing to designate about 800,000 acres of land in thirty-three Texas counties as critical habitat for the golden-cheeked warbler. She described one Texas family that fought the Fish and Wildlife Service for a year and spent $2,000 of its meager savings before being allowed to build a house on the property. This occurred even though that species of bird had never been seen on or near the property because the wildlife service said the land was habitat for that species. Hutchison protested that private property owners should not have to fight the government to build a house on their land and that they should not have to hire lawyers to convince the government that they are in compliance with regulatory laws (*Cong. Rec.* 1994).

Implementation of the ESA has triggered a public backlash among millions of large and small landowners. Even leading environmentalists specializing in the protection of wildlife acknowledge that the ESA has not worked on private lands. For example, Michael Bean of the Environmental Defense Fund said that "after 20 years of trying to make the Endangered Species Act work on private lands we don't have much to show for our efforts other than a lot of political headaches" (*Washington Times,* June 13, 1995).

Property rights proponents, plus industry criticism of the ESA and wise-use protests against restrictions on the use of federal land, exerted unprecedented pressure on Congress to reform the Endangered Species Act.

Tobin (1994) explains the backlash against the ESA in terms of the institutional nature of the act. Policies protecting endangered species violate all traditional requirements for a successful public policy. Effective policy must involve only modest changes in public behavior, should be supported by conventional opinion, and the benefits of the policy should outweigh the costs and be clear and immediate.

The ESA demands that people alter deeply ingrained habits of environmental behavior, restricts owners' use of their privately owned resources, and denies property owners the use of technologies and materials. The benefits accruing from the act are also obscure and difficult to demonstrate. And the public is asked to give up concrete immediate benefits for long-term theoretical gains in the distant future. Nevertheless, environmental SMOs and the federal agencies enforcing ESA expect the public to accept the costs and inconvenience of the act for an abstract long-term societal good.

### Arguments in Defense of the ESA

Biological, spiritual, economic, and administrative grounds exist for preserving the act. The most frequently mentioned benefit, and the one that underlies other arguments, is what biologists call the "extinction crisis."

This is the theory that biodiversity, or the variety of living species on the planet, is disappearing at a faster rate than at any time since the dinosaurs became extinct sixty-five million years ago.

Edward O. Wilson, the Harvard biologist and author of the 1993 Pulitzer prize–winning book, *The Diversity of Life*, argues that the world is in one of the great extinction spasms of all time. He has made various extinction claims, ranging from a low of four thousand to a high of fifty thousand species each year. Wilson testified before Congress that "humanity has increased the mortality rate by a factor of between 1,000 and 10,000—far too high for evolution to replace" (*Roll Call*, July 25, 1994; Mann and Plummer 1995:53—54). The scientific basis for the claim advanced by Wilson and other biologists is a mathematical equation advanced by Frank W. Preston (Mann and Plummer 1995:53–54). Preston's theory, which he advanced in 1962, has become the cause célèbre of the 1990s.

The species-area curve (see figure 6.1) is based on a mathematical formula that equates a 90 percent loss of habitat with the extinction of half of all species in that habitat. The equation is $S = cA^z$, where the number of species in a geographical area, $S$, is equal to the area of the place, $A$, raised to some power, $z$, usually 0.3 (the percentage of change in the number of a species when an area grows or shrinks) and multiplied by the number of species, $c$. This equation was used to project the number of species in areas of different sizes.

Applying Preston's theorem with these values yields the species-area curve shown in figure 6.1. Preston determined that 17,000-acre Quaker Run Valley in New York, the area he was studying, was habitat for 70 species of birds. A species-area curve of 34,000 acres (twice as large as the original area) would have 158 species of bird. The obverse would apply as well—a valley with an area of 8,500 acres would have only 40 species (or roughly half the number of species in 17,000 acres).

Wilson and most other extinction biologists have used Preston's species-area curve to make projections about the number of species threatened with extinction. For example, Wilson based his estimate of 50,000 species' becoming extinct each year on the assumption that tropical forests in the world were being cut down at a rate of 2 percent a year. In other words, Wilson assumed that species were uniformly distributed throughout an area and that they could not migrate to other hospitable habitats. Wilson and other leading conservationists have gone beyond making computer projections of species extinction. They have become advocates for the extinction crisis thesis. This activity includes appearing as expert witnesses

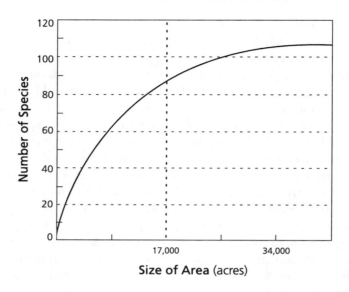

**FIGURE 6.1 The Species Area Curve**
SOURCE: MANN AND PLUMMER 1995:56.

and filing amicus briefs in support of legal suits filed by the Interior Department against property owners. For example, in 1995 Wilson and thirteen other environmentalists filed amicus briefs on behalf of the Interior Department ("Apologies" 1995). Armed with the various projections that pronounced an extinction crisis, the Endangered Species Coalition, which was the expressive group mounting the campaign to preserve the ESA, sounded the alarm. The coalition coordinates the lobbying activities of fifteen environmental and animal rights SMOs: the Center for Marine Conservation, Defenders of Wildlife, Environmental Defense Fund, Environmental Protection Information Center, Forest Guardians, Fund for Animals, Greater Yellowstone Coalition, Greenpeace, Humane Society of the United States, National Audubon Society, Sierra Club, Sierra Club Legal Defense Fund, Wilderness Society, Western Ancient Forrest Campaign, and the World Wildlife Fund. The coalition worked out of the the Washington, D.C., office of the National Audubon Society.

The coalition argued that more than six thousand species of animals and plants were at risk of extinction in the United States. However, only six hundred species were listed and protected by the ESA. About 3,700 other species were awaiting designation; of these, about 650 had been waiting more than fifteen years. In 1992 Defenders of Wildlife estimated that since 1980, 275 species had become extinct while waiting to be listed (Defenders of Wildlife 1992–93:4).

Bean of the Environmental Defense Fund argued that the ESA was vitally important for the protection and recovery of many species. He noted, for example, that actions taken under the ESA were responsible for the recovery of the bald eagle. This included protecting their nesting and roosting habitat as well as imposing heavy penalties for killing eagles and selling their feathers. In framing the issue in order to mobilize citizen support for the ESA, the coalition used what are called "charismatic animals," such as the bald eagle and panda (the mascot of the National Wildlife Federation), because of the public's emotional attachment to them. This is comparable to the use of veal calves in the animal rights campaign in Massachusetts and to the loss of family homesteads in the property rights campaign.

Other ESA success stories included whooping cranes, California sea otters, peregrine falcons, Kirtland's warblers, red wolves, brown pelicans, black-footed ferrets, Aleutian and Canada geese, and Peter's Mountain mallow wildflowers. Defenders of the ESA claimed the success stories would be more numerous if prompt action were taken to place endangered species on the protected list. Indeed, Bean argued that because the species under threat were allowed to decline to such small numbers before they were listed, their recovery was made doubly difficult, if not impossible (Bean 1994:18–22). In other words, strengthening the ESA and increasing the staffing and funding of enforcement agencies, not a weakening of the act, were urgently needed to avert an extinction crisis.

The ESA came up for renewal in 1992. Under the original legislation, which was adopted in 1972, the ESA had to be renewed every five years.[1] Pro-ESA members of Congress, including Representative Gerry Studds (D-Mass.), chair of the Merchant Marine and Fisheries Committee, which had jurisdiction over the ESA, and Senator John Chafee (R-R.I.), a strong supporter of environmental SMOs and a defender of the ESA, wanted scientific legitimation of the ESA to justify its renewal by Congress. They asked the National Research Council of the National Academy of Science to study the scientific merits of the ESA.

The research council issued its report, *Science and the Endangered Species Act,* in May 1995. It concluded that the extinction crisis was real and that the ESA had done a good job of protecting animals and plants from extinction. The report explained that at least five mass extinctions had occurred in the last 500 million years and said the major cause of the contemporary extinction crisis was human activity, including forestry, agriculture, fishing, residential and commercial development, and pollution.

According to the report, ecodisaster has economic, medical, aesthetic, and moral dimensions. For example, only 5 percent of the world's known plant species have been investigated for their medical value. Worldwide, plants are becoming extinct before their medical properties have been evaluated. The drug taxol, used for treating ovarian and breast cancer, and the rosy periwinkle, used to treat childhood leukemia and Hodgkin's disease, are examples of the medical value of plant species whose habitats are threatened.

Tom Eisner, a Cornell University chemical ecologist and chairman of the expressive groups' coalition, says the ESA has other vital medical implications for human beings (Eisner 1995). He points out that what happens to wildlife is a warning to humans. For example, the threatened extinction of bald eagles alerted scientists to the importance of keeping DDT out of the human food chain and led to a ban on the pesticide's use in crop production. This explains the often quoted expression that the ESA protects the "web of life that both people and wildlife depend on" (Endangered Species Coalition 1995:6).

The ESA is also said to make aesthetic, moral, and commercial contributions to society. It protects the quality of groundwater, rivers, wetlands, and forests on which humans depend. According to the Endangered Species Coalition (1995:6), the fishing industry knows that the act protects the habitat on which industry's future depends, business people know that protecting the ecosystem is good for business, and religious leaders know that the ESA fulfills society's moral obligation to be good stewards of "God's creation."

An example of the act's aesthetic and commercial contribution to society is Fantastic Caverns, a commercial cave attraction near Springfield, Missouri. The caverns are host to a small, blind cave-dwelling protected species called the Ozark cavefish, which lives in subterranean streams in the caves. The commercial success of Fantastic Caverns depends on clean underground water, which protects the Ozark cavefish. Clean water keeps the fish healthy and makes the cave a beautiful tourist attraction and a successful business (Endangered Species Coalition 1993).

## The Constitutionality of the ESA

Defenders of the ESA reject the criticism that the act violates the Fifth Amendment of the U.S. Constitution. They argue that no federal court has ever found that the act has resulted in a taking under the Fifth Amendment (Endangered Species Coalition 1994).

The Endangered Species Coalition offers three reasons for the absence of conflict between the act and private property rights (Endangered Species Coalition 1993). The first is that the Fish and Wildlife Service has blocked less than one-tenth of one percent of the property owners' projects reviewed because of they were found to have an adverse effect on endangered species. The coalition also notes that of the more than thirty-four thousand federal works projects from 1987 to 1991 (federal agencies are obliged to protect endangered habitat on government land), only twenty-three were halted because of threats to species. And a 1994 study by the U.S. General Accounting Office of more than 18,200 cases reviewed by the Fish and Wildlife and National Marine Fisheries Services found that 99 percent had proceeded with little or no government interference.[2]

The coalition also points out that sections 7 and 10 of the act allow property owners to engage in activities that result in incidental adverse effects on listed species under certain circumstances. For example, Section 7 allows a landowner to appeal to the Endangered Species Committee (the God squad) for an exemption. However, since its creation in 1978 the committee has been called into operation only three times. Defenders of the ESA take this as evidence of the absence of conflict. Critics argue, however, that the paucity of appeals to the God squad attests to the expense, futility, and time-consuming nature of making such appeals (Defenders of Wildlife 1992–93:14; Gordon interview 1995).

Proponents of the ESA also argue that under Section 10 landowners can harm and even kill endangered species on their property, provided that the secretary of interior has approved a long-term habitat conservation plan, which includes steps to minimize or mitigate any adverse effect on the species. In addition, landowners may apply for a permit for "incidental taking" of a specific number of endangered species in the process of using their property.

The second reason offered by defenders of the act for the absence of conflict with property rights is that much of the critical habitat for endangered and threatened species is on public lands, not private. Federal agencies are already obliged to protect the habitat of endangered species on government land. However, this ignores the millions of people who live on or near adjoining federal land, especially in the West, who have for generations enjoyed the right to use that land for commercial or recreational purposes. In fact, the wise-use movement emerged in the West expressly to protest the federal government's interference with private parties' historic right to use public land. Indeed, thousands of private properties lie within national parks, held by people who owned their land before the public parks were created (Cushman interview 1995).

The third argument is that wildlife does not belong to the owner of the land on which it lives. Wildlife is public property that must be managed for the good of society. Therefore, the government has the authority to regulate hunting on public and private lands and to sue polluters who harm wildlife. Furthermore, the government has the authority to ensure that private land is used in such a way as to protect wildlife.

### Arguments for Reforming ESA

Critics of the ESA not only question the scientific evidence of an extinction crisis but whether the ESA preserves endangered species. They contend that the act has failed to recover endangered species and that it is a powerful incentive for landowners to destroy habitat (Cushman interview 1995).

They point out that there is reason to doubt the scientific validity of the extinction crisis. The science of biodiversity is in its infancy. Not only do we not know how many species there are in the world, but the scientific community disagrees about exactly what constitutes a species. Estimates of the number of species range from a low of 10 million to a high of 100 million or more, and only about 1.4 million species have been identified and described. In other words, theories of an extinction crisis have limited application because we do not even know how many species there are in the world.[3]

For example, until the 1980s, it was estimated that only 3 million species remain in the world, half of which have yet to be found. However, Frederick Grassie, director of Rutgers University's Institute of Marine and Coastal Sciences, has estimated that the deep sea may be home to another 10 million undiscovered species. And the entomologist Terry Erwin has estimated that the world has another 30 million species, based on discoveries in the rain forest. According to Michael Smith, a senior research scientist at the Center for Marine Conservation in Washington, D.C., "The number (of species) to be discovered is greater than the number we've been able to process in the two hundred and fifty years since Linnaeus" (Huyghe 1993). Because most species have not been named or even found, it is difficult—if not impossible—to draw any firm conclusions about the state of world biodiversity.

A related flaw in extinction crises theories is that the numbers do not add up. The popular press regularly reports doomsday predictions of species extinction. For example, the media have widely reported Edward O. Wilson's prediction that at least 27,000 species of the world's 10 million species are lost each year, and Peter Raven has claimed that one-fourth of the world's plants will be extinct by the year 2010 (Mann and Plummer 1995:14, 51). However, there is no evidence to support these doomsday projections. For example, the World Conservation Monitoring Centre (WCMC) in Cambridge, England, which is sponsored by the United Nations Environmental Program, publishes an annual "blacklist" of species that have vanished since 1600. As of October 1994, the blacklist included 1,237 species. The list was comprised of 654 species and subspecies of plants, 364 invertebrates, 103 birds, 63 mammals, 33 fishes, and 20 reptiles and amphibians (Mann and Plummer 1995:50).

WCMC's blacklist does not support the doomsday projections. Using Wilson's projection of the annual extinction of 27,000 species, the world would have to lose the equivalent of the WCMC's blacklisted 1,237 species every seventeen days. Thus, if WCMC's estimates are even remotely correct, the current rate of species extinction is a slowly accumulating problem that will not become critical for centuries.

Furthermore, little scientific evidence supports the validity of extinction crisis projections. A model test case of the species-extinction crisis thesis is the Amazon delta. The Amazon is the biggest river in the world, and the Amazon delta is the largest river delta, with 2.7 million square miles, or 5 percent of the world's total land area. Until the 1960s the Amazon delta was virtually undisturbed by developers, miners, ranchers, or farmers. During the 1960s and 1970s the Brazilian government undertook a program of subsidizing logging, farming, mining, and settlement of the delta. Deforestation of the river delta set off a frenzy of extinction predictions.

For example, Norman Myers, an ecologist and author of *The Sinking Ark* (1979), claimed that logging tropical forests results in the disappearance of one species every hour. Thomas E. Lovejoy of the World Wildlife Fund estimated that 15 to 20 percent of the world's species would disappear by the year 2000. And Paul and Anne Ehrlich argue in their 1981 book, *Extinction*, that an exponential increase in human population will lead to dramatic deforestation, which, in turn, will lead to the obliteration of almost all species in the tropics by 2025. Mann and Plummer (1995:64) note that these projections fed doomsday news reports. For example, stories ranged from claims that 20 percent of all species will disappear by 2011 to the annual loss of 40,000 species to the disappearance of 5 species a day, 6 an hour, and so forth.

However, in one of the few actual studies of species in the Amazon delta, a team of biologists led by Keith S. Brown Jr. of the Universidade Estadual de Campinas in São Paulo, found no support for the extinction crisis. Brown studied the state of São Paulo where forests shrank to less than 10 percent of their original size. Given the loss of forest area, the species-area curve theory would project a 50 percent loss of species in São Paulo. To their surprise, however, the researchers found that despite the massive depletion of the forest and the destruction of habitat, they could not confirm a single known species in the area as extinct. Indeed, they actually rediscovered species that had previously been declared extinct (Brown and Brown 1992:119–42). Similar findings have been observed in Puerto Rico, which was stripped of most of its forests at the turn of the century (Lugo 1988:58–70). Nevertheless, the proponents of the species-area curve have continued to defend it on the unscientific grounds that large numbers of unknown species have disappeared or that the extinction effect is not instantaneous but will kick in at some unspecified time in the immediate future.

Applying the species-area curve to the loss of roughly 600 million acres of forest in the eastern United States also does not support extinction crisis projections. Of the approximately 160 known species of birds in the area, five extinctions have been confirmed during the past three hundred years: the ivory-billed woodpecker, passenger pigeon, Carolina parakeet, heath hen, and the Bachman's warbler. However, of these, two—the passenger pigeon and heath hen—were hunted into extinction. And the woodpecker, parakeet, and warbler lived in a tiny portion of the eastern forest—in bottomland and swamps. Thus extinction was not the result of the destruction of large areas of the forest but the destruction of small sections of the forest containing their habitat (Mann and Plummer 1995:76–77).

This suggests that projections of an extinction crisis based on mathematical equations are not supported by scientific evidence. The same observation can be made of the industry's specious projections of unemployment and economic loss as a result of implementation of the ESA.

Indeed, a study by MIT political scientist Stephen M. Meyer (1995) concludes that economic development does not suffer when the Interior Department acts to protect endangered species. Property rights proponents do not claim that species extinction has not occurred or that the rate of extinction has not accelerated since the turn of the century. They say there is no immediate extinction crisis but rather a slowly increasing threat to species from agricultural cultivation and the construction of residences, shopping centers, factories, and other buildings designed to enhance societal security and well-being (Plummer 1996). This raises a dilemma concerning species endangerment.

Plummer points out, for example, that the extinction of a species may be tragic, but it is seldom catastrophic (1996:83). Thus difficult choices must be made concerning societal progress, security for society, and threats to plant and animal species. Contrary to the ESA, which assumes that all species must be preserved regardless of the cost or feasibility, habitat preservation and economic progress for humanity must be weighed carefully and choices must be made.

Critics of the ESA argue that the act's single-minded preoccupation with saving all species is misguided. Indeed, the extinction of some species can make significant contributions to society. For example, humanity would have been better off if the deadly smallpox virus and the Ebola virus had never existed and if the species of African monkey many scientists believe was the host for the AIDS virus had become extinct. Besides, stopping evolution is impossible. Scientists estimate that species have an average lifespan of only about 100,000 years. Therefore, we are constantly losing and gaining species (Plummer 1996).

Another major criticism of the Endangered Species Act is that it does not work as intended. Plummer (1996:81, 83, 85) notes that the fundamental purpose of the ESA is the recovery of endangered species. However, few species have been removed from the list, whereas many have been added. For example, in 1973, about a year after Congress enacted the ESA, 122 species were listed as endangered. However, by the end of 1994 that list had grown to 833 species. In the twenty-one years of its existence, the list grew on average by forty species each year. But only about one species a year has come off the list (Plummer 1996).

Property rights proponents say that these numbers actually exaggerate the act's successes. For example, seven species were delisted because they were declared extinct. Twenty-one species were taken off the list because they were found not to be endangered. Six species were delisted after making a comeback because of tangential events like the ban on DDT, which predated the Endangered Species Act, not because of the act itself. The same is true of down-listing species from endangered to threatened because of improved status. For example, between 1973 and 1994 the Fish and Wildlife Service reclassified only 13 species, and of the 711 species listed as of 1992, only 69, or less than 10 percent of the total, were reported as "improving" (Plummer 1996:83).

Another problem is that some flora and fauna listed as endangered are not really species at all. The accepted scientific definition of a species is "individuals actually or potentially capable of reproducing among themselves but incapable of reproducing with other organisms"(Plummer 1996:83). Slight variations such as color or minuscule differences in size do not constitute separate species. Thus we are protecting animals and plants that may well not need protection and therefore may be causing some property owners unnecessary hardship. The clear implication of the ESA listing process is that once a species is listed as endangered, it tends to remain so indefinitely. Plummer observes that the ESA has become a permanent liability to both private landowners and federal agencies enforcing it.

Robert Gordon, the executive director of the National Wilderness Institute (a conservative lobbying organization based in Washington, D.C.) and a leading critic of the ESA, points to another failing of the act: the high cost of listing endangered species. For example, every time an animal or plant is added to the endangered species list, the government must prepare a habitat conservation plan. The HCP for the blunt-nosed leopard lizard led the government to declare that the owners of sixty thousand acres could not develop their property in order to protect the species—at a cost of at least $70 million (National Wilderness Institute 1994a:30). Eight hundred species require comparable plans, and four thousand plants and animals are under consideration for listing. The cost runs in the billions of dollars, paid by landowners who also face loss of the use of their land. Further, the adoption of an HCP would not protect a landowner if another endangered species were found on the property.

## Industry Polling Data on the ESA

In March 1995 Tom Talbot, an independent lumberman from Wisconsin who supported the Grassroots ESA Coalition, commissioned a national poll to determine public opinion of the act (Tarrance Group 1995).[4] The results circulated among opponents of the ESA.

Respondents were told that the act was designed to protect plant and animal species from extinction and were asked how important it was to keep it unchanged. Respondents divided about evenly, with 40 percent saying it was very important, and 43 percent saying it was somewhat or not very important. However, when voters were told that the act applied equally to public and private land, and that private property owners could lose the use of their land without compensation, 62 percent of respondents were against the act, whereas 30 percent were for it (Tarrance Group 1995).

The pollsters described two positions to the voters questioned. One was that the ESA was necessary to keep people from drastically harming the environment. The other was that although the ESA was a good law, its strict application by the courts led to decisions that went far beyond its original intent and good common sense. Asked which point of view came closest to their own, 54 percent said the ESA had gone too far.

But various parts of the country showed wide differences. For example, voters were asked to agree or disagree with the statement that the ESA is hurting many industries and denying people the chance to find good jobs, provide for their families, and build assets for their children's future. Sixty-two percent of voters in the mountain states said they agreed with the statement, as did 53 percent from the West and 50 percent from the Midwest. However, support for the statement dropped to 49 percent in the Northeast, and the rest of the country divided about evenly (Tarrance Group 1995).[5]

### Four Divisive Issues

The four hotly contested political issues in the fight over the future of the ESA were habitat protection, recovery of endangered species, compensation for private landowners, and species versus subspecies. Political factions have taken sharply opposing positions on these issues.

The act, backed by the U.S. Supreme Court in the 1995 *Babbitt v. Sweet Home* decision, makes it illegal to destroy areas where endangered species eat, breed, and live. Environmental SMOs and the Clinton administration strongly backed this provision of the ESA and argued that if the habitat of animals was destroyed, animals would be destroyed. Opponents insist that this provision is too broad because it prevents private property owners from making a living from their land. Critics tried to amend the act so that it extended only to preventing the direct killing or injuring of animals and so that it did not apply to their habitat.

The act requires that the federal government aid in the recovery of all endangered wildlife. Environmental groups argued that because protecting all wildlife is at the heart of the ESA, this provision should not be altered. However, critics contend that the secretary of the interior should determine which species should be preserved and which are too expensive or insignificant to save (Chase 1995:A11).

Critics also argue that the federal government should compensate private property owners who cannot develop their land because of the presence of endangered species. Environmental groups say that the federal government should not pay private individuals or companies to prevent them from destroying the habitat of endangered species. However, some environmental SMOs support tax incentives for landowners who voluntarily agree to protect the habitat of endangered species (Bean 1994).

The ESA protects not only species but subspecies of endangered wildlife. For example, if the population of certain runs of salmon in the Pacific Northwest are threatened, the ESA requires federal protection of the entire species in the Northwest, although salmon may be plentiful elsewhere. Critics argue that only entire species, not subspecies, should be protected. They point out that trivial variations in subspecies, such as pigmentation or the eye color of subspecies, or legs of subspecies that are one millimeter shorter than other subspecies' legs, are not important in their own right. Therefore, great expense should not be incurred to protect trivial differences in subspecies. They also note that all species have specific geographic ranges in which climate and habitat are congenial. Thus it is natural for species to thrive in some areas and become extinct in others. The critics say that so long as the overall population is plentiful, trying to save all species in all areas is unnecessary (National Wilderness Institute

TABLE 6.1 **Public Support for Various Levels of ESA Protection**

|  | With Cost | Without Cost Info |
|---|---|---|
| Every species and subspecies | 35% | 28% |
| Main species only | 56% | 58% |
| Neither | 4% | 7% |
| Unsure | 5% | 7% |

*Source*: The Tarrance Group, (1995).

1994a:10–13). Table 6.1 provides data from the Tarrance poll that show public support for protecting only main species.

## The Expressive Group Campaign

The expressive group that conducted the campaign to change the Endangered Species Act in 1995 was the Grassroots ESA Coalition. Its SMO supporters included the American Land Rights Association, National Wilderness Institute, Committee for a Great Northwest, Stewards of the Range, American Policy Center, Women's Mining Coalition, and the United Four-Wheel Drive Association. Its nonmovement allies were the American Farm Bureau Federation, the Endangered Species Coordinating Council, and the National Endangered Species Act Reform Coalition. The property rights campaign failed.

The campaign against the ESA was primarily inspired by the grassroots property rights movement. The principal architect of the campaign was Chuck Cushman, a former peanut vendor at Dodger Stadium in Los Angeles and later a highly successful insurance salesman who subsequently lost his money. He has been described as "a self-appointed avenging angel of private property rights" (*Sunday Oregonian*, January 1, 1995). In mobilizing opposition to the ESA, Cushman claimed to be following the tried-and-true tactics of the environmental movement—building a grassroots political structure based on a "gut cause." He learned these political tactics from Ralph Nader's citizen-action manual and publications such as *Ecotage* that emerged from Earth Day organizations in 1972 (Hamburg 1990).

Cushman's political career began in 1977 when he led a battle against a federal bill that would have removed all private property owners (called "inholders") from national parks. He succeeded, and Ronald Reagan rewarded Cushman by appointing him to a National Park Service advisory board in 1981. After that, Cushman dedicated his career to organizing grassroots property rights and wise-use protest movements around the country. The protests were against government designations of wilderness areas, wild and scenic rivers, and land use controls of all kinds (*Sunday Oregonian*, January 1, 1995).

Much of Cushman's success was attributable to his catching the waves of populist movements in the West. The first one, in the 1970s, involved the fight to preserve ownership and usage rights to private property in national parks and federal reserves. To that end, he founded the National Inholders Association in 1978. Ten years later Cushman created the Multiple Use Land Alliance, which played a prominent role in launching the wise-use movement. The alliance was an effort to forge a grassroots coalition of ranchers, farmers, loggers, miners, and inholders to resist federal regulation of public land and give these interests greater access to federal lands (Cushman interview 1995).

In 1991 Cushman founded the League of Private Property Voters to monitor congressional votes on federal regulation in such areas as wetlands preservation, conservation growth management, wilderness designation, grazing restrictions on public range land, and, most recently, the protection of endangered species (Knox 1993:28). The Private Property Congressional Vote Index, published by Cushman, is to the property rights and wise-use movements what the League of Conservation Voters' guide is to environmentalists. Cushman directed all his organizations from Battle Ground, Washington. He had a staff of six and had an annual budget of $300,000. The various organizations gave Cushman an annual income of about $35,000. He did not seek nonprofit status for any of them, a stance popular with small-scale landowners who are suspicious of any federal regulation. In addition, because large corporate landowners oppose Cushman's tactics and strategies, they do not contribute to his organizations (Cushman interview 1995). Thus, by refusing to apply for federal nonprofit status, Cushman did not risk losing the tax-deductible contributions that business likes to make.

Cushman's political targets were environmental SMOs and federal regulators. He portrayed environmentalists as devotees of "a new paganism that worships trees and sacrifices people." He characterized government regulators as careerists who got ahead by deceiving property owners while eating away at their rights. Cushman claimed that environmentalists paint those who resist government regulation of their property as being antinature (*Bellingham Herald*, May 22, 1992).

### Influence of the Property Rights Movement

The property rights movement claims it succeeded in eviscerating a key ESA-related measure in Congress, the Biological Survey Bill, and winning the rhetorical battle on the endangered species issue. These claims illustrate the political influence of the property rights movement.

When Babbitt became secretary of the interior in January 1993, he proposed an ambitious plan to create a National Biological Survey. The purpose of the survey was to create an inventory of the country's entire ecosystem in order to avoid endangered species controversies such as that enveloping the northern spotted owl in the Pacific Northwest.[6] This strategy was designed to enable Babbitt to avoid the laborious and time-consuming process of scientifically documenting the necessity of listing species individually. Critics have suggested that the survey would give the federal government greater discretion in administering the ESA. It would enable the federal government to regulate land use without having to list each species on it (Sugg 1993).

Babbitt's model for ecosystem management is Southern California's Natural Communities Conservation Plan. Under that plan developers "voluntarily" idled 200,000 acres of highly valuable real estate (as much as $800,000 per acre). They handed over the land to avoid the listing of the California gnatcatcher as endangered. The gnatcatcher is a small songbird that inhabits 400,000 acres of coastal sage scrubland with great development potential. Despite Babbitt's claim that the success of the plan was "breathtaking," the gnatcatcher was ultimately listed as endangered, and the so-called voluntary plan was transformed into a compulsory requirement (Sugg 1993).

Babbitt claimed that by making an inventory of the country's biological resources, the government could prevent species from becoming extinct. He said that the federal government was too passive in protecting species and that all too often scientific issues are decided by judges (*Washington Times*, July 22, 1993). Dr. Thomas Lovejoy, the Interior Department's scientific adviser, elaborated on the purpose of the survey by saying that it would "determine development for the whole country and regulate it all, because that is our obligation as set forth in the Endangered Species Act" (*Wall Street Journal*, November 2, 1993:A22).

While environmental SMOs were delighted with Babbitt's endorsement of a proposal they had long argued for, property rights advocates and corporate landowners were alarmed. The principal political opponent of the survey was Cushman's American Land Rights Association, formerly the Alliance for America and the National Inholders Association. In the spring of 1993 Cushman faxed about four thousand groups opposed to the ESA and about three thousand reporters to try to mobilize grassroots opposition to the survey.

Erich Veyhl of Concord, Massachusetts, who produced white papers about the survey for Cushman's American Land Rights Association, warned that Babbitt also wanted to make the National Natural Landmarks program, a biological survey implemented by the National Park Service, part of the National Biological Survey. Although Babbitt had said that he would not do so, Veyhl warned that the landmarks program could be used as a model for the National Biological Survey. This news did not sit well with Cushman, who long had inveighed against the park service's attempt to remove inholders. Veyhl cited a 1991 Interior Department inspector general's report that said that the landmarks program had illegally trampled on the private property rights of federal land users for twenty-five years (Cushman interview 1995).

Congress made the landmarks program part of the bill that would have approved Babbitt's National Biological Survey. Then Babbitt appointed Dr. Eugene Hester, the manager of the landmarks program, to head the National Biological Survey. This was like waving a red flag in front of the property rights and wise-use proponents. But despite Cushman's best efforts, he was unable to stir grassroots opposition to the survey proposal until Babbitt championed it in 1993.

The situation changed that summer. Cushman undertook a furious fax campaign, supported by a new farmers' coalition based in California called the Alliance for America.[7] He faxed press releases to four thousand property rights groups and three thousand media outlets, warning of the impending survey legislation. This time Cushman succeeded in mobilizing a grassroots network to protest the survey. The resulting protest and the effectiveness of Cushman's lobbyist, Myron Ebell, brought support from members of Congress who were committed to protecting their constituents' property rights. Representatives Charles Taylor (R-N.C.), Gary Condit (D-Calif.), Billy Tauzin (D-La.), and Richard Pombo (R-Calif.) formed a bipartisan coalition to kill the survey.

When the survey, H.R. 1845, came up for a vote in the House, the bipartisan coalition sought to defeat it by proposing amendments that would fatally handicap the bill. For example, Tauzin offered an amendment that would prevent the Interior Department from using volunteers to carry out the biological survey, and the House approved it on a vote of 217 to 212. Property rights advocates saw Tauzin's amendment as particularly important because they feared that environmentalists would volunteer to work on the survey and they would be determined to find endangered species on private property (League of Private Property Voters 1994:9).

Taylor's amendment would have required that interior's surveyors get written permission from property owners before entering nonfederal property. It also required the National Biological Survey to share its information with property owners and to file regular reports with Congress about its activities. This amendment passed by an even greater margin, 309 to 115 (League of Private Property Voters 1994:9). The bill that would have created the survey was withdrawn by pro-ESA members of Congress from consideration.

The environmental SMOs were shocked. It was the first time Congress had rejected key environmental legislation since the 1970s. Indeed, property rights advocates saw this as a turning point and a test vote for future property rights battles over the reauthorization of the Endangered Species Act (Land Rights Advocate 1994:9).

## The Anti-ESA Coalition's Legislative Strategy

The principal property rights organization opposed to the Endangered Species Act was the Grassroots ESA Coalition. The founder and chief organizer was Chuck Cushman, whom many in the movement regarded as its heart and soul. In March 1995 he convened a meeting of about thirty national grassroots leaders and twenty key congressional staff members and property rights lobbying groups in Washington, D.C. Cushman argued that the movement needed a radical statement calling for reform of the Endangered Species Act. The group responded by developing a "Statement of Principles" for ESA reform (Cushman interview 1995).

The statement of principles was predicated on the establishment of an entirely new basis for conserving endangered species. Cushman's coalition now called for rewarding people who provide good habitat for endangered species instead of punishing transgressors. Indeed, Talbot's opinion poll supported this proposition (Tarrance Group 1995).

Emboldened by what it saw as public support for its position, Cushman's coalition argued that the ESA was shackled to the idea that only Washington bureaucrats could protect species and could do so only through their federal powers of land use control. The Department of the Interior would not acknowledge that the law had failed, because doing so would mean the end of its power and influence, the coalition argued (Cushman interview 1995).

According to a 1995 press release from the Land Rights Network, a news network for Cushman's American Land Rights Association and National Inholders Association, incentives to protect species would work without wasting money and intruding on people's lives and causing problems. But the coalition's position was contradictory. On the one hand, it was arguing that the ESA was needlessly expensive; on the other, it was urging the expenditure of more federal money to encourage property owners to protect endangered species on their land.

Cushman faxed the statement of principles and a request for endorsements to twenty thousand grassroots organizations. More than three hundred groups purporting to represent four million members complied. The groups ranged from environmental organizations and private property owners to ranchers, loggers, and outdoor recreation advocates to those whose use of public land was threatened (i.e., wise-use groups) (Cushman interview 1995).

The first proposition was that the ESA had failed to conserve endangered and threatened animals and plants. Instead, it had discouraged and hindered the conservation of species and their habitat. It created a perverse incentive to destroy species habitat on privately owned land (if a species disappears, the land does not come under the ESA). It also wasted scarce funding for conservation. The ESA failed precisely because it created a heavy-handed regulatory regime that trampled individuals' property rights, destroyed jobs, and devalued property values, according to the coalition. Furthermore, the full cost of the ESA was hidden because private property owners were forced to absorb the costs, and local, county, and state governments had to pick up the tab for carrying out habitat conservation plans and losing development projects.

The coalition recommended replacing the ESA with legislation based on eight principles:

Animals and plants should be conserved for the benefit of humanity.

States, not the federal government, should have primary responsibility for protecting species.

The federal government should rely on voluntary incentive-based programs to encourage landowners to conserve species.

Federal conservation measures should encourage trade and commerce, including breeding endangered species held in captivity.

The ESA should not prevent the wise use of federal land. Federal conservation programs should cost taxpayers as little as possible.

Conservation programs should be based on sound science and should give priority to taxonomically unique and complex animals and plants that are economically and ecologically valuable.

Federal conservation programs should be limited to prohibiting killing or injuring listed vertebrate species and should not address protection of their habitat.

The coalition created an eleven-member executive committee to devise a strategy for lobbying for ESA reform. Represented on the committee were Kathleen Benedetto of the Women's Mining Coalition, Bob Boese of the Alliance for Constitutional Defense, Chuck Cushman of the American Land Rights Association, Paula Easley of the Nationwide Public Projects Coalition, Robert Gordon of the National Wilderness Institute, Dennis Hollingsworth of the Riverside County (California) Farm Bureau, Dave Hook of the United Four-Wheel Drive Association, Tom DeWeese of the American Policy Center, Mark Pollot of Stewards of the Range, Ike Sugg of the Competitive Enterprise Institute, and Bruce Vincent of Communities for a Great Northwest.

Cushman functioned as the committee's coordinator and communications hub. He faxed updates on the coalition's position to thousands of grassroots members, members of Congress, and the media. Executive committee members held weekly conference calls every Friday to coordinate the coalition's strategy (Cushman interview 1995).

The coalition formed a six-member legislative drafting committee to write an ESA reform bill. Serving on the committee were Pollot, Boese, Gordon, Benedetto, Sugg, and Myron Ebell. Ebell was an attorney and former Washington lobbyist for Chuck Cushman. He left Cushman's employ to become a legislative assistant to first-term representative John Shadegg (R-Ariz.).

The measure they produced was sponsored and introduced by Shadegg as H.R. 2364 the "Endangered Species Recovery and Conservation Act of 1995." It contained the coalition's eight principles, and the coalition issued a strong endorsement, calling it the first completely nonregulatory, incentive-based alternative to the ESA.

## Grassroots Versus Corporate Land Users

Large-scale landowners and users did not support the ESA Coalition. Instead, they asked Congress to strengthen the federal ESA decision-making process (NESARC 1995b:3). They opposed compensation for property rights takings as well as the coalition's incentives approach. For example, the major landowners said they would support a bill that "allows the federal government to do everything the law now does to bring a species to recovery" (NESARC 1995a:1).

The main concern of corporate landowners—utility, ranching, mining, agriculture, timber, and construction companies—was to establish regulatory certainty in the enforcement of the ESA. They argued that hundreds of companies and communities had been economically and socially devastated by the act's provisions. Prominently mentioned in this regard were the northern spotted owl conflict in the Pacific Northwest and the Edwards Aquifer controversy in San Antonio, Texas (NESARC 1995a:1).

Corporate landowners offered anecdotal evidence of the economic costs of the ESA. They cited a hospital in San Bernardino, California, that was forced to redesign its plans for a new wing by 150 feet and set aside eight acres as "mitigation land" for an endangered fly. This, they said, cost the hospital $3 million (NESARC 1995a:1). Like their property rights counterparts, corporate landowners used extreme examples of problems supposedly caused by the ESA in an attempt to frame the issue in a way that would make headlines and get the attention of voters and their congressional representatives.

Large landowners argued that biologists used the ESA to stop economic development, which drained hundreds of millions of dollars from the economy. While high-priced lawyers argued about the ESA in court, the affected communities and companies were shut out of the ESA decision-making process, they said. For example, the Bonneville Power Administration (BPA) in the Pacific Northwest and the National Marine Fisheries Service estimated that measures to conserve salmon on the Columbia and Snake Rivers would cost at least $350 million a year. The BPA spent more than $2 billion on salmon recovery, which passed a significant portion of this expense along to its rural customers. Escalating costs threatened to bankrupt the BPA and aggravate the already distressed economy of the Northwest, which had already suffered the loss of timber jobs because of restrictions on logging to protect the northern spotted owl.

Corporate land users said they simply wanted to streamline the ESA decision-making process to guarantee their continued commercial use of land and water resources. For example, they sought to change the act by imposing short-term deadlines requiring the secretary of the interior to determine whether federal action was required to conserve a species on this land. They wanted the secretary to have the authority to establish "conservation objectives," which ranged from full recovery to simply protecting the existing population. These changes would have shifted the act away from its "absolutist" approach, which required extraordinary measures to reach "full recovery" of species, regardless of the cost or the feasibility of doing so (NESARC 1995a).

The corporate landowners, represented by two lobbying organizations, the Endangered Species Coordinating Council (ESCC) and the National Endangered Species Act Reform Coalition (NESARC), did agree with some of the principles championed by Cushman's coalition.[8] For example, they called for an improved scientific review process before species were listed. Both groups felt that wildlife biologists had too much power in the listing process and claimed that biologists often lacked the technical ability to interpret data and had their own environmental agendas. The result, these organizations said, was an abuse in the implementation of the act. They cited as an example a report by a disillusioned former Fish and Wildlife Service biologist, W. Dean Carrier. Carrier explained the agency's alleged abuse of power in a paper entitled "The Killing of the Goose," which he presented to the Western Section of the National Wildlife Society's annual conference in 1995; NESARC subsequently introduced long excerpts from Carrier's paper during testimony before Congress:

> Suddenly, we had the power. But with power comes responsibility. We gleefully latched on to the power, but I'm not sure we lived up to the responsibility. We began to misuse our newly acquired authority in a manner no less arrogant than those who used it against us a mere decade before. We focus more on the punishment of development—any development—than on the analyzing of the real effects to biological resources or the recovery of listed species.     *(NESARC 1995c:2)*

Carrier said that the act was being used to extort huge sums of money from landowners, private utilities, and corporations. For example, he had participated in the 1989 negotiations for the renewal of the Central Nebraska Public Power and Irrigation District's license to sell electricity. In one negotiating session someone asked a lawyer representing a national environmental organization a question about a $75 million package his organization was seeking to mitigate the adverse effects on endangered species. According to Carrier, the lawyer said his client did not want to "bankrupt the District, just bring it to the brink of bankruptcy" (NESARC 1995c:2–3).

Large-scale corporate land users also disputed the U.S. Supreme Court's *Babbitt v. Sweet Home* decision (1995) by arguing that the concept of "harm" to endangered species should apply only to direct actions by persons who cause death or injury to a species. The corporate landowners argued that the ESA should not be read as protecting the habitat of species. However, they hedged on this point by supporting the secretary of the interior's designation of critical habitats as part of conservation plans. And although the corporate landowners supported federal consultation with states and local authorities in regard to ESA listing, the companies agreed that the federal government should retain its authority as the final arbiter in listing endangered species and deciding conservation plans (NESARC 1995a, 1995b, 1995c).

Corporate landowners felt that the property rights and wise-use organizations were taking an extreme position that was too negative. They argued that they wanted to repeal, not reform, the ESA. Both NESARC and ESCC believed that grassroots pressure on Congress was counterproductive and could undermine their efforts to reform the act. Corporate interests feared the all-or-nothing attitude of property rights SMOs. The act had popular support, and NESARC and ESCC feared that any effort to repeal could produce a backlash that could frustrate industry's reform efforts (Dogett interview 1995).

Cushman and his coalition wanted to turn species protection into a voluntary program comparable to the Conservation Reserve Program of the Agriculture Department, which rewards farmers who set aside farmland for conservation purposes. This program would be administered by an agency, such as the Soil Conservation Service, whose authority would be strictly advisory. By contrast, corporate land users were profit oriented and wanted only to ensure that their commercial interests were not threatened by the ESA. Corporate landowners were not concerned about the property rights of small landowners (Dogett interview 1995).

For example, a large timber company such as Boise Cascade, which owns millions of acres, could easily afford to forgo the use of fifty thousand acres for endangered species habitat. However, small-scale ranchers, farmers, home builders, and timber companies did not have the luxury of setting aside large areas of their land. Indeed, this had the potential to bankrupt small landowners and destroy family legacies (Dogett interview 1995).

The property rights movement bombarded rural members of Congress with faxes, letters, and visits of delegations of constituents to Washington. They threatened to campaign against members of Congress, especially Republican first-termers who had campaigned on a property rights platform. Cushman and his coalition took the position that they would prefer to kill any reauthorization attempt until the 105th Congress in 1997 rather than settle for a slightly reformed ESA. In other words, they banked on getting a more conservative Congress and a president who would sign a voluntary incentive-based species conservation law that would give states and local communities an equal say in species protection policy. The effect of this was to seriously weaken the efforts of corporate land users to secure a modified version of the ESA, according to Jon Dogett, senior director of government relations for the American Farm Bureau Federation, part of the NESARC Coalition.

### The Political Context

The Republican Party won control of Congress in 1994, partly by campaigning on a private property rights plank. Soon after taking control of Congress, the House approved H.R. 9, which required the government to compensate landowners whose property lost 20 percent or more of its value because of regulatory action under ESA. In the Senate Republicans Robert Dole of Kansas, Phil Gramm of Texas, and Orrin Hatch of Utah sponsored an "omnibus" property rights bill (S.B. 605) that required compensation by the government for a 33 percent loss in the value of a portion of private property affected by government restrictions.

This set the stage for the congressional battle over the future of the Endangered Species Act. The three political factions in the conflict were based on region, ideology, and perceptions of public opinion as reflected in polls leading up to the 1996 elections. The first faction was comprised of grassroots property rights proponents in Congress, primarily new Republican members and a handful of Democrats from the West and South. The second faction included large industrial landowners, represented by senior Republicans from the West and South who controlled the congressional committees with jurisdiction over the ESA legislation. And the third faction was composed of those opposed to any weakening of the ESA. This faction was led by pro-environment liberal eastern Republicans, Democratic members of Congress, Clinton, Speaker of the House Newt Gingrich, and a coalition of environmental lobbying organizations, liberal religious groups, and civil rights organizations.

The chaotic and fragmented nature of the conflict by competing interest groups is a testament to the weakness of the political parties and the ideological nature of the conflict. First-term Republicans from the West and South represented private property owners and businesses adversely affected by the ESA. By contrast, urban property owners in the East were little effected by the ESA, and their congressional representatives were more committed to environmental issues.

The environmental groups were adamantly opposed to any weakening of environmental laws, and Clinton supported this largely Democratic constituency. Gingrich had voted for earlier renewals of the ESA and was personally committed to preserving wildlife. He was a close friend of Dr. Terry Maple, director of Zoo Atlanta, to which Gingrich had contributed two Komodo dragons. Through Maple, Gingrich met privately with a cluster of pro-ESA scientists, including Edward O. Wilson and Tom Eisner, chair of the Endangered Species Coalition, which was lobbying against any reform of ESA (Kriz 1995:2265).

Gingrich also had a compelling political reason to block passage of what he once described as extreme ESA legislation. He feared it would publicly stigmatize the Republicans in the November 1996 elections. Gingrich sought to defuse the internal divisions in the Republican Congress by trying to forge a consensus between the pro-environment and antiregulation wings of the party. However, because the reasons for retaining the ESA were largely moral and religious, whereas the reasons for reforming it were largely economic, negotiating a consensus position was virtually impossible (Kriz 1995:2265).

In attempting to broker a negotiated solution, Gingrich was responding to polls that showed the public believed Republicans were rolling back air pollution, water pollution, and food safety control laws in order to appease big business supporters. For example, in a March 1995 poll Republican pollster Frank Luntz, the architect of the "Contract for America," found that 62 percent of the public wanted stricter environmental controls and only 29 percent wanted the federal government to reduce regulations. Gingrich feared that unless this public perception changed, it could hand the Democrats a potent campaign issue for 1996 (Kriz 1995:2265). Northeastern and midwestern liberal Republicans, backed by the White House and environmental lobbyists, sought to retain the ESA by reintroducing the bill with largely cosmetic changes.

## Republican Factions

Congressional Republicans also were divided into three factions during the 104th Congress. The first was a group of new members of Congress, primarily from the West, who had campaigned on a plank of property rights reform. They represented the views of Cushman and his coalition. Although this faction was not the largest in the Republican Caucus, it had the support of the grassroots property rights groups that were driving the ESA reform movement.

They were led by Shadegg, sponsor of the radical reform bill that embodied the principles set out by Cushman's coalition. The bill had only nine cosponsors, Joe Barton (R-Tex.), Barbara Cubin (R-Wyo.), Tom DeLay (R-Tex.), John Doolittle (R-Calif.), Steve Largent (R-Okla.), David McIntosh (R-Ind.), George Radanovich (R-Calif.), Lamar Smith (R-Tex.), and Bob Stump (R-Ariz.).

They took the position that the ESA must be changed from a "command and control" regulatory structure that punishes landowners with fines and imprisonment to a nonregulatory incentive-based conservation program. Instead of relying on federal punishment to protect endangered species, Shadegg's bill emphasized incentives and rewards for landowners who follow good conservation practices. Their position is an example of Lindblom's notion of the privileged position of business. It represents an attempt to associate private enterprise with political democracy and to associate the ESA with an attack on democracy.

The second and largest faction was represented by Don Young (R-Alaska), chair of the House Resources Committee, which was the committee with jurisdiction over ESA, and Richard Pombo (R-Calif.), a member of the committee. Both were outspoken critics of environmental legislation and were committed to revamping what they regarded as intrusive regulation. Shortly after taking over the chairmanship of the committee, Young asked Pombo to chair the House ESA task force on reform. Pombo had campaigned on a promise to repeal the ESA and before going to Congress in 1992 had been a member of a property rights organization in his congressional district (Pyle interview 1995).

Pombo's task force held a number of hearings on ESA reform in North Carolina, Louisiana, California, Texas, and the state of Washington, ostensibly to solicit grassroots opinion about the ESA outside the capital. In fact, they heard testimony mostly from anglers, loggers, ranchers, environmentalists, county and state officials, and property owners who attacked the ESA.

In September 1995, after the hearings, Young and Pombo introduced H.R. 2275, the Endangered Species Conservation and Management Act of 1995 with 120 cosponsors. The Young-Pombo bill retained the regulatory framework of the ESA but addressed the complaints of large landowners while making some concessions to Cushman's organization.

The Senate counterpart was the Endangered Species Act (S.R. 768), introduced by Slade Gorton (R-Wash.) and J. Bennett Johnston (D-La.) in March 1995.[9] Republican senator Dirk Kempthorne of Idaho introduced a comparable bill in September 1995 after his Subcommittee on Drinking Water, Fisheries, and Wildlife held eight hearings on ESA reform in Oregon, Idaho, and the state of Washington. Kempthorne's subcommittee was under the jurisdiction of the Environment and Public Works Committee chaired by Chafee, a strong ESA supporter.[10]

The Young-Pombo, Gorton-Johnston, and Kempthorne bills all retained the "command and control" enforcement provisions of the ESA. They rejected the voluntary approach of the Shadegg bill, which relied primarily on incentives and rewards for private landowners who protected endangered species. However, they restored the act's original, and more narrow, definition of what constitutes "harm" to endangered species, limiting it to "direct action" against a species and not extending it to protection of a species' habitat.[11]

The Young-Pombo and Kempthorne bills went beyond the Gorton bill, however, and included a key property rights principle. These bills required that private landowners be compensated financially if restrictions to protect species reduced the value of private property by 20 percent or more. Furthermore, the federal government would be required to purchase private land if its value declined by 50 percent or more because of ESA implementation.

### Environmentalists Seeking to Retain the ESA

Opposition to ESA reform was led by an expressive group called the Endangered Species Coalition (ESC), which represented about two hundred environmental, civil rights, religious, food safety, and animal rights SMOs. The Endangered Species Coalition formed an executive steering committee to direct the campaign; on it sat representatives of the Defenders of Wildlife, Sierra Club Legal Defense Fund, National Wilderness Society, Humane Society of the United States, Environmental Defense Fund, and Fund for Animals. Jim Jontz, a former Democratic member of Congress from Indiana, was appointed its executive director. He was a veteran of congressional fights to preserve the ESA. In his 1992 reelection campaign, which he lost, Jontz had unsuccessfully challenged the property rights movement and timber industry opposition to renewing the ESA.

The Endangered Species Coalition launched a national campaign in March 1995 to prevent "back door assaults" hidden in the "Contract with America" that would weaken the Endangered Species Act (Broderick 1995).

The Endangered Species Coalition refused to compromise or even acknowledge publicly that any grievances with the ESA might be legitimate. Indeed, its leaders claimed that the property rights and wise-use groups were merely fig leaves for the voracious profit-seeking appetites of the polluting industries that funded them. However, some members of the Endangered Species Coalition acknowledged that some grassroots property rights and wise-use movements were bonafide. For example, at the 1992 annual meeting of the Environmen-tal Grantmakers Association, which is comprised of large corporations that give money to environmental organizations, the grassroots basis of the wise-use movement was acknowledged. Debra Callahan, director of the W. Alton Jones Foundation's Environmental Grass Roots Program, stated that wise use is a grassroots movement active in every state. Contrary to the conventional wisdom among environmental groups, it is not a "command and control, top heavy, corporate-funded" movement, she said (Veyhl 1993). A study sponsored by the Wilderness Society, Sierra Club, Audubon Society, and the National Wildlife Fund reached a similar conclusion. The report described the property rights movement as a local movement that had found fertile ground in rural areas of the country. The movement had a strong message targeted at the "Achilles heel" of the environmental movement—its grassroots support (Wilderness Society 1993).

Nevertheless, Endangered Species Coalition said that any change in the act would result in environmental catastrophe that could only benefit big business. It rejected any reform of the act and placed its hope in Clinton's threat to veto any attempt to weaken the act (Wilderness Society 1993). This made opponents of ESA reform vulnerable to the vagaries of presidential campaign politics in the 1996 election. The electoral importance of the West, where criticism of the ESA was particularly strong, weakened the president's hand in blocking reforms of the Endangered Species Act. It also placed environmental groups in the position of relying on the minority party in Congress to block reform.

### The Newt Factor

Environmentalists were cheered when a crack appeared in the Republican reform coalition in Congress in 1995. This occurred when Gingrich had a confrontation with Young over the Young-Pombo bill that September. Gingrich argued that the bill was too extreme and did not adequately safeguard wildlife. This was at odds with Gingrich's publicly stated position favoring a laissez-faire approach to environmental regulation and his hostility toward the environmental movement as expressed in his book, *To Renew America.* He said that "national environmental organizations were all too often simply an extension of the left wing of the Democratic Party" (Gingrich 1995:215).

Gingrich recognized that gutting the ESA was unpopular with voters and had led to a deadlock between the interests of big business and the grassroots reformers. One clear implication was that if the impasse continued, future campaign contributions from corporate donors might be less generous. Gingrich threatened to block consideration of the Young-Pombo bill in the House until it was changed to satisfy liberal northeastern and midwestern Republicans. Indeed, Republican Jim Saxton of New Jersey, who chaired the Resources Subcommittee on Fisheries, Wildlife, and Oceans, was miffed that Young had passed him over in favor of Pombo to head the task force on ESA. With encouragement from Gingrich, Saxton introduced his own, largely cosmetic ESA reform bill for consideration by the full committee. Saxton later withdrew his bill, after a similar measure introduced by Wayne T. Gilchrest (R-Md.) was defeated in the full committee ("Committee OKs" 1995).

Fearing that the public would perceive Young-Pombo as antienvironment, Gingrich stalled its consideration by the full House by preventing the powerful Rules Committee from scheduling its consideration. Gingrich also weighed in on other major environmental issues, including Superfund legislation to loosen government restrictions on toxic waste cleanup and the threatened budget cuts for the EPA. Gingrich announced that he would create an environmental task force to bring together the competing factions of congressional Republicans to deal with the public perception that the GOP is an enemy of the environment. However, the 1996 presidential campaign intervened and stalled Cushman's campaign in Congress. The ESA renewal was postponed because of the deadlock. As of 1998, the act was operating on a yearly basis with contingency funding.

## Conclusion

Cushman's coalition of wise-use and property rights SMOs lobbied Congress to dismantle the Endangered Species Act. The SMOs in turn mobilized citizens throughout the country to get property rights on the Republican congressional agenda, winning its inclusion in the Contract with America. After the 1994 election, which sent a Republican majority to Congress, the coalition pressured senators and representatives to support property rights.

Cushman's group succeeded in blocking congressional reauthorization of the ESA and in defeating the establishment of the National Biological Survey, which it feared would threaten the rights of private landowners. It also succeeded in securing budget cuts for the Fish and Wildlife Service, the principal agency responsible for listing endangered species of animals and plants.

The coalition also succeeded in proposing an entirely different approach to endangered species management that would reward rather than punish landowners who had endangered species on their property. A conservative faction of House members endorsed the coalition's bill and introduced it in Congress. But the bill was stalled because of a free-rider problem involving the different interests of the grassroots property rights movement and large corporate land users.

The large commercial landowners lobbied for a moderate streamlined ESA bill, whereas Cushman's coalition was seeking wholesale reform. The Grassroots ESA Coalition insisted on a radical new approach to the Endangered Species Act and threatened to withdraw its support for new legislation if the changes proposed by large commercial landowners were in the ESA. The large landowners were represented by two large coalitions of corporations that included logging companies, utility firms, county governments, manufacturers, and the American Farm Bureau Federation.

Essentially, Cushman's coalition withdrew its support from the Young-Pombo bill as well as from Kempthorne's and Gorton's bills. because they did not satisfy the coalition's demands. This left the large corporate interests in a weakened position, with the ironic result that ESA reform legislation was stopped by the expressive group that initiated it in the first place.

### NOTES

1. The act was reauthorized in 1978, 1982, and 1988. By 1992, however, criticism of the act had grown in Congress to the point that the Clinton administration did not want to risk a reauthorization vote until it made changes in the administration of the act to placate the political opposition.

2. A study by MIT political scientist Stephen M. Meyer similarly concludes that economic development does not suffer when the Interior Department acts to protect endangered species (Meyer 1995).

3. Good catalogues of vascular plants and vertebrate animals exist for temperate and arctic areas where there are relatively few species. However, knowledge of viruses, bacteria, and soil organisms is sketchy. No detailed lists of animals and plants exist for tropical areas, where species diversity is rich. Knowledge of tropical bacteria, fungi, insects, and soil organisms is rudimentary. Marine species are the least well known but potentially the most diverse (Mann and Plummer 1995:5).

4. The telephone poll was carried out from March 25 to 27, 1995. The poll had a margin of error of plus or minus 3.1 percent. The poll was paid for by Tom Talbot, a small independent lumberman who sponsored Project CommonSense's Endangered

Species Act Task Force. Project CommonSense contracted with the Eddie Mahe Company, a top U.S. political consulting firm that hired the Tarrance Group to carry out the survey.

5. The mountain states were Arizona, Colorado, Idaho, Montana, Nevada, New Mexico, Utah, and Wyoming. The western states were Alaska, California, Hawaii, Oregon, and Washington. Midwestern states were Illinois, Indiana, Michigan, Ohio, and Wisconsin. The Northeast was comprised of Connecticut, Delaware, Maine, Maryland, Massachusetts, New Hampshire, New Jersey, New York, Pennsylvania, Rhode Island, Vermont, and Washington, D.C.

6. There is no consensus in the scientific community about what constitutes an ecosystem. According to John Fay, an Interior Department biologist, "You can't get three scientists in a room to agree on what an ecosystem is." An ecosystem can be as big as the Yellowstone National Park or as small as an acre. In the case of Yellowstone, the ecosystem is twenty million acres. It also means that about 60 percent of the country's "ecosystems" are on private property (Sugg 1993:49).

7. Farmers formed a coalition to protest the implementation of the ESA in regard to protection of the delta smelt and other species perceived as causing a hardship for farmers in California.

8. Large-scale landowners and users tended to join one of these two political coalitions lobbying Capitol Hill for modest reform of the ESA. ESCC was a federation of about 250 landowners, workers, and organizations that used or relied on natural resources. It included the Georgia Sheep and Wool Producers, Iowa Cattlemen's Association, Louisiana Forestry Association, Utah Mining Association, and Wyoming Timber Industry Association. NESARC had about two hundred members, including Alabama Electric Cooperative, Inc., Boise Cascade Corporation, the California Farm Bureau, National Association of Home Builders, Union Pacific, and the Montana Power Company. The American Farm Bureau Federation belonged to both groups.

9. Environmentalists attacked the credibility of the Gorton-Johnston bill by publicizing its drafting by industry lobbyists. Although this is a common practice on Capitol Hill, it weakened Republican support for the bill in Congress because it exposed the absence of participation by property rights advocates.

10. Despite Chafee's support for the ESA, he assured Senate Republican leaders that he would not try to block reform of the act. He deferred to Kempthorne to lead the ESA reform effort. To do otherwise would have alienated the Senate Republican leadership and risked Chafee's removal as chair of the Environment and Public Works committee (Coit interview 1995).

11. In effect, this would have severed the government's power to take action to protect the habitat of endangered species. It would also have superseded the *Sweet Home* decision, which supported the ESA's broader definition of harm, which included habitat protection.

# SEVEN

# CONCLUSION

This study of political campaigns by expressive interest groups demonstrates the continuing importance of contemporary social movements in American politics. Most studies of social movements focus on the mobilization of citizen protest activity, including how political issues are framed to mobilize voters and how social movement organizations (SMOs) provide entrepreneurial leadership in organizing protests. However, the final stage of social movement activity, political campaigns to influence public policy, has been an area neglected by scholars.

Academics have failed to recognize that SMOs function both as interest groups and as mobilizers of citizen protest. That is to say, sometimes they function primarily as interest groups, attempting to influence government policy, whereas at other times they mobilize citizen activity in social movements. However, when SMOs function as interest groups, they do not have the same characteristics as economic interest groups. Expressive interest groups differ from conventional interest groups in at least seven ways.

## Money as the Primary Resource

Scholars have tended to regard access to large sums of money to underwrite political campaigns as the determining factor in interest-group politics. Indeed, the belief that business has an advantage in political controversies stems from this premise.

Thus it is not surprising that political scientists expect less well-funded groups to fail when challenging corporate interests. Observers argue, for example, that the need to raise money interferes with interest groups' ability to fulfill their goals.

Expressive groups do not conform to the conventional wisdom regarding the critical importance of money. Even without large operating budgets, expressive groups are formidable opponents of business. For example, in the animal rights campaign discussed in chapter 3, the group sponsoring protective legislation for farm animals had a campaign budget of only $50,000. Its industry opponents had nearly twenty times that amount, yet animal rights advocates waged a highly effective political campaign. They framed the campaign by appealing to the public for collective action to ensure the humane treatment of farm animals and managed to get a lot of free publicity.

The grassroots private property rights movement, discussed in chapter 6, waged an effective lobbying campaign in Congress despite relatively meager financial resources. This movement had a strong grassroots network of supporters who volunteered time and money to lobby Congress. The antibiotechnology campaign analyzed in chapter 2 was also carried out by poorly financed expressive groups that relied instead on volunteer movement support. These food safety and animal rights groups also were good at getting free publicity and had the support of small-scale dairy farmers who felt threatened by the large pharmaceutical companies.

These expressive groups had noneconomic resources that enabled them to challenge business interests. They had a social movement of enthusiastic supporters, an effective strategy, political skill, and a reputation for wielding political influence. These factors combined to counteract the financial advantage of the large corporations. Indeed, in the Endangered Species Act (ESA) campaign, described in chapter 6, when grassroots property rights proponents withdrew their support for amending the ESA, they doomed corporate efforts to reform the legislation.

## Tax Status of Expressive Groups

An article of faith among observers of interest groups is that tax status has a powerful effect on a group's political approach. For example, corporations deduct their contributions to tax-exempt nonprofit organizations, and their trade association membership dues are deductible from taxable income. Business lobbying groups also hold the keys to the vast "soft money" resources so important to financing political campaigns. Soft money includes contributions to political parties to carry out the voter registration and "get-out-the-vote" campaigns that consist of mass mailings, advertising, polls, and fund-raising. This money does not have to be reported to the Federal Election Commission.

By contrast, tax law prohibits nonprofit expressive groups from "participate[ing] or interven[ing] in any political campaign on behalf of or in opposition to any candidate for public office" (Cerny 1996:3835). According to the Tax Reform Act of 1969, nonprofit organizations that engage in political activity may lose their tax-exempt status. They are also subject to an increasingly onerous excise tax for each infraction of the rules. For example, foundation managers who knowingly make a disbursement for political activity subject their nonprofit organization to a 10 percent initial excise tax plus a 2.5 percent tax on political expenditures. If a nonprofit organization does not cease its political activity, any manager who refuses to correct the violation is subject to another tax of 100 percent of the expenditure plus a 50 percent assessment of the amount spent (up to a maximum of $10,000).

While the tax law appears to clearly rule out any political activity by nonprofit organizations, in practice these restrictions are ambiguous and difficult to implement. For example, if an expressive group's political activity is "minimal," it is not violating the political activity prohibition. Thus a charity can engage in a "voter participation program" if the purpose is to educate the public about issues and the material does not contain a bias for or against a candidate. Moreover, a nonprofit can campaign for or against an appointed official.

Expressive groups can compile the public voting records of members of Congress or state legislators, submit questionnaires to political candidates, and publicize the results. They can use voter registration lists to identify and influence voters. They can also legally target certain segments of the electorate in their education campaigns.

A nonprofit expressive group is also allowed to carry out "public education programs" during election campaigns. For example, groups may run TV and radio ads during an election campaign if the ads explain the group's position on election issues, including urging voters to support particular legislation. These groups also are permitted to encourage people to register to vote and are allowed to emphasize the importance of an election outcome to the group. They can engage in issue advocacy even if a group's position coincides with the position taken by a well-known political candidate (Cerny 1996:3840).

The absence of any effective constraint on the political activity of non-profit expressive groups was clearly evident in this study. In all the campaigns, tax status had no discernible effect on the ability of these groups to wage political campaigns. In the secondhand smoking campaign discussed in chapter 5, business attempted to silence antismoking groups by making their tax-exempt status an issue. However, the antismoking groups ignored the companies' litigation threat and conducted a high-profile multimillion dollar campaign against the tobacco industry. The companies protested in federal court that the campaign was an abuse of the groups' tax-exempt status. But the courts sided with the antismoking groups on the ground that the campaign was educational and not legislative.

In the campaign against the chemical companies discussed in Chapter 4 nonprofit environmental groups directly supported the political campaign of a gubernatorial candidate in what appears to have been a direct violation of tax law regarding nonprofits. They also coordinated their voter registration and political strategy with a political party. Neither political activity triggered a reaction from the IRS.

Indeed, the key property rights groups in the endangered species controversy in Chapter 6 did not even apply for nonprofit IRS status. Instead, they relied on grassroots support for voluntary contributions. They knew that the major corporations would not make financial contributions to them. Therefore, these expressive groups had no incentive to even apply for nonprofit tax status.

The results of this study suggest that the tax-exempt status of expressive interest groups in political controversies is no real constraint on their political activity. Thus tax status does not appear to give business an advantage over expressive groups in a political campaign.

## Hiring Public Relations Firms

Another area of consensus among observers of interest groups is that only well-financed organizations can afford to hire public relations firms to conduct costly campaigns. The techniques of public persuasion and mobilization involve major expenses for TV, radio, and newspaper ads, mass mailings, public opinion surveys, and hiring experts to design an effective media campaign. It is also widely believed that expressive groups, as a rule, cannot afford to pay for expensive media campaigns, that they are forced to rely instead on publicity from media supposedly sympathetic to their cause.

The results of this study do not support the belief that expressive groups cannot afford to hire public relations firms. For example, the antichemical and secondhand smoke campaigns discussed in chapters 4 and 5 received major donations from movement and nonmovement supporters to carry out elaborate and expensive media campaigns with the aid of public relations firms. Although the expressive groups' budgets were not big enough to pay for the media campaigns, they had no difficulty raising the money they needed from their social movement supporters.

The antichemical groups received large contributions and assistance from Hollywood celebrities. And the antismoking groups received millions of dollars from a nonprofit health foundation to finance a media campaign against protobacco legislation. This suggests that, contrary to conventional wisdom, business interests do not necessarily have a monetary advantage over expressive groups in hiring public relations firms.

### Sensationalism

According to conventional wisdom, interest groups tend to sensationalize political controversies. They are said to use advertisements and emotional rhetoric to exploit public fears, anger, and frustration to gain support for their policy positions. For example, photographs of baby calves chained to their pens in darkness produce a gut-wrenching public reaction.

Students of interest groups believe that distortions of fact, and exaggerated or manufactured threats to public health and safety, are counterproductive. This belief is rooted in the traditions of interest-group lobbying, which relies on the trustworthiness and reputations of groups' representatives.

However, expressive groups follow a different philosophy. They believe that it is necessary to shock the public in order to get its attention and mobilize citizens to protest. They also believe that the long-term effects of hyperbolic advocacy ads are innocuous. They feel that their supporters will tolerate sensationalism, whereas only those who disagree with the message will be offended.

I found that both business and expressive groups tend to sensationalize their causes in waging their campaigns. However, large corporations are more sensitive to charges of distortion and misrepresentation than are expressive groups. Business groups depend heavily on a personal working relationship with government elites. To maintain that relationship business lobbyists must maintain a professional reputation for honesty and trust-worthiness.

In the antipesticide campaign discussed in chapter 4, business was highly sensitive to criticisms that the industry was exaggerating the potential economic losses. For this reason business elites deliberately suppressed one of their own reports that projected high economic losses as a result of environmental legislation. They did this because they feared losing credibility with legislators.

By contrast, expressive groups rely heavily on citizen protests to back their efforts. This makes it imperative that they get the attention and support of the public. However, when mobilizing voters, expressive groups invariably overstate and exaggerate dangers to the public.

In the antipesticide campaign, expressive groups ran ads that featured questionable claims that the use of pesticides in the production of fruits and vegetables causes cancer. Similarly, in the antibiotechnology campaign discussed in chapter 2, food safety groups asserted that the Food and Drug Administration is too reliant on industry drug studies in determining whether a new drug is safe. They claimed that the injection of growth hormones in dairy cows would contaminate the country's milk supply.

Although the risks to the credibility of business lobbying groups from sensationalized claims are very real, the same practice by expressive groups seems to be of less risk to them. Although both economic and expressive interest groups are inclined to sensationalize their cases in political campaigns, the risks to business are greater than they are for expressive groups.

### Political Parties and Interest Groups

Observers of expressive interest groups believe that political parties are not important in achieving interest-group goals. The conventional wisdom is that environmental and consumer groups overlap and compete with political parties. They overlap insofar as both organizations select political candidates, campaign for their election, and have political agendas. They compete with parties for supporters' time, money, and loyalty. In other words, the policy goals of expressive groups are more appealing to some voters than the broad-based policy agendas of political parties.

This book has demonstrated that expressive groups tend to work closely with political parties in campaigns of importance to both. For example, chapter 6 shows that the property rights groups coordinated their political campaign closely with the conservative wing of the Republican Party in Congress. The antichemical groups in the Big Green campaign joined a broad coalition of interest groups under the leadership of the Democratic Party. Antismoking groups also worked closely with key legislative leaders in the Democratic Party. Indeed, in each campaign the objective was to win the support of party leaders as the first step in realizing the expressive group's objectives. Therefore, in terms of time, money, and loyalty of supporters, parties and expressive groups work toward common policy objectives.

However, during the Big Green and property rights campaigns, free-rider problems weakened both. Political party elites took control of these campaigns and subordinated the SMOs to a secondary role. This tended to discourage the mobilization of citizen support. Indeed, the SMOs tended to transfer responsibility for running the campaigns to party leaders and nonmovement allies—Hollywood celebrities in Big Green and large corporate landowners in the property rights campaign.

This suggests that when political parties displace expressive groups in political campaigns, the result is a weakening of the SMOs' ability to mobilize citizen support. In contrast with conventional economic interest groups, therefore, political party alliances with expressive groups may weaken, not strengthen, the campaigns.

## Business Unity in the Face of Environmental Challenge

It is widely believed that the traditional antagonism between business and labor is overshadowed by conflict between business and environmental-consumer groups. Related to this is the notion that business and union interests unite when challenged by these expressive groups. The reasoning is that although unions are active only in particular industries, environmental, occupational, and consumer safety regulations affect all sectors of business and their workers. Thus businesses are more inclined to unite in the face of increased government regulation than when confronted by union opposition.

But my findings do not support this proposition. In two campaigns, antibiotechnology in chapter 2 and property rights in chapter 6, small-scale farmers and landowners opposed the large corporations. To protect their economic interests during the antibiotechnology campaign farmers joined food safety groups against corporate agribusiness and drug companies. In the property rights campaign small landowners united with public land users to lobby a congressional faction of the Republican Party to block a proposal sponsored by another Republican faction that was backed by large corporate landowners.

In the animal rights campaign in chapter 3 agribusiness did not support the small livestock farmers when they were under attack. The companies feared that they would become targets of the animal rights movement if they were involved in a losing campaign. In the antipesticide campaign in chapter 4 agricultural producers disassociated themselves from the chemical industry. Farmers and the timber industry sponsored separate campaigns against environmental legislation, despite warnings that doing so would weaken the overall business response to antichemical groups.

These findings challenge the conventional belief that business is more united when challenged by environmental and consumer groups. It suggests that business groups, like all other economic interest groups, will act on the basis of their own perceived commercial interests, regardless of how that decision affects other business groups or business as a whole.

### The Free-Rider Problem

Contrary to the conventional wisdom of the social movement literature, my findings suggest that expressive groups, like large economic interest groups, do have free-rider problems. Movement scholars have tended to deny that movements have such problems largely because people join movements out of deeply held beliefs and group solidarity. Although this is undoubtedly true, it does not exclude social and political goals from a movement's collective goods. In other words, if the members of a movement believe that a cherished goal of their campaign is being compromised or subordinated, they will tend to withdraw their support. This is precisely what happened in the Big Green and property rights campaigns, discussed in chapters 4 and 6.

In the Big Green campaign environmental and food safety SMOs felt that the movement had been co-opted by party politicians to advance their political agendas. The SMOs reluctantly continued to support the campaign but without any real enthusiasm. Indeed, they did not even provide the promised financial contributions or signatures to get the initiative on the ballot. In this situation the SMOs had a relatively free ride on the efforts of a political party and a nonmovement ally, Hollywood celebrities.

In the property rights campaign SMOs withdrew their support from efforts to reform the Endangered Species Act when it appeared that non-movement allies—the large corporate landowners—were prepared to jettison key demands of the property rights movement. The property rights SMOs were not prepared to accept partial concessions and therefore refused to campaign for an ESA reform bill backed by large commercial landowners.

### Expressive Group Campaigns and Social Movements

These case studies reveal several distinctive characteristics of expressive group campaigns (see table 1.1). With the exception of the biotechnology campaign, expressive groups formed coalitions of SMOs to mobilize support. Indeed, the failure of SMOs to form such a coalition in the biotechnology campaign was a weakness. The differing leadership styles and strategies of the antibiotech SMOs made it difficult for them to agree on a single campaign strategy. It also made it difficult to frame the issue in a way that would arouse citizen protest. This split the campaign into factions and thereby weakened the mobilization effort.

What is noteworthy about SMOs in successful campaigns is that despite differing priorities and objectives, the organizations are united under the leadership of an expressive group. For example, in the second-hand smoke campaign a wide range of SMOs and nonmovement allies submerged their agendas and mobilized citizens to defeat the Philip Morris initiative. Chuck Cushman and his coalition also coordinated hundreds of property rights groups to mobilize protest of the Endangered Species Act. The protest had a discernible influence on rural and western members of Congress. However, when the coalition's nonmovement allies, corporate landowners, withdrew their support, the campaign stalled. This suggests that for expressive campaigns to be successful, they need the support of both SMOs and nonmovement allies.

Expressive campaigns also need political allies. In the three successful campaigns—secondhand smoke, preserving the Endangered Species Act, and antibiotechnology, expressive groups had the backing of political elites in Congress, some regulatory agencies, and some state legislatures. Without political allies the campaigns probably would have had failed outright. By contrast, the animal rights campaign's lack of political allies was a critical weakness. This alienated SMOs that feared the loss of their access to political elites.

Business opponents of expressive campaigns likewise played a key role in the outcome. With the exception of Big Green and animal rights, industry opposition to the various campaigns was a failure. In both cases, industry opponents did not directly challenge the campaign issues. They recognized that they could not win unless they reframed the issues. In other words, the expressive campaigns tapped widely popular support within the electorate. This placed opponents on the defensive. Indeed, the only way that they could challenge the expressive campaigns was to reframe the issues. In the case of Big Green, industry personalized the campaign by turning it into a vote against the controversial director of the expressive group mounting the campaign. In the animal rights campaign, industry opponents decided not to contest the campaign because they feared the political fallout if they lost. That left individual farmers to defend what they saw as their livelihoods and way of life.

The framing process was critical in all the campaigns. Expressive groups that were successful in this regard had an advantage over their opponents. For example, the animal rights, secondhand smoke, and endangered species campaigns were effective in framing the issues in a way that mobilized citizen protest. The animal rights campaign framed the issue as guaranteeing the humane treatment of farm animals, the secondhand smoke campaign as protecting the health of children, and the endangered species campaign as guaranteeing the property rights of all citizens. Opponents of these campaigns recognized that they could not challenge the issues as framed and hope to win. This forced them to attempt to reframe the issues. In the most ironic attempt to reframe a campaign issue, the tobacco companies sponsored an antismoking initiative.

The biotechnology and Big Green campaigns were weakened from the outset by a failure to frame their campaign issues clearly. In the case of biotechnology, two interests—food safety and farmers' economic security—competed to frame the issue. The failure to resolve who would frame the campaign dogged it until late in the day. In the case of Big Green, the initiative was so ambitious that reducing the issue to one that the electorate could understand and support was impossible.

### Expressive Interest Groups and Democracy

Finally, my findings suggest that the role of expressive groups is important to the health of the American democratic system. Observers of expressive interest groups are divided on this point. Proponents argue that these groups have created new opportunities for participation in the political system. They are part of a long historical process of democratic enfranchisement in the United States, from the freeing of slaves and the suffrage movement to the protection of environmental, consumer, and property rights. This has enabled the democratic system to accommodate new and diverse groups of participants in policy making. In other words, expressive groups have enriched and revitalized the American democracy.

Critics argue that the wave of new expressive groups since the 1970s has paralyzed the democratic system by overloading it with shrill and uncompromising demands. The sheer number of interest groups has exceeded the ability of politicians to cope with them, the critics say. Senator Edward Kennedy has observed, for example, that the "Senate and the House are awash in a sea of special-interest campaign contributions and special-interest lobbying" (*Newsweek*, November 6, 1978:48–50). And Judis argues that Washington is awash with "professional movement groups," a phenomenon that has undermined popular political institutions (1996:159, 177–78). The critics also argue that expressive groups are led by single-issue zealots whose extremist rhetoric has poisoned public discourse and made more difficult the compromise that is an intrinsic part of democratic policy making.

Although both arguments may be valid to some degree, many observers of interest groups have ignored a larger issue. That is the role of expressive interest groups in balancing the power of economic interest groups in public policy. Contrary to the conventional wisdom that business dominates interest group politics, the expressive groups we have examined here were able to compete with business organizations regarding public policy. This finding is consistent with several other studies, including those by Hadwiger (1982), Browne (1995), Vogel (1996), Heinz et al. (1993), Woliver (1993:21–23), and Costain (1992:134).

This observation takes us back to Madison's warnings about the "mischief of factions" in *Federalist* 10. He feared that a dominant private economic interest or class would emerge to tyrannize society. By emphasizing economic interest groups in their theorizing, scholars have tended to overlook what we might call the "cure" for the mischief of factions. Although Lindblom's insight regarding the "privileged position" of business in capitalist societies is undoubtedly correct, this study shows that expressive groups have emerged as a counterweight to economic power. Madison's warnings may have been heeded.

# BIBLIOGRAPHY

Abler, David G. 1989. "Vote Trading on Farm Legislation in the U.S. House." *American Journal of Agricultural Economics* 71 (August).

Adams, Charles Francis. 1851. *The Works of John Adams, Second President of the United States: A Life of the Author*, vol. 6. Boston: Charles C. Little and James Brown.

Adler, Jonathan. 1995. "Property Rights and Wise-Use Activism." In *Environmentalism at a Crossroads: Green Activism in America*. Washington, D.C.: Capital Research Center.

AFBF (American Farm Bureau Federation). 1991. *Meeting the Animal Rights Challenge*. Park Ridge, Ill.: AFBF.

———. 1997. *Farm Bureau Policies for 1997*. Park Ridge, Ill.: AFBF.

AFT (American Federation of Teachers). 1994. *What College-bound Students Abroad Are expected to Know about Biology*. Washington, D.C.: AFT.

Aguinaga, Stella, Heather Macdonald, Michael Traynor, Michael E. Begay, and Stanton A. Glantz. 1995. "Undermining Popular Government: Tobacco Industry Political Expenditures in California, 1993–1994." Pamphlet. University of California—San Francisco, School of Medicine, Institute for Health Policy Studies and University of Massachusetts—Amherst, School of Public Health. May.

AHA (American Heart Association). 1988. *Annual Report, 1988*. Dallas: AHA.

AHI (Animal Health Institute). 1992. "Backgrounder." Press release. Washington, D.C. December.

———. 1993. *AHI Bovine Somatotropin (BST) Public Information Program Annual Report, 1987–1991*. Washington, D.C.: AHI.

American Cancer Society of California. 1994. "American Cancer Society Releases Poll Results: Californians Say Tobacco Company Should Not Set Smoking Policy." Press release. March 15.

American Hospital Association. 1998. *Hospital Statistics*. Chicago: AHA.

American Society of Heating, Refrigerating, and Air Conditioning Engineers. 1989.

"ASHRAE Standard 62–1989: Ventilation for Acceptable Indoor Air Quality." Report issued by ASHRAE, Washington, D.C.

Andrade, Anthony J. and Patrick R. Tyson. (legal counsel for Philip Morris Corporation). 1994. Letter to John Vitton, administrative law judge, U.S. Department of Labor, from Andrade and Tyson, legal counsel for Philip Morris Corporation. November 22.

Anthan, George. 1994. "Debating Property Rights: Farmers Are at the Heart of What's Being Called 'The Civil Rights Issue of the 1990s.'" *Des Moines Register*, November 28, p. 1.

"Apologies to the Alligators." 1995. *Washington Post*, April 22, p. A17.

Arbogast, Nicole. 1995. "Public Versus Private Land Management: Which Is Better for the Environment?" In Jonathan Adler, ed., *Property Rights Reader*. Washington, D.C.: Competitive Enterprise Institute.

Arnold, Ron and Alan Gottlieb. 1994. *Trashing the Economy*. Bellview, Wash.: Free Enterprise Press.

*Babbitt v. Sweet Home,* 515 U.S. 687 (1995).

Balzar, John. 1993. "Creatures Great and Equal?" *Los Angeles Times*, December 25, p. A1.

Baumgartner, F. R. and B. D. Jones. 1993. *Agendas and Instability in American Politics*. Chicago: University of Chicago Press.

Beall, Gary A. and James H. Hayes. 1991. "Big Green and Careful: How Major California Newspapers Covered Two Ballot Initiatives in the 1990 General Election." Unpublished manuscript.

Bean, Michael J. 1994. "Symposium: On Species Conservation." *Insight*, May 30.

Begay, Michael E., Michael Traynor, and Stanton A. Glantz. 1994. "The Twilight of Proposition 99: Reauthorization of Tobacco Education Programs and Tobacco Industry Political Expenditures in 1993." Pamphlet. University of California— San Francisco, School of Medicine, Institute for Health Policy Studies and University of Massachusetts—Amherst, School of Public Health. March.

Begley, Sharon, Mary Hager, and Judy Howard. 1989. "Dangers in the Vegetable Patch." *Newsweek*, January 30.

Bennett, James and Thomas DiLorenzo. 1994. *Unhealthy Charities: Hazardous to Your Health and Wealth*. New York: Basic Books.

Bentley, Arthur F. 1908. *The Process of Government*. Chicago: University of Chicago Press.

Berry, Jeffrey M. 1977. *Lobbying for the People: The Political Behavior of Public Interest Groups*. Princeton, N.J.: Princeton University Press.

——. 1980. "Public Interest Versus Party System." *Society* (May–June).

——. 1989. *The Interest Group Society*. 2d ed. Glenview, Ill.: Scott, Foresman/Little, Brown.

——. 1993. "Citizen Groups and the Changing Nature of Interest Group Politics in America." *Citizens, Protest, and Democracy*, ed. Russell J. Dalton, special issue of *Annals of the American Academy of Political and Social Science* 528 (July): 30–41.

———. 1996. "The Rise of Postmaterialism in American Politics." Unpublished manuscript presented at the 1996 annual meeting of the American Political Science Association, San Francisco, August 29–September 1.

———. 1997. *The Interest Group Society.* White Plains, N.Y.: Longman.

Bonafede, Dom. 1983. "Interest Groups Pressing for Earlier, More Active Role in the Electoral Process." *National Journal,* May 14, pp. 1005–17.

Bosso, Christopher J. 1987. *Pesticides and Politics: The Life Cycle of a Public Issue.* Pittsburgh: University of Pittsburgh Press.

———. 1994. "After the Movement: Environmental Activism in the 1990s." In Norman J. Vig and Michael E. Kraft, eds., *Environmental Policy in the 1990s.* 2d ed. Washington, D.C.: Congressional Quarterly Press.

———. 1995. "The Color of Money: Environmental Groups and the Pathologies of Fund Raising." In Allan J. Cigler and Burdett A. Loomis, eds., *Interest Group Politics.* Washington, D.C.: Congressional Quarterly Press.

Boyte, Harry C. 1980. *The Backyard Revolution.* Philadelphia: Temple University Press.

Brambell, F. W. R. 1965. *Report of the Technical Committee to Enquire into the Welfare of Animals Kept Under Intensive Livestock Husbandry Systems.* London: Her Majesty's Stationery Office.

Brich, Philip. 1995. "Taking Back the Rural West." In John Echeverria and Raymond Booth Eby, eds., *Let the People Judge.* Washington, D.C.: Island Press.

Broderick, Brian. 1995. "Senate Judiciary Committee Approves Omnibus Takings Bill." *Daily Environment Report,* no. 256 (December 22): A-2.

Brookes, Warren T. 1991. "EPA's Misguided Hysteria over Pesticide Risk." *Farm Chemicals* 154, no. 2 (February).

Brown, K. S. and G. G. Brown. 1992. "Habitat Alteration and Species Loss in Brazilian Forest." In T. C. Whitmore and J. A. Sayer, eds., *Tropical Deforestation and Species Extinction.* New York: Chapman & Hall.

Brown, Phil. 1991. "Popular Epidemiology and Toxic Waste Contamination: Law and Professional Ways of Knowing." *Journal of Health and Social Behavior* 33 (September).

Brown, Phil and Edwin J. Mikkelsen. 1990. *No Safe Place: Toxic Waste, Leukemia, and Community Action.* Berkeley: University of California Press.

Browne, William. 1988. *Private Interest, Public Policy in American Agriculture.* Lawrence: University of Kansas Press.

———. 1990. "Organized Interests and Their Issue Niches: A Search for Pluralism in a Policy Domain." *Journal of Politics* 52 (May).

———. 1995. *Cultivating Congress: Constituents, Issues, and Interests in Agricultural Policy Making.* Lawrence: University of Kansas Press.

Brownson, Ross C., Michael C. R. Alavanja, Edward T. Hock, and Timothy S. Loy. 1992. "Passive Smoking and Lung Cancer in Nonsmoking Women." *American Journal of Public Health* 82, no. 11 (November): 1525–30.

Bruce-Briggs, B. 1988. "The Health Police Are Blowing Smoke." *Fortune,* April 25.

Burnham, Walter Dean. 1970. *Critical Elections and the Mainsprings of American Politics.* New York: Norton.

Buttel, Frederick H. and William L. Flinn. 1978. "The Politics of Environmental Concern: The Impacts of Party Identification and and Political Ideology on Environmental Attitudes." *Environment and Behavior* 10 (1).

California Legislative Analysts Office. 1990. "128 Environment, Public Health, Bonds, Initiative Statute." Sacramento.

California Manufacturers' Association. 1990. Report on a strategy for dealing with Proposition 128 (Big Green) to the California Coordinating Council. May 22.

California Wellness Foundation. 1993. "The Future of Tobacco Control, California Strategic Summit: Conference Report." Paper presented at the Western Consortium for Public Health. San Francisco. December 15–16.

——. 1995. "Preemption in Tobacco Control: History, Current Issues, and Future Concerns." Report. Brentwood.

——. 1996. Revised general grants program brochure. July 16.

Cambridge Reports. 1988. "Appendix A: The Questionnaire." Report no. CR 2530, prepared for the Massachusetts Farm Bureau. February.

——. 1989. "Survey Results on How Americans View Modern Livestock Farming." Report no. CR 2765, prepared for the Animal Industry Foundation and BMc Strategies, representing industry. April.

Caplin, Arthur L. 1990. "Moral Community and the Responsibility of Scientists." *Ethics of Animals in Our Lives.* St. Paul: Minnesota Extension Service of the University of Minnesota.

CEASE (Coalition to End Animal Suffering and Exploitation, Somerville, Mass). 1988a. *CEASE Synopsis* (Spring–Summer).

——. 1988b. "Humane Farming Initiative: Questions and Answers." May.

Center for Science in the Public Interest. 1990. Press release of text of testimony by Michael Jacobson, director, during U.S. House hearings on FDA's regulation of animal drug residues in milk. February 6.

Cerny, Milton. 1996. "Advising Charities in Avoiding the Pitfalls of Political Activity." *Tax-Exempt Organizations Tax Review.* Vols. 1 and 2. Washington, D.C.: Research Institute of America.

Charlton Research Company. 1989. "Van De Kamp/Hayden Initiative." Report prepared for the anti–Proposition 128 campaign. San Francisco.

——. 1990. "The Hayden Initiative (Proposition 128) Postelection Survey." Report prepared for the anti–Proposition 128 campaign. San Francisco. November.

Chase, Alston. 1995. "What's the Point of Endangered Species Act?" *Detroit News*, May 31.

Cheatham, Ken. 1991. Press release by Cheatham, executive director of the American Veal Association: "Veal Industry Commitment Is Strong Amid Challenges." July 27.

Cigler, Allan J. and Burdett A. Loomis. 1995. *Interest Group Politics.* 4th ed.

Washington, D.C.: Congressional Quarterly Press.

Clemens, Elisabeth S. 1997. *The People's Lobby.* Chicago: University of Chicago Press.

Coit, Janet L. 1995. Interview by author. July 26. Coit was counsel to the Senate Committee on Environment and Public Works.

Colleton, Don. 1993. Interview by author. December 12.

"Committee OKs Young-Pombo Bill; Gingrich Seeks Moderate Reform." 1995. *Water Policy Report,* October 25.

Colvin, Gregory L. 1995. "A Case Study in Using Private Foundation Funds to Educate Voters." *Journal of Taxation of Exempt Organizations* 6 (5). May/June, pp. 276-280.

Commoner, Barry, 1990. *Making Peace with the Planet.* New York: Pantheon.

Comstock, Pam. 1988. Letter to Susan Sellew from Comstock, director of public relations, Massachusetts Farm Bureau. February 3.

———. 1989. "Working with Editorial Boards." Analysis of the Massachusetts animal rights referendum presented at meeting sponsored by the American Farm Bureau Federation and Massachusetts Farm Bureau. April 6. Chicago.

Competitive Enterprise Institute. 1995. "Property Rights, Regulatory Takings, and Environmental Protection: Proposals for Statutory Compensation." Press release of text of statement submitted by Jonathan Adler, senior research fellow, to Committee on Environment and Public Works, U.S. House of Representatives. July 12.

Computer-Aided Research and Media Analysis (CARMA). 1992–1993. "Executive Summary of U.S. Media Coverage of the Beef Industry." Report prepared for the American Veal Association. October 1, 1992–September 30, 1993.

Conda, Cesar V. and Mark D. LaRochelle. 1994. "The New Populism: The Rise of the Property Rights Movement." *Commonsense* 1, no. 4 (Fall).

*Congressional Record.* 1993. July 15. S8842.

*Congressional Record.* 1994. September 22. S13285.

Consumers Union. 1993a. Press release of text of testimony by Michael K. Hansen before the (FDA's) Veterinary Medicine Advisory Committee on Potential Animal and Human Health Effects of rbGH Use. March 31.

———. 1993b. Press release of text of testimony by Michael K. Hansen before the joint meeting of the Food Advisory Committee (U.S. Department of Health and Human Services) and the Veterinary Medicine Advisory Committee of the FDA on whether to label milk from RBGH-treated cows. May 6.

Costain, Anne N. 1992. *Inviting Women's Rebellion: A Political Process Movement.* Baltimore: Johns Hopkins University Press.

Council on Environmental Quality. 1993. *Environmental Quality.* Washington, D.C.: U.S. Government Printing Office.

Crabo, Bo G. 1990. *Swedish Government Rules for Animal Protection.* Minneapolis: University of Minnesota, Minnesota Extension Service.

———. 1991. English translation of the Swedish government's "accompanying" law governing animal welfare (SFS 1988 539 L 2).

Crooker, Brian A. 1990. "The Animal Welfare, Animal Rights Movement, and Animal

Agriculture: A Research and Education Perspective." Paper presented at the 51st Minnesota Nutrition Conference, Bloomington, September 18–19.

Curtis, Stan. 1993. Interviews by author. November 11 and 19. Curtis was professor of animal science and headed the Department of Dairy and Animal Science at Pennsylvania State University.

Cushman, Chuck. 1995. Interview by author. August 23.

Dahl, Robert A. 1956. *A Preface to Democratic Theory*. Chicago: University of Chicago Press.

———. 1982. *Dilemmas of Pluralist Democracy*. New Haven, Conn.: Yale University Press.

"Dairy Farmers Fewer and Farther Between." 1988. *Accent*, August 18.

Dao, James. 1992. "Ted Weiss, Stalwart Conscience of Liberals in House, Dies at Sixty-Four." *New York Times*, September 15, p. D22L.

Deakin, Robert. 1990. "BST: The First Commercial Product for Agriculture from Biotechnology." In Peter Wheale and Ruth McNally, eds., *The BIO Revolution: Cornucopia or Pandora's Box?* London: Pluto Press.

Defenders of Property Rights. 1995. Press release of text of statement submitted by Nancie G. Marzulla, president and chief legal counsel, Agricultural Committee of the Subcommittee on Research Conservation, Research, and Forestry, U.S. House of Representatives, February 15.

Defenders of Wildlife. 1992–1993. *Saving Endangered Species: A Report and Plan for Action*. Washington, D.C.: Defenders of Wildlife.

Devall, Bill. 1970. "Conservation: An Upper-Middle Class Social Movement: A Replication." *Journal of Leisure Research* 2 (2).

———. 1980. "The Deep Ecology Movement." *Natural Resources Journal* 20 (2).

Dillow, Gordon L. 1981. "The Hundred-Year War Against the Cigarette." *American Heritage*, February–March.

Dogett, J. Jon. 1995. Interview by author. July 25. Dogett was senior director of government relations for the American Farm Bureau Federation.

Dowie, Mark. 1995. *Losing Ground: American Environmentalism at the Close of the Twentieth Century*. Cambridge, Mass.: MIT Press.

Doyle, Jack. 1985. *Altered Harvest*. New York: Viking.

Easterbrook, Gregg. 1995. *A Moment on the Earth: The Coming Age of Environmental Optimism*. New York: Viking.

Ecenbarger, William. 1991. "Tobacco's Long and Winding Road." *Chicago Tribune Magazine*, December 29.

Eckerly, Susan M. 1994. "The Triple Threat to Government Red Tape." *Commonsense* 1, no. 4 (Fall).

Ehrlich, Paul and Anne Ehrlich. 1981. *Extinction: The Cause and Conscience of the Disappearance of Species*. New York: Random House.

Eisner, Tom. 1995. "Endangered Species Coalition for Our Health." Press release from the Endangered Species Coalition.

Eliason, Robert. 1995. Interview by author. January 16. Eliason was a research chemist.

Endangered Species Coalition. 1993. "Property Rights and Endangered Species Protection." Press release. September.

———. 1994. "The Endangered Species Act Protects Us." Press release.

———. 1995. "Early Summer Alert." Press release.

Environmental Defense Fund. 1995. "A Moment of Truth: Correcting the Scientific Errors in Gregg Easterbrook's *Moment on the Earth*, Part I." Press release.

Fairfield, Roy P., ed. 1981. *Federalist Papers*. Baltimore, Md.: Johns Hopkins University Press.

Feagin, Joe R., Anthony M. Orum, and Gideon Sjoberg. 1991. *A Case for the Case Study*. Chapel Hill: University of North Carolina Press.

*Feedstuffs*. 1994. *Feedstuffs* (Minneapolis, Minn.), November 14.

Feinstein, Alvan. 1992. "Critique of Review Article, Environmental Tobacco Smoke: Current Assessment and Future Directions." *Toxicologic Pathology* 20 (2).

Feldman, Paul. 1994. "The Times Poll; Anti-Illegal Immigration Prop. 187 Keeps the Two-to-One Edge." *Los Angeles Times*, October,p. A1.

Fox, Michael W. 1983. *Farm Animals: Husbandry, Behavior, and Veterinary Practice— Viewpoints of a Critic*. Baltimore: University Park Press.

———. 1990. "Why BST Must be Opposed." In Peter Wheale and Ruth McNally, eds., *The BIO Revolution: Cornucopia or Pandora's Box?* Winchester, Mass.: Pluto Press.

———. 1992. *Superpigs and Wondercorn*. New York: Lyons & Burford.

Fumento, Michael. 1993. *Science Under Siege*. New York: Morrow.

"Fur Industry Seeking Friends." 1990. *Animals' Agenda*, October, pp. 28–29.

Gallup Organization. 1989. "Californians' Perceptions and Concerns About Animal Production Practices." Report on poll prepared for the California Beef Council during the animal rights campaign. March.

———. 1991. "A Gallup Study of Scientists' Opinions and Understanding of Global Climate Change." Report on poll prepared for the Center for Science, Technology, and Media, Washington, D.C. November.

Gans, Herbert J. 1980. *Deciding What's News*. New York: Random House.

Garner, Robert. 1993. *Animals, Politics, and Morality*. Manchester, England: Manchester University Press.

Gingrich, Newt. 1995. *To Renew America*. New York: HarperCollins.

Gladwell, Malcolm. 1989. "Some Fear Bad Precedent in Alar Alarm." *Washington Post*, April 19, p. A12.

Glantz, S. A. 1987. "What to Do Because Evidence Links Involuntary (Passive) Smoking with Lung Cancer." *Western Journal of Medicine* 140, no. 4 (April): 636–37.

Glantz, S. A. and R. A. Daynard. 1991. "Safeguarding the Workplace: Health Hazards of Secondhand Smoke." *Trial* 27, no. 6 (June): 36–40.

Glantz, S. A. and William W. Parmley. 1991. "Passive Smoking and Heart Disease: Epidemiology, Physiology, and Biochemistry." *Circulation* 83, no. 1 (January):

1–12.

Goffman, Irving. 1974. *Frame Analysis.* Cambridge, Mass.: Harvard University Press.

Gordon, Robert E. 1994. "Symposium: On Species Conservation." *Insight,* May 30.

———. 1995. Interview by author. July 20. Gordon was executive director of the National Wilderness Institute, Washington, D.C.

Grassie, Linda. 1998. Interview by author. Grassie was a member of the communications staff of the Center for Veterinary Medicine, U.S. Food and Drug Administration. July 7.

"Green but Not Growing." 1994. *USA Today.* October 19, p. 8A.

Grommers F. J. 1988. "The Animal Welfare Movement–European Perspective." *Animal and Health* 1 (1).

Gross, Paul R. and Norman Levitt. 1994. *Higher Superstition: The Academic Left and Its Quarrels with Science.* Baltimore. Md.: Johns Hopkins University Press.

Guest, Gerald B. 1991. Letter to Fred R. Holt, president, Animal Health Institute, Washington, D.C., in which Guest informs AHI that the National Dairy Board, U.S. Department of Agriculture, can no longer join the drug companies in promoting BST. February 14.

Guither H. D. and S. E. Curtis. 1983. "Animal Welfare: Developments in Europe–A Perspective for the United States." Unpublished report no. ASE 4536 AS 675. University of Illinois–Urbana-Champaign, College of Agriculture, Illinois Agricultural Experiment Station.

Hadwiger, Don F. 1982. *Political Agricultural Research.* Lincoln: University of Nebraska Press.

Hair, Jay D. 1994. "Statement by Jay D. Hair, President and CEO National Wildlife Federation." Press release. December 21.

Hamburg, Jill. 1990. "The Lone Ranger." *California Magazine,* November.

Hamilton, Edith and Huntington Cairns. 1961. *The Collected Dialogues of Plato.* Princeton, N.J.: Princeton University Press.

Hansen, Michael and Jean M. Halloran. 1993. Letter to Jerry Mande, Office of the Commissioner, Food and Drug Administration, describing what the writers saw as the health hazards of BST. May 24.

Hanson, John Mark. 1991. *Gaining Access.* Chicago: University of Chicago Press.

Harris, Mark. 1995. "The Threat from Within." *Vegetarian Times* 177 (February).

Harrison, Ruth. 1964. *Animal Machines: The New Factory Farming Industry.* New York: Ballantine.

Harry, Joseph, Richard Gale, and John Hendee. 1969. "Reply to McEvoy: Organized Conservationists an Upper-Middle Class Social Movement." *Journal of Leisure Research* 1: 246–54.

Hays, Samuel. 1987. *Beauty, Health, and Permanence.* Cambridge, Mass.: Cambridge University Press.

Heinz, John P., Edward O. Laumann, Robert L. Nelson, and Robert H. Salisbury. 1993. *The Hollow Core: Private Interests in National Policy Making.* Cambridge,

Mass.: Harvard University Press.

Helvarg, David. 1994. *The War Against the Greens.* San Francisco: Sierra Club Books.

Hershey, Marjorie Randon. 1993. "Citizens' Groups and Political Parties in the United States." In *Citizens, Protest, and Democracy,* ed. Russell J. Dalton, special issue of *Annals of the American Academy of Political and Social Science* 528 (July).

Hiscock, Ed. 1988. "Will Livestock Farms Survive Massachusetts Vote?" *Drovers Journal* (August 18).

Holden, Constance. 1987. "Animal Regulations: So Far, So Good." *Science* 238 (November 13): 880–82.

Holt, Thomas H. and Robert Pambianco. 1994. "The Antismoking Movement." Studies in Organization Trends, occasional paper issued by Capital Research Center, a conservative research center, Washington, D.C. September.

Humane Society of the United States. 1989. Press release of text of testimony of Michael W. Fox, vice president for large animals, during hearings before Committee on Agriculture, U.S. House of Representatives, on H.R. 84, the Veal Calf Protection Act. June 6.

Huyghe, Patrick. 1993. "New-Species Fever." *Audubon* 95, no. 2 (March–April).

Imig, Doug. 1996. *Poverty and Power.* Lincoln: University of Nebraska Press.

Imig, Doug and Sidney Tarrow. 1996. *The Europeanization of Movements? Contentious Politics and the European Union, October 1983–1995.* Ithaca, N.Y.: Cornell University, Institute for European Studies.

Ingersall, Bruce. 1989. "Milk Is Found Tainted with a Wide Range of Drugs Farmers Give Cattle." *Wall Street Journal,* December 6, pp. A1, A3.

Inglehart, Ronald. 1977. *The Silent Revolution: Changing Values and Political Styles Among Western Publics.* Princeton, N.J.: Princeton University Press.

——. 1981. "Postmaterialism in an Environment of Insecurity." *American Political Science Review* 75 (4): 880–900.

——. 1990. *Culture Shift in Advanced Industrial Society.* Princeton, N.J.: Princeton University Press.

——. 1992. "Public Support for Environmental Protection: Objective Problems and Subjective Values." Paper presented at the meeting of the American Political Science Association, Chicago, September 3–6.

Jamison, Wesley V. and William M. Lunch. 1992. "Rights of Animals, Perceptions of Science, and Political Activism: Profile of American Animal Rights Activists." *Science, Technology, and Human Values* 17, no. 4 (Autumn).

Japenga, Ann. 1989. "Livestock Liberation: A Revolution May Be Brewing as Animal-Rights Activists Challenge Conditions Down on the Farm." *Harrowsmith,* no. 24 (November–December).

Jasper, James M. and Dorothy Nelkin. 1992. *The Animal Rights Crusade.* New York: Free Press.

Judis, John B. 1996. *Ticking Time Bomb,* ed. Robert Kuttner. New York: New Press.

Kenny, Charles. 1986a. "The Antismoking Guerrillas: The Tobacco Wars," part 1 of two-part series, *Boston Globe Sunday Magazine*, May 4.

———. 1986b. "The Antismoking Guerrillas Face Their Biggest Battle Yet: Taking the Industry to Court," part 2 of two-part series, *Boston Globe Sunday Magazine*, May 11.

Key, V. O. Jr. 1958. *Politics, Parties, and Pressure Groups*. New York: Thomas Y. Crowell.

Keystone Center. 1995. "The Keystone Dialogue on Incentives for Private Landowners to Protect Endangered Species: Final Report." Unpublished report for corporate landowners. Keystone, Colorado. July 25.

Kingdon, John W. 1984. *Agendas, Alternatives, and Public Policies*. Boston: Little, Brown.

Kluger, Richard. 1996. *Ashes to Ashes: America's Hundred-Year Cigarette War, the Public Health, and the Unabashed Triumph of Philip Morris*. New York: Knopf.

Knepprath, Paul. 1994. Memo to Jack Nicholl regarding the Philip Morris initiative in Calfornia. September.

Knox, Margaret L. 1993. "The World According to Cushman." *Wilderness* 56, no. 200 (Spring).

Kopperud, Steve. 1988a. Memo to Farm Animal Welfare Coalition from Kopperud, senior vice president of the American Feed Industry Association.

———. 1988b. "Last-Minute Contributions to Massachusetts." Memo to all members of the Farm Animal Welfare Coalition. October 28.

———. 1993a. Interview by author. March 3.

———. 1993b. "What's Animal Agriculture Doing About Animal Rights?" *Agricultural Engineering* 74, no. 3 (May).

Kraft, Michael E. and Diana Wuertz. 1995. "Environmental Advocacy in the Corridors of Government." Unpublished manuscript.

Kriesi, Hanspeter. 1996. "The Organizational Structure of New Social Movements in a Political Context." In Doug McAdam, John McCarthy, and Mayer Zald, eds., *Comparative Perspectives on Social Movements*. New York: Cambridge University Press.

Kriz, Margaret. 1995. "The Green Card." *National Journal* 27, no. 37 (September 16): 2265, 2432.

Ladd, Everett Carll Jr. 1982. "Clearing the Air: Public Policy on the Environment." *Public Opinion* 5 (February–March).

Ladd, Everett Carll Jr. with Charles D. Hadley. 1978. *Transformations of the American Party System*. 2d ed. New York: Norton.

Lambert, Thomas and Robert J. Smith. 1994. "The Endangered Species Act: Time for a Change." Policy Study No. 119, March. Center for the Study of American Business, Washington University, St. Louis.

Land Rights Advocate. 1994. "The National Biological Survey History and Background." Report by the American Land Rights Association/National Inholders Association (Battle Ground, Washington). January–February.

Landy, Marc and Mary Hague. 1992. "The Coalition for Waste: Private Interests and

Superfund." In Michael S. Grieve and Fred L. Smith Jr., eds., *Environmental Politics: Public Costs, Private Rewards*. New York: Praeger.

Lasley, Paul and Gordon Bultena. 1986. "Farmers' Opinions About Third-Wave Technologies." *American Journal of Alternative Agriculture* 1, no. 3 (Summer).

League of Conservation Voters. 1994. "National Environmental Scorecard." Report on votes of the 103d Cong., 1st sess., February.

League of Private Property Voters. 1994. "Private Property Congressional Vote Index" for the 103d Cong., 2d sess. September.

Lee, P. N., J. Chamberlain, and M. R. Alderson. 1986. "Relationship of Passive Smoking to Risk of Lung Cancer and Other Smoking-Associated Diseases." *British Journal of Cancer* 54.

Letto, Jay. 1992. "One Hundred Years of Compromise (The Changing Environmental Movement)." *Buzzworm* 4, no. 2 (March–April).

Lewis, Martin W. 1992. *Green Delusions: An Environmental Critique of Radical Environmentalism*. Durham, N.C.: Duke University Press.

Lindblom, Charles E. 1977. *Politics and Markets*. New York: Basic Books.

——. 1982. "The Market as Prison." *Journal of Politics* 44 (May).

Lipset, Seymour M., Martin Trow, and James S. Coleman. 1956. *Union Democracy: The Internal Politics of the International Typographical Union*. Glencoe, Ill.: Free Press.

Loew, Franklin M. 1993. "Animals and the Urban Prism." *Journal of the American Veterinary Medical Association* 202, no. 10 (May).

Lowi, Theodore J. 1964. "American Business, Public Policy, Case Studies, and Political Theory." *World Politics* 16 (July).

——. 1969. *The End of Liberalism: Ideology, Policy, and the Crisis of Public Authority*. New York: Norton.

——. 1972. "Four Systems of Policy, Politics, and Choice." *Public Administration Review* 32 (July–August): 298–310.

Lowrey, A. H. and J. L. Repace. 1980. "Indoor Air Pollution, Tobacco Smoke, and Public Health." *Science* 208: 464–72.

Lubenow, Gerald C. 1991. *California Votes: The 1990 Governor's Race*. Berkeley: University of California, Institute of Governmental Studies.

Lucas, Gregory. 1991. "Health Groups Blast Tobacco-Industry Bill." *San Francisco Chronicle*. September 6.

Lugo, A. E. 1988. "Estimating Reductions in the Diversity of Tropical Forest Species." In E. O. Wilson, ed., *Biodiversity*. Washington, D.C.: National Academy Press.

Luttrell, Martin. 1988a. "Talk for the Animals: Farm Petitioners: We're Misunderstood." *Middlesex (Mass.) News,* August 26, pp. 1A–2A.

——. 1988b. "Farmers Flex Political Muscle." *Middlesex (Mass.) News,* October 21, pp. 1A–2A.

Lyons, James M. and Frank G. Zalom. 1990. "Progress Report: Vice President's Task Force on Pest Control Alternatives—Overview." *California Agriculture* (July–August).

Macdonald, Heather R., Stella Aguinaga, and Stanton A. Glantz. 1997. "The Defeat of Philip Morris's 'California Uniform Tobacco Control Act." *American Journal of Public Health* 87, no. 12 (December): 1989–1996.

Macdonald, Heather R., Michael Traynor, and Stanton A. Glantz. 1994. "California's Proposition 188: An Analysis of the Tobacco Industry's Political Advertising Campaign." Pamphlet. University of California—San Francisco, School of Medicine, Institute for Health Policy Studies. November.

Mallia, Joseph. 1988. "Farmers Worry About Question 3." *Greenfield (Mass.) Recorder*, November 3, pp. 1, 22–23.

Mann, Charles C. and Mark L. Plummer. 1995. *Noah's Choice: The Future of Endangered Species.* New York: Knopf.

Marttila and Kiley. 1994. "A Survey of Voter Attitudes in California." Poll prepared for Coalition of a Healthy California, which fought the Philip Morris initiative. August.

Mayes, Elizabeth. 1994. "Proposition 188 Stokes Debate on Whose Rights Prevail." *Contra Costa Times,* October 16.

Mazmanian, Daniel and David Morell. 1992. *Beyond Superfailure: America's Toxics Policy for the 1990s.* Boulder, Colo.: Westview.

McAdam, Doug. 1982. *Political Process and the Development of Black Insurgency, 1930–1970.* Chicago: Chicago University Press.

——. 1988a. *Freedom Summer.* New York: Oxford University Press.

——. 1988b. "Micromobilization Context and Recruitment to Activism." In Bert Klandermans, Hanspeter Kriesi, and Sidney Tarrow, eds., *From Structure to Action: Comparing Social Movement Research Across Cultures,* pp. 125–54. Vol. 1 of *International Social Movement Research.* Greenwich, Conn.: JAI Press.

McAdam, Doug, John D. McCarthy, and Mayer N. Zald. 1988. "Social Movements." In Neil J. Smelser, ed., *The Handbook of Sociology.* Newbury Park, Calif.: Sage.

——., eds. 1996. *Comparative Perspectives on Social Movements.* New York: Cambridge University Press.

McCarley, William R. 1990. "Report re: Environmental Protection Act of 1990." Report on costs of implementing Proposition 128 prepared for the California Legislative Analysts Office, California Secretary of State. April 30.

McCarthy, Bruce. 1989. "Developing a Plan." Analysis of Massachusetts animal rights referendum presented at meeting sponsored by the American Farm Bureau Federation and Massachusetts Farm Bureau. April 6. Chicago.

McCarthy, John D. and Mayer N. Zald. 1973. *The Trends of Social Movements in America: Professionalization and Resource Mobilization.* Monograph. Morristown, N.J.: General Learning Press.

——. 1977. "Resource Mobilization and Social Movements: A Partial Theory," *American Journal of Sociology* 82: 1212–41.

McFarland, Andrew S. 1976. *Public Interest Lobbies: Decision Making on Energy.* Washington, D.C.: American Enterprise Institute.

———. 1984. *Common Cause: Lobbying in the Public Interest.* Chatham, N.J.: Chatham House.

———. 1993. *Cooperative Pluralism: The National Coal Policy Experiment.* Lawrence: University Press of Kansas.

Meehan, Martin T. 1994. "Prosecution Memorandum: Requesting a Formal Investigation by the United States Department of Justice of the Possible Violation of Federal Criminal Laws by Named Individuals and Corporations in, or Doing Business with, the Tobacco Industry." Memo. December 14.

"Mexican Food Tips Fat Scale to 'Mucho.'" 1994. *USA Today,* July 19, p. 1A.

Meyer, John A. 1992. "Cigarette Century." *American Heritage,* December.

Meyer, Stephen M. 1995. "Endangered Species Listings and State Economic Performance: Project on Environmental Politics and Policy." Massachusetts Institute of Techology. March.

Meyerhoff, Al, Lawrie Mott, and Tom Hayden. 1990. "'Big Green' and Pesticides: Let's Get Tough!" *EPA Journal* 16, no. 3 (May–June): 45–46.

Milbrath, Lester W. 1984. *Environmentalists: Vanguard for a New Society.* Albany: State University of New York Press.

Miles, Robert. 1982. *Coffin Nails and Corporate Strategies.* Englewood Cliffs, N.J.: Prentice-Hall.

Miller, Jill Young. 1996. "Congressional Inaction May Make 237 Species Extinct." *Sun-Sentinel* (Fort Lauderdale, Fla.). March 3.

Mitchell, Robert Cameron. 1979. "Silent Spring/Solid Majorities." *Public Opinion* 2 (August–September): 16–22, 55.

———. 1980. "How 'Soft,' 'Deep,' or 'Left'? Present Constituencies in the Environmental Movement for Certain World Views." *Natural Resources Journal* 20, no. 2 (April): 345–58.

Mitchell, Robert C. and J. C. Davies. 1978. "The United States Environmental Movement and Its Political Context: An Overview." Discussion paper D-32, prepared for the Conservation Foundation, Washington, D.C.

Mitchell, Robert C., Angela G. Mertig, and Riley E. Dunlap. 1991. "Twenty Years of Environmental Mobilization: Trends Among National Environmental Organizations." *Society and Natural Resources* 4: 219–34.

Moseley, James. 1993. "Think Like an Environmentalist!?" *Farm Journal,* February.

Myers, Norman. 1979. *Sinking Ark.* New York: Pergamon.

National Academy of Science. National Research Council. 1986. *Environmental Tobacco Smoke: Measuring Exposures and Assessing Health Effects.* Washington, D.C.: National Academy Press.

———. 1989. *Diet and Health.* Washington, D.C.: National Academy Press.

———. National Research Council. 1993. *Pesticides in the Diets of Infants and Children.* Washington, D.C.: National Academy Press.

———. National Research Council. 1995. *Science and the Endangered Species Act.* Washington, D.C.: National Academy Press.

National Association of Animal Breeders. 1986. *Proceedings of the Animal Conference on Artificial Insemination and Embryo Transfer in Beef Cattle.* January 11, 1986. Denver, Colo. (Columbia, Missouri).

National Wilderness Institute. 1994a. "Going Broke?" Report. Washington, D.C. March 23.

———. 1994b. "NWI Resource: Endangered Species Blueprint." Vol. 5. Report.

National Wilderness Society. 1993. "The Wise Use Movement: Strategic Analysis and Fifty State Review." Pamphlet. Washington, D.C., March.

Nelson, Nancy L. 1987. "Farmers, State Oppose Animal Care Referendum." *Springdale (Mass.) Union News,* December 28, pp. 12–13.

NESARC (National Endangered Species Act Reform Coalition). 1995a. "Point/Counterpoint: The Gorton/Johnston ESA Reform Bill." Press release. May 9.

———.1995b. Press release of text of testimony by Glenn English, vice chair of NESARC, to U.S. House of Representatives during hearings on Endangered Species Act Reauthorization. May 18.

———. 1995c. Press release of text of testimony by David F. Mazour, NESARC director, on behalf of Endangered Species Act Reauthorization before Subcommittee on Drinking Water, Fisheries, and Wildlife, Committee on Environment and Public Works, U.S. House of Representatives. July 13.

NHC (National Health Council). 1991. *Report on Voluntary Health Agency Revenue and Expenses, Fiscal Year 1990.* Washington, D.C.: NHC.

Nicholl, Jack and Paul Knepprath. 1994. "Preliminary Campaign Plan to Defeat Philip Morris Initiative." Confidential memo for the Coalition for a Healthy California. June 27.

No on 135 Campaign. 1990. Summary of Marttila and Kiley polling results between October 14 and 17. October 29.

NRDC (Natural Resources Defense Council). 1990. "Lies, Damned Lies, and Statistics: A Critique of Spectrum Economics, Inc.'s Analysis of Proposition 128." Press release. San Francisco. September 19.

Oliver, Daniel T. 1993. *Animal Rights: The Inhumane Crusade.* Studies in Organization Trends, no. 7, occasional paper issued by Capital Research Center, a conservative research organization, Washington, D.C.

Olson, Erik. 1994. "Draft Legislative Strategy Paper Developed by Environmental Group Lobbyists." Prepared for environmental organizations. March 4.

Olson, Mancur Jr. 1965. *The Logic of Collective Action.* Cambridge, Mass.: Harvard University Press.

Opinion Dynamics. 1990. "American Attitudes Toward Farmers and Farm Animal Issues." Confidential report on survey of public attitudes toward farmers and the treatment of farm animals prepared for American Farm Bureau Federation. Cambridge, Mass. November.

Parsons, Talcott. 1978. *Action Theory and the Human Condition.* New York: Free Press.

"People Are Looking at Animals with Greater Respect." 1988. *Sunday Eagle-Tribune*

*(Lawrence, Mass.)*, August 21, p. C5.

Peter D. Hart Research Associates. 1992. "A Nationwide Survey of Attitudes Among Consumers and Opinion Leaders Toward the Bean Industry." Poll prepared for environmental organizations. July.

———. 1994. "Key Findings from a Postelection Voter Survey Conducted for the National Wildlife Federation." Study #4315, prepared for the National Wildlife Federation. Washington, D.C. December.

Pierce, John P. and Robert M. Kaplan. 1994. *Tobacco Use in California: An Evaluation of the Tobacco Control Program, 1989- 1993.* Prepublication copy of a report to the University of California–San Diego, California Department of Health Services, Cancer Prevention and Control Program, March.

Plummer, Mark L. 1996. "Pro and Con: Is the Endangered Species Act Fundamentally Sound?" *Congressional Digest: Saving Endangered Species* 75, no. 3 (March).

Polsby, Nelson W. 1980. *Community Power and Political Theory.* 2d ed. New Haven, Conn.: Yale University Press.

Porter/Novelli. 1990. "A National Survey of Americans' Attitudes Toward Farmers, Farm Practices, and Food Safety." Survey of poll results prepared for the American Farm Bureau Federation. February.

Prindle, David F. and James W. Endersby. 1993. "Hollywood Liberalism." *Social Science Quarterly* 74, no. 1 (March).

"Progress on the Hill: NCA Official Pushes Issues from Public Lands to Private Property Rights." 1994. *AgWeek*, June 13.

Public Media Center. 1995. "Environmental Health Risks: Activists, Scientists, and the Public." Preliminary report on research in progress prepared for anti–Proposition 188 campaign. San Francisco.

*Public Media Center v. Californians for Statewide Smoking Restrictions*, No. C-94-3854-SBA, slip op. (N.D.Cal. Nov. 3, 1994).

Pyle, Tom. 1995. Interview by author. Pyle was legislative assistant to Representative Richard Pomba (R-Calif.).

Rapp, David. 1988. *How the U.S. Got into Agriculture and Why It Can't Get Out.* Washington, D.C.: Congressional Quarterly.

Rausch, Jonathan. 1994. *Demosclerosis.* New York: Times Books.

Regan, Tom. 1983. *The Case for Animal Rights.* Berkeley: University of California Press.

Rempel, Bill. 1991a. "Agriculture Close to Losing Animal Rights War." *Feedstuffs*, February 4.

———. 1991b. "Animal Rights Beliefs: Are They on Target?" Paper presented at the University of Nebraska, Lincoln. April 10.

Repace, J. L. and A. H. Lowrey. 1985. "A Quantitative Estimate of Nonsmokers' Lung Cancer Risk from Passive Smoking." *Environmental International* 11: 3–22.

"Return of Organization Exempt from Income Tax, and Form 990EZ." 1996. *Statistics of Income Bulletin* 16, no. 1 (Summer).

Richards, Rebecca Templin. 1990. "Consensus Mobilization Through Ideology,

Networks, and Grievances: A Study of the Contemporary Animal Rights Movement." Unpublished Ph.D. diss., Utah State University.

Richardson, Jason and Rick Kushman. 1991. "Advice to Tobacco Firms Admitted." *Sacramento Bee*, August 30.

Roper Organization. 1978. "A Study of Public Attitudes Toward Cigarette Smoking and the Tobacco Industry in 1978." Vol. 1. Poll and report prepared for the Tobacco Institute. May.

Rosen, Joseph D. n.d. "The Death of Daminozide." Unpublished report. Department of Food Science, Cook College, Rutgers University, New Brunswick, N.J.

Rosenbaum, Walter A. 1995. *Environmental Politics and Policy.* 3d ed. Washington, D.C.: Congressional Quarterly Press.

Rothman, Stanley and S. Robert Lichter. 1996. "Is Environmental Cancer a Political Disease?" *Annals of the New York Academy of Science* 775: 231.Rubin, Charles. 1994. *The Green Crusade: Rethinking the Roots of Environmentalism.* New York: Free Press.

Rucht, Dieter. 1996. "The Impact of National Contexts on Social Movement Structures: A Cross-Movement and Cross-National Comparison." In Doug McAdam, John McCarthy, and Mayer Zald, eds., *Comparative Perspectives on Social Movements.* New York: Cambridge University Press.

Rural Vermont. 1991. *Rural (Montpelier) Vermont Report* 2, no. 1 (February).

———. 1993. *Rural (Montpelier) Vermont Report* 4, no. 1 (Winter).

Russell, Dick. 1988. "Prop. 65 Goes to the Market." *Nation*, June 4.

Sale, Kirkpatrick. 1986. "The Forest for the Trees: Can Today's Environmentalist Tell the Difference?" *Mother Jones*, November.

Samuels, Bruce and Stanton A. Glantz. 1991. "The Politics of Local Tobacco Control." *Journal of the American Medical Association* 266 (October 16).

Sanders, Connie and Patrick Lippert. 1990. Memo to the Steering Committee of the Entertainment Industry Coalition: "Schedule of Upcoming Events." March 8.

Schattschneider, E. E. 1960. *The Semisovereign People.* New York: Holt, Rinehart and Winston.

Schlozman, Kay Lehman and John T. Tierney. 1986. *Organized Interests and American Democracy.* New York: Harper and Row.

Schwartz, Harry. 1994. "Stop the Scaremongering of Cigarettes." *USA Today*, June 23, p. 10A.

Seasholes, Brian. 1995. "Appendix: Are Property Rights Popular?" In Jonathan Adler, ed., *Property Rights Reader.* Washington, D.C.: Competitive Enterprise Institute.

Sewell, Bradford and Robin Whyatt. 1989. "Intolerable Risk: Pesticides in Our Children's Foods." Report for Natural Resources Defense Council, New York. February.

Shabecoff, Philip. 1993. *A Fierce Green Fire.* New York: Hill and Wang.

Shaiko, Ronald G. 1993. "Greenpeace U.S.A.: Something Old, New, Borrowed." *Annals of the American Academy of Political and Social Science* 528 (July): 88—100.

Shurland, Elizabeth. 1990. *The Politics of Farm Animal Welfare: The Massachusetts 1998 Debate on Initiative Petition 3—Should Farm Animal Husbandry Standards Be Set by the State?* Report no. 7, North Grafton, Mass.: Tufts Center for Animals and Public Policy.

Silverman, Jennifer. 1996. "Environmental Groups Sue U.S. Government over Failure to Pursue Lynx to ESA List." *Daily Environment Report*, no. 20 (January 31): 1060, 2976.

Singer, Peter. [1975] 1990. *Animal Liberation: A New Ethics for Our Treatment of Animals.* New York: Avon Books.

Slattery, Jay. 1989. "A Detailed Presentation on How Issue Got Started, Obstacles Faced, and Assets of Agriculture." Analysis of Massachusetts animal rights referendum presented at meeting sponsored by the American Farm Bureau Federation and Massachusetts Farm Bureau. April 6. Chicago.

Slattery, Jay and John Bragg. 1989. "Step by Step Analysis." Analysis of Massachusetts animal rights referendum presented at meeting sponsored by the American Farm Bureau Federation and Massachusetts Farm Bureau. April 6. Chicago.

Smith, T. Alexander. 1969. "Toward a Comparative Theory of the Policy Process." *Comparative Politics* 1 (July).

——. 1975. *The Comparative Policy Process.* Santa Barbara, Calif.: ABC-Clio Press.

——. 1978. "A Phenomenology of the Policy Process." *International Journal of Comparative Sociology* 23 (1–2): 1–16.

Snow, David A. and Robert D. Benford. 1988. "Ideology, Frame Resonance, and Participant Mobilization." In Bert Klandermans, Hanspeter Kriesi, and Sidney Tarrow, eds., *From Structure to Action: Social Movement Participation Across Cultures.* Greenwich, Conn.: JAI Press.

Snow, David A., E. Burke Rochford Jr., Steven K. Worden, and Robert D. Benford. 1986. "Frame Alignment Processes, Micromobilization and Movement Participation." *American Sociological Review* 51: 464–81.

Solis, Suzanne Espinosa. 1994. "Poll Finds Few Voters Know About Fall Initiatives." *San Francisco Chronicle* (East Bay edition), July 28, p. A17.

Spectrum Economics. 1990. "California Environmental Protection Act of 1990, Working Paper One: Initiative Requirements and Preliminary Interpretations." Report prepared for the anti–Proposition 128 campaign. January 16.

Starr, Paul. 1982. *The Social Transformation of American Medicine.* New York: Basic Books.

Stauber, John. 1993. Interview by author. July 15.

Stitzenberger, Lee. 1994. Interview by author. July 11. Stitzenberger was chairman and CEO of the Dolfin Group, a Los Angeles Republican political consultancy.

Stull, Carolyn and Duncan A. McMartin. 1992. *Welfare Parameters in Veal Calf Production Facilities.* Visual Media, Video Cassette No. 2130. Davis: School of Veterinary Medicine, University of California.

Sugg, Ike C. 1993. "Babbitt's Ecobabble." *National Review*, September 20, pp. 48–49.

———. 1995. "Property Wrongs: The Growth of Federal Land-Use Control." In Jonathan Adler, ed., *Property Rights Reader* Washington, D.C.: Competitive Enterprise Institute.

Szasz, Andrew. 1994. *EcoPopulism: Toxic Waste and the Movement for Environmental Justice.* Minneapolis: University of Minnesota Press.

Tarrance and Associates. 1989a. "Food Safety Initiative II: Survey Overview—A Confidential Report." Poll prepared for the CAREFUL campaign. Alexandria, Va. December.

———. 1989b. "Research Report: Food Safety Initiative." A confidential polling report prepared for Agricultural/Food Study Group, a conservative research organization. Alexandria, Va. September.

Tarrance Group. 1995. "A Survey of Voter Attitudes in the United States: Endangered Species Nationwide Survey." Poll prepared for Project CommonSense. Alexandria, Va. March 25–27.

Tarrow, Sidney. 1983. *Struggling to Reform: Social Movements and Policy Change During Cycles of Protest.* Western Societies Program Occasional Paper no. 15. Ithaca: Cornell University, New York Center for International Studies.

———. 1994. *Power in Movement: Social Movements, Collective Action, and Politics.* New York: Cambridge University Press.

Tatalovich, Raymond and Bryon W. Daynes, eds. 1988. *Social Regulatory Policy: Moral Controversies in American Politics.* Boulder, Colo.: Westview.

Tate, Cassandra. 1989. "In the 1800s Antismoking was a Burning Issue." *Smithsonian,* July.

Taylor, Verta. 1989. "Social Movement Continuity: The Women's Movement in Abeyance." *American Sociological Review* 54 (5): 761–75.

Tesconi, Tim. 1991. "Milk-Boosting Chemical Opposed." *Empire (Santa Rosa, Calif.) News,* November 13, pp.

Tesh, Sylvia. 1984. "In Support of 'Single-Issue' Politics." *Political Science Quarterly* 99, no. 1 (Spring).

Tesh, Sylvia and Bruce A. Williams. 1996. 'Identity Politics, Disinterested Politics, and Environmental Justice." *Polity* 18, no. 3 (Spring).

TFA (Tobacco Free America). 1990. "Blueprint for Success: Countdown 2000—Ten Years to a Tobacco-Free America." Washington, D.C.

Tilly, Charles. 1978. *From Mobilization to Revolution.* Reading. Mass.: Addison-Wesley.

Tobin, Richard. 1990. *The Expendable Future: U.S. Politics and the Protection of Biological Diversity.* Durham, N.C.: Duke University Press.

Traynor, Michael P., Michael E. Begay, and Stanton A. Glantz. 1993. "New Tobacco Industry Strategy to Prevent Local Tobacco Control." *Journal of the American Medical Association* 270, no. 4 (July 28).

Traynor, Michael P. and Stanton A. Glantz. 1995. "The Development and Passage of Proposition 99, California's Tobacco Tax Initiative." Report for the San Francisco Institute for Health Policy Studies.

Truman, David. 1951. *The Governmental Process.* New York: Knopf.

Tucker, L. 1978. "The Environmentally Concerned Citizen: Some Correlates." *Environment and Behavior* 10 (3).

Tucker, William. 1982. *Progress and Privilege: American in the Age of Environmentalism.* New York: Anchor.

U.S. Congress. Office of Technology Assessment. 1986. *Technology, Public Policy and the Changing Structure of American Agriculture.* Washington, D.C.: U.S. Congress, OTA.

———. 1990. *Agricultural Research and Technology Transfer Policy for the 1990s.* Washington, D.C.: U.S. Congress, OTA.

———. 1992. *A New Technological Era for American Agriculture.* Washington, D.C.: U.S. Congress, OTA.

University of Wisconsin. 1990. *News and Features,* publication of the School of Family Resources and Consumer Sources, University of Wisconsin, Madison.

U.S. Department of Agriculture. Food Safety and Inspection Service. 1992. *Domestic Residue Monitoring Program Results.* Red Book. Washington, D.C.: U.S. Government Printing Office.

U.S. Department of Health and Human Services (HHS). 1986. "The Health Consequences of Involuntary Smoking: A Report of the Surgeon General." Washington, D.C.: HHS.

———. Office of Inspector General. 1994. "Follow-Up Review of Possible Improper Preapproval Promotion Activities." Report no. A-15–93–00018 by June Gibbs Brown. Washington, D.C. September.

U.S. Environmental Protection Agency. 1982. *Environmental Monitoring at Love Canal.* Report No. EPA-600/4–82–030, May, vol. 1.

———. 1990. *Health Effects of Passive Smoking: Assessment of Lung Cancer in Adults and Respiratory Disorders in Children.* EPA report no. 600/6–90/006A.

———. Office of Research and Development. 1992. "Respiratory Health Effects of Passive Smoking: Lung Cancer and Other Disorders." EPA report no. EPA/600/6–90/006F. December.

———. 1993. *Respiratory Health Effects of Passive Smoking: Lung Cancer and Other Disorders.* Washington, D.C.: Government Printing Office.

U.S. Food and Drug Administration (USFDA). 1990. Press release of text of testimony by Gerald B. Guest, veterinarian and director of FDA's Center for Veterinary Medicine, during U.S. House hearings on FDA's regulation of animal drug residues in milk. February 6.

———. Veterinary Medicine Advisory Committee. 1993. *Whether to Label Milk from RBGH-Treated Cows: Hearings.* Joint hearing with Food Advisory Committee of U.S. Department of Health and Human Services. May 6–7.

U.S. General Accounting Office (USGAO). 1990. "Food Safety and Quality: FDA Surveys Not Adequate to Demonstrate Safety of Milk Supply." Report to the chairman, Human Resources and Intergovernmental Relations Subcommittee,

Committee on Government Operations, House of Representatives. GAO/RCED-91–26. November 1.

———. 1992a. "Food Safety and Quality: FDA Needs Stronger Controls over the Approval Process for New Animal Drugs." Report to the chairman, Human Resources and Intergovernmental Relations Subcommittee, Committee on Government Operations, House of Representatives. GAO/RCED-92–63. January 17.

———. 1992b. "Food Safety and Quality: FDA Strategy Needed to Address Animal Drug Residues in Milk." Report to the chairman, Human Resources and Intergovernmental Relations Subcommittee, Committee on Government Operations, U.S. House of Representatives. GAO/RCED-92–209. August 5.

———. 1992c. "Food Safety and Quality: FDA Strategy Needed to Address Animal Drug Residues in Milk." Testimony before the Intergovernmental Relations Subcommittee, Committee on Government Operations, U.S. House of Representatives. GAO/T-RCED-92–89. August 5.

———. 1992d. "Recombinant Bovine Growth Hormone: FDA Approval Should Be Withheld Until the Mastitis Issue Is Resolved." Report no. GAO/PEMD-92–26, prepared at the request of Congress. August 6.

———. 1992e. *Food and Agriculture Issues.* GAO/OCG-93–15-TR. December.

———. 1994. "Endangered Species Act: Information on Species Protection on Nonfederal Lands." GAO/RCED-95-16. December 20.

U.S. House of Representatives. Committee on Government Operations. Human Resources and Intergovernmental Relations Subcommittee. 1985. *Human Food Safety and Regulation of Animal Drugs.* Report 27. 99th Cong., 1st sess.

———. Committee on Agriculture. 1989. *Joint Hearing before the Subcommittee on Livestock, Dairy, and Poultry and the Subcommittee on Department Operations, Research, and Foreign Agriculture on H.R. 84, the Veal Calf Protection Act.* 101st Cong., 1st sess., June 6.

———. Subcommittee on Livestock, Dairy, and Poultry. Committee on Agriculture. 1990. *Formulation of the 1990 Farm Bill.* Hearings. 101st Cong., 2d sess., January 8–10, 16–18, February 21, March 8.

———. Committee on Energy and Commerce. 1993a. *Compilation of Selected Acts Within the Jurisdiction of the Committee on Energy and Commerce: Food, Drug, and Related Law.* 103d Cong., 1st sess., February. Committee Print 103-D.

———. 1993b. *Environmental Tobacco Smoke: Hearing before the Subcommittee on Health and the Environment of the Committee on Energy and Commerce.* 103d Cong., 1st sess., July 21, serial No. 103–51.

Vamos, Mark and Stuart Jackson, eds. 1989. "The Public Is Willing to Take Business On." Business Week/Harris Poll no. 3107, May 29, p. 29.

"Van de Kamp, Ecologists Unveil Initiative." 1989. *San Jose Mercury News,* October 11.

Van de Kamp, John. 1994. Interview by author. July 15.

Vanderbeek, Debra. 1989. "What MBc Strategies Showed." Analysis of Massachusetts animal rights referendum presented at meeting sponsored by the American Farm Bureau Federation and Massachusetts Farm Bureau. April 6. Chicago.

Vermont Biotechnology Working Group. 1991. "Biotechnology: An Activists' Handbook." Paper. Montpelier, Vt.:

Veyhl, Erich. 1993. "Special Supplement: Preservationists Acknowledge Growing Grass Roots Opposition, Plan Strategy." *Land Rights Letter*, January–February.

Vig, Norman J. and Michael E. Kraft. 1997. *Environmental Policy in the 1990s: Reform or Reaction?* 3d ed. Washington, D.C.: Congressional Quarterly.

Vogel, David. 1978. *Lobbying the Corporation: Citizen Challenges to Business Authority.* New York: Basic.

——. 1989. *Fluctuating Fortunes.* New York: Basic Books.

——. 1995. *Trading Up: Consumer and Environmental Regulation in a Global Economy.* Cambridge, Mass.: Harvard University Press.

——. 1996. *Kindred Strangers: The Uneasy Relationship Between Politics and Business in America.* Princeton, N.J.: Princeton University Press.

Walker, Jack L. 1983. "The Origins and Maintenance of Interest Groups in America." *American Political Science Review* 77 (June).

Walters, Dan. 1989. "'Big Green' or big bust?" *Sacramento Bee*, September 12, pp.

——. 1991. "Tobacco Firms Blowing Smoke." *Sacramento Bee,* July 15.

Webb, Gary. 1991. "Speaker Disguised Smoking Bill, Memo Says." *Mercury News*, August 27.

West, Kirk. 1994. Interview by author. July 11. West was president of the California Chamber of Commerce during the Big Green campaign.

Wheale, Peter and Ruth McNally. 1990. "Introduction." In Peter Wheale and Ruth McNally, eds., *The BIO Revolution: Cornucopia or Pandora's Box?* London: Pluto Press.

Whelan, Elizabeth M. 1984. *Smoking Gun: How the Tobacco Industry Gets Away with Murder.* Philadelphia: George F. Stickley.

Wildavsky, Aaron. 1995. *But Is It True?* Cambridge, Mass.: Harvard University Press.

Wilson, Edward O. 1993. *The Diversity of Life.* New York: Norton.

Wilson, Lowell L. 1992. Letter to the Editor. *Time*, September 10, p.

Wirthlin Group. 1989. "National Survey of Consumer Attitudes." Poll #599–36–01 #4773–08,prepared for the National Cattlemen's Foundation. September.

——. 1991. "Survey of Opinion Influencers." Poll #599–36–05 #5354–12, prepared for the National Cattlemen's Association. March.

Woliver, Laura R. 1993. *From Outrage to Action: The Politics of Grassroots Dissent.* Urbana: University of Illinois Press.

Woodward, Bob. 1994. *The Agenda: Inside the Clinton White House.* New York: Simon and Schuster

Woodward, Richard and Jack McDowell. 1990. "Campaign Plan to Defeat the Hayden Initiative." Confidential document presented to California Coordinating Council. June 8.

Woodward, Richard S. 1994. Interview by author. July 14. Woodward was president of Woodward and McDowell.

Wright, Pamela A. 1992. "Perceived Structure of the Environmental/ Conservation Organization Market." Unpublished Ph.D. diss., Ohio State University.

Yankelovich, Skelly and White/Clancy, Shulman, Inc. 1992. "The American Vegetarian: Coming of Age in the '90s." Study of the vegetarian market conducted for *Vegetarian Times.*

Young, Alvin L. 1990. "Role of the Federal Government in Agricultural Biotechnology Research and Regulation." In Indra K. Vasil, ed., *Biotechnology: Science, Education, and Commercialization.* New York: Elsevier.

Zeff, Robbin L., Marsha Love, and Karen Stults. 1989. *Empowering Ourselves: Women and Toxics Organizing.* Arlington, Va.: Citizen's Clearinghouse for Hazardous Wastes.

Zeller, Mitch. 1993. "FDA Responsibilities in Regulation of Drugs for Use in Animals: Congressional Perspective." *American Journal of Alternative Agriculture* 202, no. 10 (May).

Raitt, Bonnie, 103
Raven, Peter, 183
Redistributive arena of organized interest activity, 5–6
Referenda and initiatives: in animal
rights campaign, 66, 70–84; in antismoking campaign, 150–52, 167*n*12;
in Big Green campaign, 91–94, 108,
109, 116, 117–20; and counterinitiatives, 116, 117–20, 126*n*14, 153; his-
tory in California, 124*n*; reflecting
emotional issues, 17; reflecting
grassroots social movement support,
17; secondhand smoke
campaign, 148–49, 153–57,
159–60, 167*n*13
Regan, Tom, 58, 85*n*3
Regulative arena of organized interest
activity, 5
Regulatory policy making, 2
Rempel, Bill, 60–61, 62, 64, 65
Repace, James L., 145–46, 147
Reynolds Co., R. J., 149, 167*n*11
Richardson, Jason, 153
Rifkin, Jeremy, 28–29, 42, 47, 48, 49
Rochford, E. Burke Jr., 20
Ronan, Stephen, 69, 70
Roosevelt, Theodore, 172
Roper Organization, 138, 139
Ross, Richie, 96
Rucht, Dieter, 18, 19
Rural Vermont (expressive group), 32–34
Ruth, Lee, 117

Salisbury, Robert H., 10, 217
Salmon, 196
Samuels, Bruce, 138, 152
Sanders, Bernard, 42, 51*n*4, 52*n*9
Sanders, Connie, 103
Sarandon, Susan, 103
Saxton, Jim, 204
Scenic Hudson Preservation

Conference, 90
Schattschneider, E. E., 2, 3, 10
Scheuplein, Robert, 107
Schlozman, Kay Lehman, 4, 7, 12, 13, 16
Science: animal biotechnology, 30–31;
and antismoking movement,
141–48; biodiversity and "extinction
crisis," 176–80, 182–86; causes of
cancer, 125*n*11; challenge to BST,
35–37; and genetic engineering, 27;
"instrumentalism" questioning,
53–54; "meta-analysis" research
method, 144; pesticide risk statistics,
107–8, 111, 121, 126–27*n*12; progress
identified with national interest,
129; questions on definition of
ecosystem, 206*n*6; species-area
curve, 177–78; use/misuse by grassroots campaigns, 22, 139–41; *see also*
Antibiotechnology campaign; Big
Green campaign; Secondhand
smoke campaign
Secondhand smoke campaign: advan-
tages of antismoking infrastructure, 164–65; background in modern health movement, 129–34;
comparison of smoking laws,
150*table*; criterion of consistency of
association, 143–44; economics of
tobacco growing, 131; expressive
group reaction to tobacco's campaign, 158–61; expressive groups'
coalition strategy change, 161–64;
expressive groups involved in,
24*table*, 160–61; framing of issues,
153–56, 157, 161; funding, 136, 137,
149, 151–52, 157, 160, 162, 163,
166*n*6&10; gender gap in antismoking opinion polls, 155; grassroots antismoking campaigns,
135–37, 138–49; illustrative of diffi-
culties faced by expressive groups,